PERFORMANCE
HANDLING

Don Alexander

Motorbooks International
Publishers & Wholesalers ®

First published in 1991 by Motorbooks International Publishers & Wholesalers, P O Box 2, 729 Prospect Avenue, Osceola, WI 54020 USA

Motorbooks International books are also available at discounts in bulk quantity for industrial or sales-promotional use. For details write to Special Sales Manager at the Publisher's address

Library of Congress Cataloging-in-Publication Data
Alexander, Don.
    Performance handling / Don Alexander.
        p.   cm.
    Includes index.
    ISBN 0-87938-418-2
    1. Automobiles—Handling Characteristics. I. Title.
TL154.A54 1990
629.28'72—dc20
90-49035

On the front cover: The IMSA Firestone Firehawk Endurance Chevrolet Camaro of MainLine Racing, driven at the March 1991 West Palm Beach race by team owner Will Barclay of Glenmoore, Pennsylvania, and John Kohler of Bradford, Pennsylvania. *Geoffrey Hewitt*

Printed and bound in the United States of America

Contents

Acknowledgments

Many individuals have assisted in the preparation and completion of this work. My sincere thanks to all of them for their input and expedient assistance:

Mike Walker
Shane Lewis
Phil DeLorm
Bob Ryder
Bob McClurg, *Mustang Illustrated*
Dan Sanchez, *All Chevy*
John Pentelai-Molnar, *Grassroots Motorsport*
Rick Titus, Special Editions
Olga Vernon, General Tire
Mary Jo Thomas, General Tire
Kathy Thomas, General Tire
Skip Pipes, Skip Pipes Racing
Tom Culbreth, Skip Pipes Racing
Bob Brezinski, Skip Pipes Racing
Bruce Foss, Hoosier Tires
Kevin Wilkerson, Bob Thomas & Associates
Mike Burroughs
John Taylor, Bridgestone
Rick Brennan, Bridgestone
Geno Effler, Pirelli
Rick Shaffer, BFGoodrich
Ed Jacobs, BFGoodrich
Al Speyer, Firestone
Bob Roberts, Firestone
Carolyn Ashby, Goodyear
Rodney Girolami, Ford SVO
Bill Huth, Willow Springs International Raceway
Necie Kelly, Willow Springs International Raceway

Michael Coates
Dave Dinger, Vista Group
Tom Huxie, Chevrolet
Pete Magnuson, Consulier
Don Preito, Preative Group
Greg Woo, Eibach
Richard Janieck, Eibach
Gary Peek, Suspension Techniques
Jeff Cheechov, Suspension Techniques
Don Bunker, Energy Suspensions
Ray Bartlett
Bob Zecca, Driving Impressions
Mike Shield, Shoei Helmets
Kurt Tucker, Team Tech Safety Equipment
John Thawley
Dairn Johi, Toyota Racing Development
Gerald Blum, Cobra Seats
Anson Lisk, Bilstein Shocks
Richard Meyer, Tokico
Tim Clark, Tokico
Chuck Blaney, Shelby Wheels
Bill Cobb, Revolution Wheels
Richard Small, Flowmaster
Joe Ruggles, Ruggles'cales
John Covan, Reb-Co
Art Galliot, Koni Shocks
Bob Eckhardt
Craig Stanton
Bill Follmer
Jim Vial

A special thanks to my wife, Christie, for her support and tolerance.

Foreword by Rick Titus

A car that handles well is a joy to drive. Be it a race car or a street machine, the balance, poise and reflexes of a finely honed chassis are a delight to work with. A car that handles well doesn't react, it responds. It can be played like an instrument. Like a good sound system, once you've experienced it, you'll never be satisfied with anything less. And bear in mind that a car that handles well is smoother, faster and safer to drive in either a street or racetrack environment.

I continue to be amazed at the absolute ignorance of a driver, any driver, who thinks he can drive around a handling deficiency. Twenty years ago, some of this world's top race drivers could "carry" a poor-handling car, but not today, not with any hope of running up front. Yet with alarming frequency I hear some uninformed or lazy driver tell his crew, "Don't sweat it, I'll just drive around it." Sure, to last place. Competition today is so tight nobody can afford to not sweat it. Suspension engineering advances and fundamental tire development have given production-line automobiles of today handling characteristics that would leave a full-out racing machine of twenty years ago panting in jealousy.

That development has forced a change in driving style and required today's competition driver to know far more about the engineering make-up of his car. Walk the pit lane of any racetrack in the world, be it a Formula 1 event or a local Pro Solo meet, and you'll hear drivers and crew talking roll centers, toe figures, roll rates, bump steer, tire temperatures, antiroll bar settings and dampner firmness. And the one who understands it best runs up front.

Good handling is not a black art, but rather an exacting science fraught with compromises. To de-velop a basic understanding of it requires a knowl-edge of the fundamental components and the role they play in a performance chassis. Feel, as much as know-how, is an essential ingredient. This book was written with that thought in mind.

I am considered by some to be a good "sorting" race driver. Simply put that means I have both the desire and the knowledge to work at fine tuning a race car's handling. Hence my winning SCCA's Professional Endurance Driver's Championship. Don Alexander taught me a lot of what I know, and more importantly, all of what I understand about suspension technology. I've called him my "sus-pensionologist" for over fifteen years. More ac-curately he is my friend.

It was because of my enormous faith in Don, that my partner Chuck Beck and I hired him as the suspension engineering consultant on the Sho-gun. His input proved invaluable, and Don shares with you the outcome of that effort in part of this book.

Don's approach to this subject is the result of his teaching both performance driving and perfor-mance handling for years. That combination of skills gives him a real advantage when it comes to a task as challenging as explaining handling to the newcomer. His shirt-sleeve style and by-chapter project approach makes for a perfect comparative when it comes time for you to start sorting your chassis. You will learn a great deal about perfor-mance handling, and as an added bonus, you'll be-come a better driver for it.

Remember: He with the most information, wins!

Rick Titus

Chapter 1

What is Handling?

In 1950, the first year of the World Driving Championship in Grand Prix racing, the fastest Formula One cars were cornering at less than 1.0 g. Today, the average Formula One car is capable of exceeding 4.5 g cornering power. One g is equal to the force of gravity, and is today's benchmark measurement for performance handling. Tires and aerodynamics are the keys to the staggering improvements in handling.

Even more significant is the change in performance on the street. In 1969, Trans-Am series race cars, custom-built Camaros, Mustangs, Firebirds and so on using racing tires, could barely achieve 0.90 g cornering power. Just twenty years later, street cars can be set up on DOT (Department of Transportation approved) tires that exceed the magical 1.0 g cornering power barrier. A mini truck

has even been developed that generates more cornering power than a stock Corvette—and this was accomplished with off-the-shelf, bolt-on components and the tuning techniques described in this book. From a component standpoint, tires are the biggest factor in the dramatic improvement in handling. But controlling the tire contact patch takes on an even more important role as the tire grows wider and stickier.

Handling is not a specific point, but rather a spectrum or a range. At one end lies ride comfort, at the other maximum traction. In 1950, the spectrum was wide, with ride comfort worlds apart from good traction. Today, the spectrum is much narrower. Good ride and good traction are no longer opposites. Both can exist in the same vehicle if the right compromises are made.

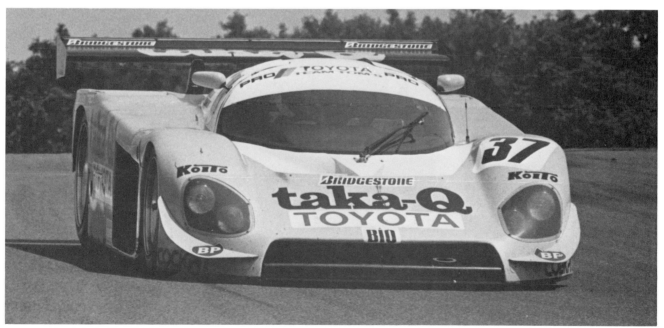

Today's road race cars are capable of exceeding 3.0 g in cornering power, whereas the race cars of the 1950s were cornering at less than 1.0 g. (One g is equal to the force of gravity.) In the old days, suspension systems were set up for a hard ride with little travel and the hard rubber compounds provided little grip, so drivers were *forced to slide cars through corners. Today, racers like the Toyota 88C Group C car of the World Sports Prototype Championship have lots of suspension travel and soft-compound tires that stick like glue to the road. Toyota Motorsports*

Author Don Alexander at work plotting suspension geometry upgrades on a computer for a project car. Bob Ryder

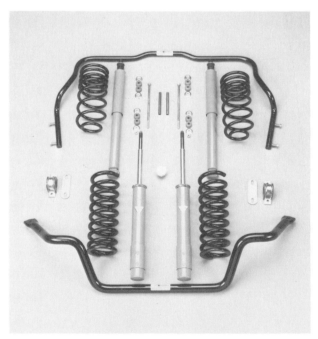

Aftermarket suspension upgrade packages are available from a variety of suppliers. This kit is designed specifically for 1979-1990 Mustangs and Capris, and uses struts and shock absorbers from Koni along with springs and antiroll bars from Suspension Techniques. Suspension Techniques

So what is handling? It can be any point on the spectrum. The individual use of a vehicle and the needs to be filled by the vehicle are the only real considerations to be made.

Handling Parameters

In the definition of handling, four parameters form the core. Each of these must be considered when determining the goal for a specific vehicle and application.

Testing plays a crucial role in developing performance handling. Here the author tests an IROC Camaro on the Willow Springs skid pad. Suspension Techniques

In the early days of sports car racing, cars like this 289 Shelby Cobra ran with stiff chassis, little suspension travel and hard-compound tires. The wire-spoke wheels—usually of large diameter with long spokes— provided some of the car's suspension due to the wire wheel's natural tendency to flex. This was performance handling circa 1963; quality handling tuning was pure black magic.

On the other side of the spectrum are Winston Cup NASCAR stock car racers, set up primarily for the left-hand turns that dominate the superspeedways. Suspension stiffness is balanced against aerodynamic downforce; with the aerodynamic bodywork, suspension travel is also limited, often to between 0.5 to 1.0 in.

Today's sports cars, such as the 1989 Corvette ZR-1, come from the factory with handling packages that are much more advanced than the race cars of the past. Straight from the dealer's showroom, this Corvette offered cornering power in excess of 1.0 g. Chevrolet

Traction

Traction is the ability of the tire contact patch to grip the road surface and is the most important of the handling parameters if higher cornering power is a consideration for a specific car or application. In any form of auto competition, increased traction is the most important consideration. Increases in traction may not be high on the priority list for street applications, however.

The most obvious way to increase traction is to increase the effective size of the tire contact patch. In addition to using a wider tire, the effective size of the tire contact patch can be increased by changing suspension settings to allow the entire tire contact patch to lie flat on the road surface during cornering.

Traction can also be increased by using a softer tire compound. The stickier tire provides more grip, but the tire will wear more quickly. A stickier tire may also provide less traction on slippery surfaces, such as wet roads.

Tires are a quick way to improve traction, but any change in tire will also affect responsiveness, balance and ride.

Responsiveness

For a vehicle to exhibit good handling qualities, it must respond quickly to driver inputs. Some of the factors that improve responsiveness include shock absorber rates, tire aspect ratio, sidewall construction, hard suspension bushings and available tire traction. Stiff shock absorbers have a reputation for improving handling. Stiffer shocks do make a car more responsive, but if the shocks are too stiff for a given application, they can deteriorate traction in many instances.

Low-profile tires improve response because the sidewalls flex less, thereby allowing the tire to steer more quickly when the driver turns the steering wheel. Virtually all factors that improve responsiveness will increase ride harshness.

Balance

For a car to exhibit good handling characteristics, the front-to-rear traction balance must be close to neutral. If the front tires lose traction first, the car pushes and the rear tires are just along for the ride, not really working to their maximum potential. In the opposite case, where the rear tires loose traction first, the car is loose. Neither condition is desirable in anything exceeding small quantities. The most important factors that dictate balance are the tires and the relative contact patch areas at the front versus the rear, the rates of the springs and the rates of the antiroll bars.

Achieving a good handling balance will improve the handling characteristics of the car. And in most instances, cornering power will improve also, with no detrimental effects on ride or responsiveness. Often, simple alignment settings can improve the balance of a car. On the other hand, changing springs or antiroll bars can have a major effect on the balance.

Selecting the correct spring rates and antiroll bar rates requires engineering expertise and experience. If the front and rear rates are not compatible, the handling balance can be out of the ballpark and the vehicle can become absolutely diabolical to drive, either trying to go straight on when the steering is turned, or attempting to spin out on every corner. Great care must be taken here.

Ride

Many people, including some in the suspension business, equate harsh ride qualities with improved handling. Quite the opposite is true. While improved handling requires stiffer suspension systems, excessively stiff suspension can hurt cornering power and handling quality. Handling improvements are not necessarily made at the expense of ride quality.

Spring rates, shock absorbers, bushing material, tire aspect ratio and sidewall construction, and tire pressure all affect ride quality.

Handling Goals for the Racer

For the average automotive performance enthusiast, improved handling requires some jug-

Setting up handling for the street is based on a different set of variables than for a race car of any sort. Ideally, skid pad or racetrack testing is a must, but you can also test your car on the street in everyday driving by paying close attention to both your testing and to traffic. Bob McClurg

gling of parameters. For the competitor, the goal is substantially more concise.

For the racer, only one real goal exists: to reduce lap times. Achieving this requires maximum tire traction, quick response and close to neutral handling characteristics. This applies to any form of competition.

The tire is the key to maximum traction. Everything we do to the suspension is to make the tire

Even sophisticated cars, such as the Ford Thunderbird Super Coupe, with state-of-the-art handling packages can be improved upon with aftermarket equipment. The place to start is with new wheels and tires. Ford Motor Company

Autocrossing Solo II offers classes for many types of cars. This stock Toyota pickup runs in the Sport Truck class.

The Prepared category gets radical for production-based equipment. The Mazda RX-7 is a quick, demanding ride through the pylons.

The Street Prepared autocross category is popular because it allows many modifications, but the cars are still reasonable on the street. National champion Bob Endicott gets ready to start in his Honda CRX front-driver in C Street Prepared at a SCCA Pro Solo event in California.

Another form of competition for your daily transportation is Time Trials. Many clubs hold events all over the United States. Here a pair of Porsche 911s sandwich a Mustang 5.0 liter. Bob McClurg

work more efficiently. Ride is the least important concern; the driver is usually too busy to notice ride harshness, anyway.

While the job of reaching these goals is arduous, the goals themselves are straightforward. Not so for the street performer.

Handling Goals for the Street

The picture for improved handling on the street is indeed bright. Tremendous improvements can be achieved easily and with a relatively small expenditure. Reaching the heights of handling performance takes more effort, money and some sacrifices in creature comfort and convenience, however. Here are some worthy goals to achieve for any street set-up.

Ride

It is not necessary to sacrifice ride comfort to achieve improved handling. When a street vehicle is sprung too stiffly, the tires will not maintain good contact with the road over bumpy surfaces, which are likely to be encountered on the streets and highways.

Convenience

A vehicle that becomes inconvenient to drive soon becomes little fun. Convenience refers to ease of maneuvering, ground clearance over dips and driveways, isolation of unnecessary road vibration and noise, and ease of maintenance.

The more aggressively the handling envelope is pushed, the less convenient a vehicle becomes: steering effort increases; great care must be exercised over speed bumps, dips and driveways lest undercarriage damage results; interior noise and vibration increase; and routine maintenance intervals shrink and wear increases. All of these are part of the price of improved handling performance. The level of performance, and inconvenience, is the individual's choice.

The Trans-Am series offers the ultimate form of production-based racing in the United States. The front-engine, all-wheel-drive Audi 200 Quattro was a rocketship in the 1988 Trans-Am series. Audi of America

Traction, Balance and Responsiveness

All of these parameters require similar attention as they do for the racer; only their relative priority changes.

Defining Good Handling

When creating a handling package you need to ask yourself a series of questions. This should be done to determine the best possible package to suit your individual needs. Here is a general list of questions that everyone should ask themselves when handling improvements are sought.
- How is the car to be used?
- What types of roads (racetracks) do you drive on most often?
- What are the road (racetrack) conditions where you drive most?
- What is your level of driving experience relative to the intended use of the vehicle?
- What is your goal with this project?
- What kind of performance improvements do you expect?
- What compromises are you willing to accept to achieve this level of performance?
- What is your budget range for such a project?

These questions help determine what is needed and expected for a given project. Let's look more closely at each question.

Vehicle Application

How is the vehicle to be used? This is a crucial question. There are many possible answers, but we will examine three general categories and a few more specific ones.

Competition

If the vehicle is going to be used solely for competition, we approach the project from a different perspective. To effectively create a package for a competition vehicle, we must know what form of competition is planned, and what the class rules are for the type of competition. There are several forms of competition to consider as well.

Autocrossing

Autocrossing is not wheel-to-wheel competition. Drivers negotiate a pre-determined course defined by construction cones. Times are registered per lap, and each lap time is used individually to determine standings. The lowest lap time wins. In addition, each cone is marked. Knocking a cone down or moving the cone outside it's pre-

A popular form of competition in Europe is rallying, and the sport is gaining ground quickly in the United States. This Toyota is typical of rally cars in the United States where all SCCA Rally vehicles must be street legal. Toyota Motorsports

marked box will result in a penalty of anywhere from one to three seconds added to your time. In a sport where victory is often measured in thousandths of a second, a cone penalty is tantamount to stopping for lunch while on course. Most clubs give competitors anywhere from three to eight runs depending on format.

Most autocross clubs require the use of a helmet, functioning seatbelts, safe tires and a well-maintained vehicle to participate. Car classification is determined by the degree of modification, if any. This means that, whether you drive a Yugo or a tube-frame Porsche 930, meeting these basic safety requirements assures you a spot on the grid.

For the purpose-built autocross race car, traction is critical, responsiveness and balance are extremely important, and ride quality is not a consideration at all.

Time Trials

Time trials or Solo I is similar to autocrossing in that cars compete for the lowest lap time, but time trial events are held on racetracks with several cars on the track at the same time. Passing is limited to specified areas, and the intent is to keep cars evenly spaced from one another. The purpose of Solo I is to allow drivers to experience the thrill of high racing speeds without the added danger of wheel-to-wheel competition.

Vehicle requirements for time trials are more stringent than for autocrossing. All vehicles must have an SCCA-approved roll bar, although roll cages are recommended. Six-point harnesses are needed as well as a fire extinguisher and a window net. Drivers must have an approved driving suit, gloves and shoes, as well as the appropriate Nomex underwear.

For time trials race cars, responsiveness is less important, traction and balance are critical, aerodynamics becomes important and ride is somewhat more important.

Road Racing

Road racing combines the skill of autocross, the speed of Solo I and the bravado of wheel-to-wheel competition. Road races are usually held at racetracks, although the popularity of street circuits has been resurrected in recent years. Most races last anywhere from fifteen to twenty-four laps, while certain racing series like the Escort Endurance Series and the Firehawk Endurance Series run three- to twenty-four-hour races. There are classes for virtually every type and configuration of car, with the only controlling factor being the depth of the budget. Road racing occurs at both

A car's design will affect how you tune its handling characteristics. Setting up the suspension and choosing wheels and tires will be different for this front-engined, rear-wheel-drive Modified Corvette autocrosser versus for the mid-engined, rear-wheel-drive Fiat X1/9 following it to the starting grid.

the amateur level (SCCA, RCCA) and the pro level (SCCA, IMSA, CART). Because of the complexity of these numerable classes, the stakes are higher, and the importance of reading the rules becomes especially critical.

Participation in road racing comes many ways, but there are several basic requirements. All vehicles must have roll cages, the drivers must have full drivers suits, shoes, gloves and underwear, with fire-extinguishing systems being mandatory in the cars. There are many other safety requirements, each varying with the type and class of vehicle.

Road race cars require the same consideration as time trials cars, but more emphasis is placed on safety due to the wheel-to-wheel competition.

Pro Rallying

Pro Rallying is like autocrossing in that the lowest time is used to determine the winner. Add unpaved "roads," usually lined with trees, rocks, cliffs, and so on, as well as horrible weather conditions, often at night. The challenge is to complete these rough-and-tumble courses in a minimum of time without crashing. These courses are divided into a series of stages. Each stage is a certain length, and drivers must travel between stages on public roads, all the while keeping within local traffic laws. The time for each stage is then added up, and the competitor with the lowest overall time wins.

Rally cars require totally different handling parameters than road cars with traction, suspension travel and balance being critical. Ride is not important.

Each of these competition categories requires a different approach due to the nature of the event and the rules for a given class.

Combined Street and Competition Cars

When a vehicle is driven on the street, but also used to compete, new compromises enter the equation. On certain cars in certain classes the compromises are small. On other cars in certain classes, the compromises can render the car uncompetitive. The more the rules deviate from pure Stock, the more difficult it becomes to create a competitive dual-purpose vehicle.

Autocrossing

Most of the Stock category cars are used as daily transportation, with only wheels and tires changed for an event. The Street Prepared category allows many modifications, making it difficult to compete for a class win in anything but a purpose-built vehicle. Some classes of Street Prepared are less of a problem, however. On the other hand, the Street Prepared autocrosser driven on the street is a phenomenal street performer, and offers great fun on the autocross course.

Some of the pioneers of modern aerodynamics were the Formula 1 cars of the late 1960s. This 1968 Lotus ran with a wing mounted high above the car on carriers attached to the suspension so that the wing moved with the suspension. Side wings were added to the nose to balance the effect of the rear wing by providing downforce to the front of the racer as well as the rear.

By the early 1970s, Formula 1 aerodynamics had progressed radically to the point where, with this 1971 Lotus, the rear wing and the front side wings were incorporated into the bodywork, which was in turn smoothed as much as possible to make it slip through the air.

Time Trials

There are so many different rules for different clubs in time trials that a set answer is impossible. The rule of thumb is that the fewer modifications allowed in a given class, the more streetable the car will remain. Many competitive time trial cars are used as daily transportation.

Road Racing

To be competitive in road racing, even in Showroom Stock or Improved Touring, a purpose-built vehicle is needed. In Showroom Stock, it is reasonable to race your car and drive it on the street. But at the national level, it is unlikely that such a car would be competitive.

Street Use Only

The street use category is actually the hardest to design for, because the range of needs covers such a broad spectrum. Other questions come to mind here: Does your mother-in-law ever ride in the back seat? Is the vehicle ever driven to the limit of the tire traction available? Is visual image more important than actual performance? How important is tire wear? Are you willing to drive slowly over bumps, driveways and so on to avoid damage to the undercarriage of your vehicle? Is increased noise and vibration acceptable? Is increased maintenance acceptable?

Use Conditions

Questions in the use category are important for specific selection of parts. Spring and shock rates are calculated based on road conditions and intended use. If you drive on city streets with many potholes, ruts and driveways, an acceptable set-up will differ greatly from a set-up where roads are relatively smooth.

Engine-Drivetrain Layout

How a car is laid out in terms of the engine and drivetrain will also have an impact on handling. Your handling goals will be the same whether you have a front-wheel-drive or rear-wheel-drive car. How you set up your car to achieve those handling goals will differ, however, depending on your car's layout, whether it is front-engined with front- or rear-wheel drive, or rear- or mid-engined with rear-wheel-drive. This book will explore the different layouts and handling tuning considerations.

Driving Experience

Driving experience is especially important when a car is to be used for competition. Balance and responsiveness relate to driver experience. An experienced driver will likely want a different handling balance compared to an inexperienced driver. An experienced driver will also be able to utilize quicker vehicle response. Often, a newer driver in a responsive car cannot feel the feedback from the car quickly enough. It is possible to slow the response of the vehicle slightly so that a newer driver can keep up with the vehicle.

Project Goal and Expectations

Your goal for a project dictates the approach to creating the appropriate handling package. It is also a time to analyze the performance potential from the project.

Your goal may be to win in an autocross class, but you may have a car that doesn't stand a chance of being competitive. If your goal is to modify a street vehicle to achieve 1.0 g cornering power, with no competition class limitations, the approach is dictated by the type of car. Some cars are easier than others; some are impossible without extensive modifications.

What type of vehicle you start with and where you want to go are major considerations in the process of creating an effective handling package. Price is also dictated by these factors.

As with setting any goal, a good dose of reality makes a project more likely to be completed with the anticipated results.

Compromises

Just what are you willing to sacrifice to reach your desired level of performance? For pure competition, a purpose-built vehicle minimizes compromises, other than those dictated by budget restraints and rules. For dual-purpose vehicles, the compromises usually favor performance over comfort. For the street-only vehicle, compromises are more difficult to make. How much of the time do you drive your car for work, or commuting, compared to pleasure driving? If most of the time spent behind the wheel is for commuting, ride comfort becomes much more important, or will quickly! The important point is to consider the price you pay, not just in dollars, but in comfort for the driver as well as passengers, increased wear and higher maintenance costs.

Budget

It is always a good idea to set a budget before you begin a project. The cost for improved handling can cover a broad range, from $100 for a good alignment to many thousands for wheels, tires and so on. For each of the project vehicles in this book I've included approximate cost to achieve specific levels of handling performance. This will act as a guide to establish a budget for your project.

Coordinated Handling Packages

Hopefully, three important points have become evident from the exploration of these handling goals. First, if you change one item, everything else is affected. Second, it is extremely easy to do more harm than good if all the components and adjustments are not coordinated. Finally, the best components and tires available will improve handling only if they are tuned for the vehicle, the combinations and the conditions. This is important on the street, crucial on the racetrack.

When a professional race team designs a handling package, they follow a specific program of design and development. The first step is to determine the final use of the vehicle. The next steps include computer analysis of the suspension of a given vehicle. Then changes are specified to achieve the predetermined goals. The parts are installed, and the suspension is set up to baseline figures. The package is then skid pad and track tested. Final adjustments are made to achieve the original goals.

The same procedure is used for all types of applications, street and race. Tuning the tires and components on the skid pad and test track yields the largest performance gains. If tire brands, sizes, compounds or even pressures are altered, many of the other suspension settings must be changed to gain maximum traction from the new set-up combination.

To achieve maximum handling performance, careful planning of the project and a fully coordinated component package are required. Then, tuning the tires and components for peak performance integrates all of the elements into the ultimate handling package.

Three Steps to Good Handling

As you delve into this book, keep in mind that there are three phases to good handling. The first requires the right pieces; the second requires tuning the pieces to their maximum potential; the third requires the use of good driving skills, both to extract maximum enjoyment from the improved handling of your vehicle, but also to live up to the potential of the vehicle from a safety point of view.

Improved handling translates into improved safety, but only in the hands of the prudent, considerate driver. It is reasonable that if you improve vehicle performance, you should also improve driving skills to match the vehicle's potential.

Chapter 2

Tires and Traction

The most important aspect of handling is improved traction for the vehicle as a whole. While improved traction is the key, the goal is to increase cornering speed, reduce braking distance and enhance acceleration. The tire is the link to the road and, by itself, is the most important factor in the handling equation. Additionally, everything else you change in the suspension system will ultimately have an effect at the tire contact patch. Thus, understanding the basics of the tire and how it develops traction is paramount to making handling improvements.

Start off by thinking as if you were a rubber molecule at the tire contact patch. The goal of this exercise allows you to understand an important point: what happens at the tire contact patch is all that counts.

When you attempt to increase traction, the only factor that matters is the increase in traction, not what was done to increase traction. The rubber molecules at the tire contact patch do not know how they were made to work harder (nor do they care). They only know that they are now working harder, helping your vehicle brake, accelerate and corner more quickly.

Car manufacturers and tire manufacturers work closely to design compatible components for optimum performance handling packages. Starting in 1986, Porsche worked with Bridgestone to design a tire capable of handling speeds up to 200 mph and still give cornering power exceeding 1.0 g. The result was the Bridgestone RE71 17 in. tire, used as original equipment on the Porsche 959.

Increasing Tire Traction

There are three factors that increase tire traction:

- Increasing the friction between the tire and the road.
- Increasing the number of rubber molecules at the tire contact patch.
- Increasing the vertical load on the tire.

These are rather general statements, requiring further explanation.

Increasing Friction Between Tire and Road

This can occur in two ways. First, the coefficient of friction of the road surface can increase. The coefficient of friction is an arbitrary measurement of grip created by a surface. The higher the coefficient, the greater the grip. Roads of varying materials—such as asphalt, concrete, dirt and so on—and in different states of repair will have different coefficients of friction. This will let the tires grip the road more firmly. We have no control over this, short of choosing specific roads to drive on.

Second, we can increase the coefficient of friction of the tire. This is done by choosing a softer rubber compound tire. The softer rubber molecules will grip the road more firmly, but will also wear more quickly.

Increasing Amount of Rubber at Contact Patch

This can be accomplished in three ways. First, and most obvious, is a wider tire. Second, we can choose a tire with fewer grooves in the tread, thus increasing the area of the tire contact patch. This has obvious flaws on wet, slippery surfaces, however.

Finally, and most importantly, the existing contact patch area can be more efficiently utilized by properly tuning the tires and suspension system so that the maximum number of rubber molecules available are actually working to their fullest potential.

Increasing Vertical Load on Tire

The traction a given tire can generate increases with vertical load on the tire. Vertical load is the combination of vehicle weight resting on the tire contact patch, plus any aerodynamic downforce that may be present. The rubber molecules at the tire contact patch are further pushed into the road surface as the vertical load increases. This allows the rubber molecules to do more work.

Contrary to popular belief, the increase in vertical load does not cause the tire contact patch to grow larger to any significant degree—at least for the modern, low-profile high-performance or racing tire. The traction increase is due to the pressure on the rubber molecules. Try pushing a rubber eraser across a smooth surface. It will slide easily with no downward pressure being applied (vertical load). Now push down on the eraser while sliding it. The effort needed to move the eraser increases. The harder you push down, the more traction the eraser is able to generate.

Vertical load can be increased by adding weight to the vehicle, so that the tire contact patch sees more vertical load. While this will increase traction, the *work* that each rubber molecule at the tire contact patch must do also increases. Cornering speed, braking distances and acceleration will not improve. In fact, performance in these categories will actually deteriorate.

Aerodynamic Downforce

Aerodynamic downforce also increases the vertical load on the tire contact patch. For cars on the street, this is not a factor worth serious consideration, but on any competition vehicle, aerodynamics must be considered. Aerodynamic downforce adds to the vertical load on the tire, but *does not* add to the weight of the vehicle. The tire contact patches are pushed harder into the road surface, thus creating more traction. Since the vehicle weighs the same as before, the tires have no increase in workload, but have a greater capacity to do work (more traction) so the vehicle can corner at a higher rate of speed. Traction for braking and acceleration also increases. This is the reason wings and ground effects bodywork have appeared on race cars over the last twenty-plus years.

Aerodynamic forces increase with the square of speed. In other words, if the vehicle speed is doubled, then the aerodynamic forces are four times greater. This relates to downforce, lift and drag. Aerodynamics have a much greater effect at high speed than at low speed. For production-based race cars and, to a much lesser extent for the street, one of the keys to improved handling is improved aerodynamics. First, it is important to reduce or eliminate aerodynamic lift. Lift reduces the vertical load on the tires, and hence the amount of traction. This is best accomplished by reducing the airflow under the vehicle. Rear spoilers can also reduce lift or even create a small amount of aerodynamic downforce. Reducing aerodynamic drag is the second area for improved aerodynamics.

Vertical Load Effects on Tire Traction

Tire traction increases as vertical load increases. We have already explored how this works, but that is not the entire story. While traction does increase as vertical load increases, it is not a linear relationship. The vertical load increases more quickly than the traction. For example, if we increase the vertical load by 100 percent, traction may increase by only eighty percent. This principle is crucial to fully understand how tire traction works on a vehicle.

Keep this relationship in mind: an increase in vertical load will increase traction, but the traction increase is proportionally smaller than the in-

How Performance Tires Are Designed
By Rick Brennan, Bridgestone Tire
high-performance marketing manager

What makes a tire a performance tire? Many people automatically think about tread design, but there are many more important parts of the equation. One of the most important is compounding.

The rubber compound chosen for use in a tire plays a large part in tire performance levels in terms of durability and mileage, traction, speed rating and handling capabilities of the tire.

The rapid growth of the performance vehicle market in recent years has resulted in an expansion of demands on the performance of the tire. Concentrated research and development efforts toward performance tires have produced great advances in performance capabilities. A major focus of these developments has been rubber compounding.

Compounding

Rubber and plastics are polymers. Rubber consists of macromolecules, or strings of molecules made up of chains of repeating monomers. If you could view rubber molecules through a microscope, they would resemble cooked spaghetti. These long chains of molecules would be intertwined like strings of spaghetti lying on a plate. To strengthen these strings of molecules, chemical bonds between each string are made. This is accomplished by adding sulfur and producing a chemical reaction through the addition of heat.

The most noticeable tire characteristic to the driver which can be attributed to rubber is the tire's grip on the road surface. Unfortunately, tires must operate on a wide variety of surfaces under a wide variety of conditions, from smooth roads, to rough roads, to no roads, and through heat, rain and snow.

Ten years ago, tires had to be either all-season or high-performance. They could not be both. This was largely due to the way rubber reacts to temperature. As the temperature goes down, rubber tends to stiffen and harden, reducing its traction-producing capability. Compounds were designed to work in the cold, but then could not stand up to running in the heat. Thus, two separate tires were made.

New construction techniques and rubber compounding technology are chipping away at the limitations of the past.

For instance, Bridgestone has developed technology which enables us to put two separate rubber compounds in the cap-and-base tread construction. The rubber compound on the bottom, just on top of the tire casing, is formulated to resist generating heat. The rubber on top of the base rubber, or cap rubber, is what touches the road. This cap compound is softer than the base rubber, thereby creating a better grip on the road.

Cap-and-base tread construction has made it possible to build tires which have competent bad-weather traction, like the Bridgestone Potenza RE71 in the rain or the Potenza HP41 in the snow, and still give great dry grip and handling when it's nice and sunny.

By varying the amount of base rubber to cap rubber, or vice versa, and by using different compounds, tires can now be better tailored to the needs and wants of the high-performance car owner.

Tread Design

The same can be said about tread design. For instance, the new continuous center rib pattern on the Potenza RE71 is specifically designed to reduce noise. The previous RE71 tread pattern had segmented blocks in the center tread rows. As each block came into contact with the road surface, it generated an impact noise like tiny footsteps.

By replacing these segmented blocks with a solid rib, the center of the tire runs on a smooth surface, virtually eliminating the impact noise of the previous pattern, resulting in a more quiet, smoother ride.

Another new arrival on the tread pattern scene is the unidirectional design. This pattern offers maximum water drainage without sacrificing dry handling and grip. The design allows for the use of large outside shoulder blocks necessary to generate high cornering forces, while the angled grooves across the tread act like a water pump, pushing the water from under the tire's contact patch. With the unidirectional design, you no longer have to tip-toe through the rain on your way home from the racetrack.

Something extremely new in the industry is the asymmetrical tread pattern. This design generally has extremely large ribs of rubber on the outside shoulders of the tire, with smaller ribs on the inside of the tread. These large outside ribs greatly stiffen the tread where the highest lateral load is concentrated during cornering, offering maximum cornering effectiveness. Asymmetrical patterns in use today enhance dry handling, but may not offer the wet traction efficiency of unidirectional patterns.

The Informed Consumer

Are you interested in a smoother ride on your Porsche? Do you want your ZR-1 to have ultimate handling in dry weather, with little concern for snowy roads? You should know the answers to these and similar questions when it's time to shod your performance car with new rubber.

With the recent advances in compounding and tread design, there is, without question, a tire that is perfectly suited for your vehicle and driving conditions.

There are still trade-offs, of course. There is no one tire that performs best in the dry and wet and provides ultimate durability at high speeds. But high-performance and all-season are no longer mutually exclusive terms. It all depends on what you desire as the driver; and no one knows that better than yourself.

crease in vertical load. If the load increase is due to aerodynamic downforce, the work that the rubber molecules at the tire contact patch must perform is reduced for a given cornering force (lateral acceleration). Since the capacity for work done by the rubber molecules is the same as before, the cornering force (lateral acceleration) can be increased.

In the same way, increasing vertical load on a tire contact patch by adding weight to the vehicle will increase the traction available. But here is the big-time glitch. Remember, the traction increase is proportionally smaller than the weight increase. Since the work required of the tire contact patches is increasing at a rate proportional to the weight increase, but traction is increasing at a *slower* rate, the lateral acceleration or cornering speed of the now heavier vehicle is *less*. The extra weight also hurts acceleration and braking performance. This fact is why Trans-Am teams yell and scream over a 50 lb. weight increase. It might appear that 50 lb. in a 2,200 lb. car with 600 hp is insignificant, but it is incredibly important.

For any 2,200 lb. car capable of cornering at a lateral acceleration of 1.0 g, the addition of 50 lb. to the total weight of the vehicle would reduce the lateral acceleration (cornering force) to 0.984 g. On a 200 ft. diameter skid pad, the time needed to negotiate one lap at 1.0 g is 11.04 seconds. The time needed to negotiate one lap at 0.984 g is 11.16 seconds, a one-percent increase in lap times. Since about forty percent of a lap is spent cornering at the limit, for a lap time of 1 minute, 30 seconds for the example car at 1.0 g, 36 seconds is spent cornering at the limit. For the car with fifty extra pounds of weight added, the time spent cornering at the limit would increase to 36.36 seconds. This does not take into account the effect on braking performance and acceleration, which would be about the same loss in time. Top speed is the only factor not affected by the weight increase. So the 50 lb. costs about 0.75 second per lap in this example. In racing terms, that is an eternity.

One factor that helps to explain this phenomenon is the relationship between vertical load on the tire and the coefficient of friction of the tire. The coefficient of friction tells us the relative amount of grip that a tire (in our case) is capable of generating. As vertical load increases, the coefficient of friction decreases. This is a relatively minor loss in grip, more than offset by the increase in grip as load increases. It is, however, one factor that explains why the total traction increase with increasing load is not a linear relationship.

Tire Slip Angle

The pneumatic tire is a marvelous invention. Its characteristics have allowed phenomenal performance from the automobile. One of the characteristics of a tire is the twist in the carcass of the tire

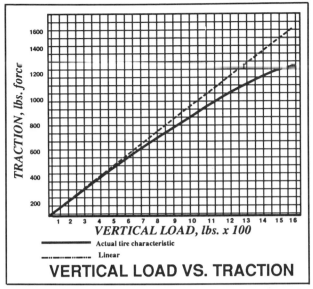

VERTICAL LOAD VS. TRACTION

The traction of a tire increases as the vertical load on the tire increases. In this graph, the dotted line shows a linear relationship between vertical load and traction. If this relationship was the actual relationship, then weight transfer during cornering, braking and acceleration would be of little consequence. However, the actual tire characteristics are represented by the solid line, and this graph shows that the relationship is not linear. Traction increases with load, but at a slower rate. This affects total vehicle traction during cornering, braking and acceleration, reducing the total amount of traction available. This tire characteristic is the most important to understand when tuning the suspension of a car.

when it corners. A tire does not have to be rotated by the steering for this twist to occur. When a vehicle is steered, all four tires experience this twist in the carcass. Slip angle is the technical name for this.

When a tire is rolling in a straight line, the rubber molecules at the tire contact patch trail one in front of the other as the tire rotates. In a left turn, for example, each molecule, as it reaches the leading edge of the tire contact patch and begins to touch the road surface, moves farther to the left than the previous molecule. As the molecule moves farther to the rear of the contact patch (as the tire rolls forward), it scribes an arc to the left. If you could trace the path of a single molecule as it moved across the road surface, it would make a smooth arc approximating the arc of the vehicle through the turn. It is like placing your right foot slightly ahead and to the left of your left foot as you walk; the feet point forward, but you "steer" to the left. At the tire contact patch, this movement to the left is caused by the twist in the tire between the tire contact patch and the tire sidewall.

The tire sidewall is then pointing in a different direction than the molecules at the tire contact patch. The top of the sidewall, where the wheel rim

Ferrari's F40 used Pirelli P Zero tires that were specially designed for the car by Pirelli.

meets the tire bead, is one point of measurement. The other point of reference is the instantaneous path of the rubber molecule at the tire contact patch. The difference in direction between the reference points, measured in degrees, is the slip angle. The wheel always points farther into the turn than the tire contact patch. This is true at both ends of the car.

Tire Slip Angle and Cornering Force

When a vehicle is steered into a turn by the driver, the wheel begins to turn first. The steering force is then transmitted to the tire sidewalls of the front tires. The force, which begins twisting the sidewall, moves to the tire contact patch and the vehicle begins to change direction. As soon as the steering force reaches the wheel, the twisting motion begins on the front tire sidewalls. The front of the vehicle begins to change direction. The vehicle then develops a yaw angle, which allows the rear tires to experience a load on the tire contact patch, with the same twisting force as at the front tires. The rear tires then develop a slip angle and follow the front tires through a turn. The yaw angle of the car is approximately the same as the slip angle of the tires.

At low cornering forces, the slip angles are small. As cornering forces increase, so does the slip angle. Maximum cornering force – the limit of the tire – is reached at a given slip angle. If the slip angle is forced to increase beyond that point (more cornering speed or more steering lock applied by the driver), the cornering force reduces and the tire will begin to slide.

Understeer and Oversteer

If the tires begin to slide at one end of the car before the other, the handling balance is out of whack. The front and rear slip angles are different, and want to follow different paths along the road. When the front slip angles are larger, the vehicle will push or understeer. When the rear slip angles are larger, the vehicle is loose or oversteers. If both front and rear slip angles are equal, the car handling is neutral, and perfect balance has been achieved. When a car understeers, the path of the rubber molecules at the front is a larger radius than the path of the rubber molecules at the rear; the opposite is true for oversteer.

When a vehicle oversteers, the rear of the car will slide out when the limit of adhesion is reached (maximum cornering force). The car will try to continue in a straight (or straighter) line if understeer is encountered.

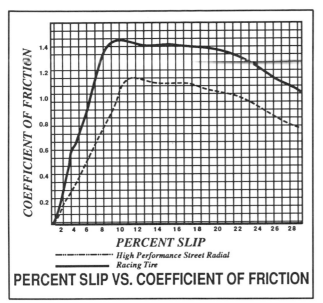

PERCENT SLIP VS. COEFFICIENT OF FRICTION

--------- High Performance Street Radial
———— Racing Tire

Percent slip is the amount of slippage between the tire contact patch and the ground during straightline acceleration and braking. One hundred-percent slip would be wheel lock-up during braking. The graph shows that maximum coefficient of friction (which is proportional to traction) occurs at some percent of slippage, usually about ten percent. More or less slippage means less traction.

Percent Slip of a Tire

We have looked at tire slip angle and how it relates to cornering force. Percent slip of a tire relates to straight-line traction while accelerating and braking in the same way that slip angle relates to cornering. Maximum traction, and therefore maximum braking force or acceleration, is directly related to the amount of slip at the tire contact patch and road surface interface during braking and acceleration. Zero percent slip means that the vehicle travels the distance of exactly one tire circumference for every revolution of the tire. One hundred percent slip means that the vehicle travels no distance for every revolution of the tire (massive wheel spin during acceleration, probably on ice), or the vehicle travels any distance without wheel rotation (wheel lock-up under braking).

Maximum traction occurs at around five to ten percent slip for most tires, meaning that for every 100 in. the vehicle travels under braking, the tire rotation is equal to only 90 to 95 in. of travel. The tire contact patch actually slides for 5 to 10 in., not in one spot, but equally over the 100 in. of travel. Beyond about ten percent slip, traction diminishes, and acceleration or deceleration rates deteriorate.

Tire Contact Patch Area

How large should the area of each tire contact patch be? This is an important question. The initial

A small amount of wheelspin will allow for maximum coefficient of friction during straightline acceleration.

obvious answer is: as large as possible! But that is not true. Yes, we want a large tire contact patch, but if it is too large for a given car, rolling resistance increases, and may negate any performance improvements added by traction gains. Additionally, as a tire increases in tread width, it becomes more difficult to keep the tire contact patch flat on the ground when it is most needed.

A basic rule of thumb is that as engine horsepower increases, the need for larger contact patches also increases. A corollary to this is: If the tires fit in the stock fender wells without rubbing during suspension travel or body roll, then the tire is probably not too large.

Traction Circle

One of the interesting aspects of tire traction is that the rubber molecules at the tire contact patch do not care what direction they are working in. The forces can come from any direction, or more than one direction at a time. The tire will generate a specific amount of traction before it begins to slide across the track surface. Traction can be 100 percent from the side or 100 percent rearward or any combination of the two.

In the case of a tire, the rubber molecules at the tire contact patch do not care in which direction they generate a force. They can do only so much work, and the direction does not matter. The total amount of work done by the rubber molecules at the tire contact patches is represented by the radius of the circle on the traction circle diagram. The resultant force is the maximum work done by the tires, and is represented by any line from the center of the circle to the circumference. If the radius of the line is shorter than the radius of the circle, the tires could do more work. In other

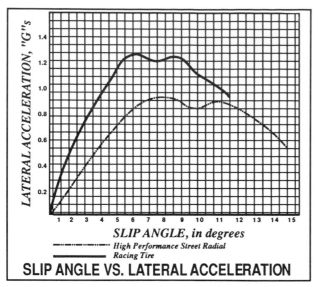

SLIP ANGLE VS. LATERAL ACCELERATION

Lateral acceleration, which is proportional to traction, increases as the tire slip angle increases up to a point, then diminishes. The characteristic is the same for all tires; only the shape of the curve and the peak lateral acceleration will change. Low-profile tires will have peak cornering force at lower slip angles. Higher tire pressures will also cause the peak cornering force to occur at lower slip angles. In both cases the tire sidewalk is stiffer, allowing operation at smaller tire slip angles. The slope of the curve tells us how responsive the tire is, with steeper curves meaning more response. The flatness of the curve at the top tell us if a tire is forgiving. In the above example, the high-performance street tire generates peak cornering force at a higher slip angle for a longer period of time than the racing tire. It is easier to drive on the street at the limit, because it will not break away as quickly as the racing tire. Another important consideration in this graph is the slip angle where the peak cornering force occurs. Using the racing tire as an example, peak cornering force occurs at 6 degrees slip. Near peak cornering force is maintained up to 9 degrees slip. While cornering force will be relatively consistent through this range, it is best if the driver can maintain peak cornering force at 6 degrees slip instead of a higher number. Why? Heat build-up in the tires is the key. Driving at the higher slip angle causes more heat in the tires. In a race car, this is crucial. Drivers often complain of the tires going off, and overheating the tire is often the cause of this. Overheating is not a problem for highway driving. In some cases, like autocrossing where run time is short, operating at high slip angles may build heat in the tires more quickly, increasing traction.

words, the car is not at the limit of traction. However, the tires are not capable of doing more work than shown by the circle, so the length of the line cannot exceed the circumference of the circle. In reality, the tire can create slightly more traction in the longitudinal direction than in the lateral, or cornering, direction. This would make the circle an ellipse rather than a true circle, with a longer radius in the acceleration and braking directions.

If the force line is along the horizontal axis of the circle, all of the tires' traction is used for cornering. If the line is along the vertical axis, all of the tires' traction is used for straight-line traction as in braking or acceleration. If the force line is not on one of the axes, then we have two forces at work, and can break down the component forces along the vertical and horizontal axes.

In the traction circle diagram, the numbers represent forces in g. The circumference of the circle represents the theoretical limit of traction for a given set of tires. Any data point not on the vertical or horizontal axis indicates a combination of forces acting in more than one direction relative to the car. In this vector diagram of one point on the traction circle, the vehicle is turning left and braking at the same time. The limit of traction is 1.20 g in any direction. The vehicle is neither cornering nor braking at the limit, but is doing both at the same time at a rate of 0.81 g, or seventy-one percent of the maximum of each. By combining functions, the tire's total tractive capacity is being utilized. The same principle applies to acceleration while exiting a turn.

Handling Horsepower

Everyone knows that more horsepower means more performance. When an engine creates more power, it accelerates the car faster. Tires create "handling horsepower" in a similar way. Larger tire contact patch areas are the equivalent of increased engine power; softer rubber compounds are like changing camshafts; aerodynamic downforce is like adding a turbocharger or supercharger.

Each molecule for a given rubber compound is capable of doing a certain amount of work for a given vertical load. For cornering, the work the rubber molecule must perform is to carry a given weight around a turn at a given speed. When a vehicle is driven around a corner as fast as possible (at the limit), each molecule at the tire contact patch is working to its maximum. To increase cornering speed, we can either increase the vertical load on the tire (but not increase the weight on the tire since it then has more work to accomplish), or we can increase the number of rubber molecules doing the work (larger tire contact patch area).

To state this more scientifically, the cornering speed of a vehicle around a given radius turn is proportional to the total tire contact patch area of the vehicle divided by the total weight of the vehicle. We can decrease the weight of the vehicle, which allows an increase in cornering speed. We can increase the tire contact patch area, which also allows an increase in cornering speed. While these statements always hold true, two glitches muddy the waters slightly.

The first is getting *all* of the rubber molecules in the tire contact patch working. This is the classic management (driver, test engineer and so on) versus union (the United Rubber Molecules, we will call them) conflict. The second is getting the front URM workers to go on strike at the same time the rear URM workers decide to leave the job. The old balancing act rears It ugly head again. Most of our development time is spent managing rubber molecules. Consequently, we will spend considerable time exploring the methods of rubber molecule management within these pages.

So, if you want more handling horsepower, either use a softer compound tire, grow wings or buy more rubber molecules. Just be prepared! They take considerable time to keep under control.

Front Versus Rear Tire Contact Patch Area

There is a way to determine how large the front tire contact patch area should be relative to the rear tire contact patch area. Begin by asking, How much work do the front tire contact patches perform compared to the work done by the rear tire contact patches? That is difficult to say, but let's start with cornering.

If a car has perfect fifty-fifty front-to-rear weight distribution, then in a steady state turn (no change in cornering speed) the workload is equally split between front and rear tires. If we look at deceleration, the front tires do more work than the rear because weight will transfer from the rear tires to the front tires under braking. How much weight transfers depends on a number of factors we will explore later. During straight-line acceleration, the opposite is true. Weight will transfer to the rear. If the drive wheels are at the rear, then the rear tire contact patches will do more work during acceleration. So, if we have a rear-drive car with fifty-fifty weight distribution and not much horsepower, the total work (that is, work performed while cornering, braking and accelerating) is about equal front and rear.

If you surmised that the front tire contact patch area should equal the rear tire contact patch area in this example, you are correct. In theory, the contact patch area of a tire should be proportional to the total amount of work done by that tire. If the front tires do sixty percent of the work, then they should have sixty percent of the total tire contact patch area, or thirty percent on each front tire.

But wait, you say! Almost all cars come with the same size tire front and rear, but few have fifty-fifty weight distribution. In fact, most cars are front heavy. And wouldn't a front-wheel-drive car have even more work performed by the front tires because they drive the car? Right again! So why don't most cars have larger tires in the front? Two reasons. First is convenience, both for the manufacturer and for the consumer. Who wants to carry two different-sized spares? Second, it would look kind of dumb. Besides, with the rear tire contact patch area proportionately larger than necessary, this car would never oversteer. It would have a ba-

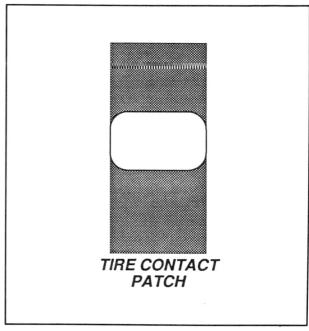

TIRE CONTACT PATCH

The area of the tire contact patch is one factor that determines the handling horsepower of a car. The area of the contact patch should be proportional to the load on the tire. If the load at the front is equal to the load at the rear, then the contact patch areas should also be equal to each other. If they are not, then the end of the car with larger tire contact patches will have more traction capability than the other end, and handling balance will be affected.

sic understeer tendency, which offers improved stability and increased safety margins for the average driver.

Let's look at the technical reason for this. If the front tires carry more load, so that while cornering they are doing more work, they will operate at a higher slip angle for a given cornering speed. This means the front tire slip angles exceed those at the rear, and understeer occurs.

When a designer begins to create a purpose-built race car, the known parameters are outlined. Many of these stem from class rules for tire size, rim width, minimum weight, expected horsepower, track width and so forth. Combined with some educated guesswork, the designer can estimate the workload on each tire contact patch. The approximate tire contact patch area for the front and rear tires can be specified. Then it is matter of testing to fine-tune everything, hopefully, or to return to the drawing board (or more likely a CAD/CAM computer program).

This method applies to all race cars. If a car generates aerodynamic downforce, the estimated aerodynamic load on each tire is calculated for a range of speeds, and the tire contact patch sizes are planned accordingly. Obviously, the design parameters for a production car are very different.

Compare the outside front tires in these photos: the tires in the first photo show little sidewall rollover during limit cornering; the tires in the second photo are rolling over severely. Same car, same driver, same day. The difference is about 10 psi lower pressure in the second photo. The reduction in pressure causes a loss in side-wall rigidity and a substantial reduction in cornering power. The reduction in rigidity allows for a smoother ride. For hard driving, the tire can be inflated to optimum pressure for maximum traction and reduced for more sedate highway driving. Never exceed the mini-mum or maximum pressure recommended by the tire manufacturer. And don't try to drive hard on an underin-flated tire, at least if you wish to stay on the road. Bob Ryder

The only difference in the car in these two photos is the front tire pressure: the car on the left has optimum tire pressure. Note that the steering angle is less for the same radius turn. The car on the right has the front tires underinflated by about 10 psi. Note the tire sidewall roll-over and the increased steering angle needed to negoti-ate the same radius turn. The lower tire pressure also causes more body roll.

Effect of Tire Pressure on Traction

The pressure in a tire has a big effect on tire traction. The pressure doesn't really affect the grip of each rubber molecule, but it certainly can affect how many of the molecules at the tire contact patch are in contact with the ground. A specific tire on a given car with a given load will have only one correct tire pressure. In practice it is a narrow range of pressure, within about 3 pounds per square inch (psi). If the tire pressure is outside this range, the tire contact patch is deformed and not fully contacting the road surface. In other words, fewer than the possible number of rubber molecules are in contact with the surface of the road.

If the tire is overinflated, the edges of the tire will lose contact with the surface, and traction is reduced. Fewer rubber molecules are carrying the same load, so the tire will operate at a higher slip angle for a given cornering force, and the maximum cornering force will be lower. If the tire is underinflated, the center of the tire contact patch will not maintain optimum contact with the road surface, and again, fewer rubber molecules than possible will be doing the same work, resulting in higher slip angles for the same load and reduced cornering power.

Many autocrossers will chalk their tires to see if they are getting sidewall rollover. If the chalk wears off the tire in the shoulder area where the tread and sidewall meet, then the tire is rolling over onto the sidewall. If this occurs, the solution to the problem is to increase tire pressure until the rollover ceases. While increasing tire pressure will reduce or eliminate tire rollover, it is unlikely that the problem is being solved. The real reasons for the rollover usually do not relate to tire pressure. Wheel width and camber are usually the real causes.

High-performance tires are denoted by their series or aspect ratio, which compares the tire's section height to its section width. While most street cars come stock with 70 or 80 series tires, low-profile, wide tires will have a lower series number. This Pirelli P Zero tire is a 245/45ZR16: divide the section height of 4.3 in. by the section width of 9.5 in. to obtain 0.45, which is the aspect ratio, translated as a 45 series tire.

The 45 series tires on the Mustang show little sidewall flex, while the 60 series tires on the Corolla show considerably more flex. Less flex translates into quicker response to steering inputs and improved traction, although less negative camber is required to keep the tire contact patch on the ground in the turns. The price one pays for the quicker response rate of the 45 series tires is a harsher ride. The short, stiff sidewalls of the 45 series tires do not absorb bumps as well as the 60 series tires.
Bob McClurg

Study the Yokohama A-008R-TU tires on the Corolla GT-S and you can actually see deformity in the sidewall near the tire contact patch. This slight twist in the sidewall is caused by the slip angle of the tire. The Corolla is cornering near 1.0 g, and the handling balance is nearly neutral. The front and rear slip angles are virtually identical, as shown by the amount of twist in the sidewall. These 60 series tires show more twist in the sidewall than a 50 series tire would, even at the same cornering force and slip angle.

Tire Aspect Ratio and Traction

The aspect ratio of a tire is the percentage of section height (the sidewall) compared to the section (tread) width. If the tread width is 10 in. and the sidewall section height is 5 in. the aspect ratio is 50.

The aspect ratio has little direct effect on traction. The aspect ratio does affect the slip angle, however. A lower profile tire (lower aspect ratio) is usually stiffer, and operates at a lower slip angle for the same load and cornering force. Assuming the tire contact patch size stays the same, the lower aspect ratio tire will operate at a lower slip angle under the same load and cornering conditions. This will affect handling balance if the aspect ratio is changed at only one end of the vehicle.

Tire Camber and Traction

One of the most important suspension settings is camber, or the inclination of the wheel and tire from vertical. Camber is measured in degrees from vertical, with zero camber occurring when the tire is perpendicular to the ground. Negative camber occurs when the top of the tire tilts toward the center of the vehicle; positive camber occurs when the top of the tire tilts away from the center of the vehicle.

The first question to ask is, what camber angle

While this photo shows a BFGoodrich Comp T/A R-1 tire at rest, the slight amount of negative camber seen here is actually the amount of negative camber that is ideal in the dynamic cornering state. Radial ply tires generate more cornering force with a slight amount of negative camber while cornering. This will show when tire temperatures are taken: the inside tire temperature should be 5 to 7 degrees Fahrenheit hotter than the outside temperature after a skid pad test.

will keep all of the rubber molecules working the hardest? The obvious answer is zero camber. When we need the tires to work, we want the maximum number of rubber molecules in contact with the road surface. For braking, we want all four tire contact patches flat on the road surface; for acceleration, we want the tire contact patches of the drive wheels flat; for cornering we want all four (but especially the two outside) tire contact patches flat on the road. Anything other than zero camber will reduce the effective size of the tire contact patch area and change the loading on each of the rubber molecules at the tire contact patch.

Some molecules will have greater loads, some less. The ones with more load have more work to do, but the rubber molecules' capacity for more traction does not keep up with their increased workload, hence, less traction. This is the single most important area for tuning the suspension to improve handling power.

We have been talking about camber angles in

This Stock class IROC-Z Camaro needs more negative camber or less body roll at the front to keep from running at the positive camber angle shown.

The correct rim width and offset for a given application is crucial for optimum handling. The widest rim for a given tire size will help maintain a good footprint during cornering. If the rim is too narrow, the tire contact patch will crown, and the tire will try to roll over to the outside; tire temperatures will read as if the car needs more negative camber. Wheel offset is important for clearance, but even more important for optimum track width and scrub radius. Large offsets can increase track width, but can also cause large scrub radiuses. The scrub radius is the distance from the center of the tire contact patch to the point where the steering axis intersects the tire contact patch when viewed from the front of the vehicle. A large scrub radius will increase steering effort and cause the tire to scrub in a turn, which will increase drag and reduce cornering power. A small scrub radius is beneficial as it gives important feedback through the steering to the driver, and it contributes to the self-centering effect of the steering, called aligning torque.

the dynamic state, that is, when we need traction during cornering, braking and accelerating. The other state is called static. The static settings—for instance, when the vehicle is at rest—affect the dynamic settings, but in themselves are not very important. Also, the optimal dynamic camber for different functions is slightly different. For braking and accelerating, zero camber is ideal. For cornering, however, a small (⅛ to ¼ degree) amount of negative dynamic camber actually increases cornering force. The differing needs of straight-line performance and cornering make the set-up job even more difficult. The real problem, however, is controlling camber change during suspension travel and body roll. This problem will receive more scrutiny in the suspension chapter.

Wheel Size and Tire Traction

The diameter of the wheel has no direct effect on traction, but it can change the tire contact patch area size if a lower aspect ratio tire is used on a larger diameter rim, with the overall tire rolling radius remaining constant. This will also affect ride and responsiveness.

The width of a wheel, however, can have a major effect on traction. If the rim is too wide for a given tire, the bead will not seat properly. This can also happen if the wheel is too narrow. All tire manufacturers specify a range of rim widths for every tire. It is crucial to stay within this range for safety reasons.

But what effect does the width of the rim have on the tire contact patch? The rim width will affect the contour of the tire tread, and therefore affect the shape of the tire contact patch. If the rim is too narrow, the tire tread will bow out, and less than the maximum tire contact patch area will meet the road surface. It is unlikely to have a rim too wide within the specified range of rim widths for a given tire size.

After considerable testing, we have found that it is best on most tires to use the widest rim width recommended by the manufacturer for a specific tire. This will optimize the tire contact patch area for that tire, and allow the highest cornering force

Selecting Tires and Wheels

Tires

Just what are the important parameters for selecting the best tires and wheels for your purpose? That can be a tough call, especially considering the vast numbers of products to choose from. Here are some simple guidelines to assist in the process.

The first step is to determine *how* your car is to be used—or more specifically, how the wheel and tires are to be used. If the car is driven for your daily commute, wear may be a major consideration. The ultra-high-performance tires have plenty of grip, but wear rapidly when used for daily driving. And the minimal tread pattern on these ranges of tire is less than desirable for wet conditions. Forget mud and snow.

If you drive in wet weather but not in a four-season environment, one of the three-season tires is a good bet and excellent compromise between wet traction and dry grip. They usually look more high-performance, as well. If snow and mud are in your driving picture, select an all-season tire rated for snow and mud use.

A final factor, but one that is usually high on the priority list when making a purchase, is cost. All high-performance tires are expensive; some are just more expensive. Good prices are available in many instances, but use discretion as you often get what you pay for. Remember that tires are your link to the road and a lot rides on them. There are better places to save money on your project car than with your tires.

Wheels

Wheels are another story altogether. First, the wheel must be compatible with the tire. When selecting wheel width, be sure to use the widest wheel (within ½ in. narrower) that the tire calls for.

The aspect ratio is an important part of the tire selection process. The shorter tire has a lower aspect ratio, a shorter diameter but the same tread width. Dan Sanchez

Rim width and offset are two important parameters of wheel selection. The offset is measured by subtracting half the rim width from the back space measurement (as shown, from the hub face to the edge of the rim). If the backspace measurement is greater, then the rim is inset. If they are equal, the offset is zero. Dan Sanchez

This improves the tire contact patch interface with the road and gives you more bite for the buck.

Second, the offset must be correct and for two reasons. The obvious one is tire clearance in the wheelwell. The second is steering geometry and wheel bearing wear. Large wheel offset can cause changes to the steering geometry (castor offset), which causes tire wear, drag and heavy steering effort. Extreme wheel offset will place high radial loadings on the wheel bearings, which can increase wear and even cause failure.

When increasing tire and wheel size, great care must be taken to be sure that there are no clearance problems. Wheels and tires that rub in the wheelwells can be a major hassle, one best avoided. Many aftermarket suppliers can help answer your questions concerning clearance if the answers cannot be found in the wheel manufacturer's catalog.

Wheel price is usually related to weight and construction methods. Weight is everything in competition, so be prepared to spend big bucks. If you invest in a set of competition wheels, pop for a spare set of rims (or use the stock rims) for your daily driving if you have a dual-purpose car. Racing wheels are fragile in some respects, especially to curb, rut and bad weather contact.

For the street, weight is not a major consideration, but materials and construction are. Cheap wheels are mass produced and use inferior materials. In normal driving, stress on the wheel is usually in the rim section from hitting bumps. Most wheels are beefy in this section, but if you drive hard, as in corners, braking and launch starts, stress is placed in different areas of the wheel, such as the lug holes and hub face. If these areas are weak, wheel failure is a likely possibility. And they usually happen at inopportune times.

Tire and wheel clearance are crucial for safety and sanity. If you're not certain, ask a pro at an aftermarket wheel and tire shop for advice. If you're not going to buy from him, offer to pay for his time; he probably saved you a bundle. Dan Sanchez

A coordinated wheel and tire package can enhance the look of your car and improve the handling considerably. This package for the Geo Storm project features American Racing wheels and Bridgestone Potenza RE-71 ultra-high-performance tires. Dan Sanchez

The front-wheel-drive Volkswagen Jetta in stock trim shows considerable deflection in the tire contact patch. Note, however, that the tire contact patch is relatively flat on the road surface even though there is considerable positive camber caused by body roll. While the contact patch is relatively flat on the surface, the outside edge of the tire is loaded much more than the inside edge. This will show in the tire temperatures: the outside temperature will exceed the inside temperature by 20 to 30 degrees Fahrenheit. Ideally, the temperatures should be nearly equal across the surface of the tread, with the inside slightly hotter than the outside for maximum traction.

for that tire. Narrower rims tend to crown the tire too much, hence reducing the contact patch area.

Let's look at the problem from the other side. If you are limited to a maximum rim width because of rules, budget and other factors, then it is usually best to use the smallest-diameter tire that will fit on the rim. In most, but not all, cases, the smaller tire will have a larger tire contact patch area. This will increase cornering force, improve tread wear and allow better suspension settings for overall performance.

We have found that most brands of tires respond in this fashion. However, some tires, due mostly to stiffer sidewall construction, are less sensitive to rim width differences within the manufacturer's specified range. Since high-performance tire manufacturers are constantly changing designs and compounds, it is probably reasonable to follow this rule of thumb.

Rubber Compound and Tire Traction

The compound of the rubber on the tread of a tire makes a large difference in the traction capability of the tire. If the compound is softer, the coefficient of friction is higher and each rubber molecule at the tire contact patch can generate more grip. Overall tire traction will increase, but only if the tire does not overheat.

A softer compound tire will also wear more

quickly. In racing, selecting the compound that offers the best grip without overheating, and the best wear characteristics, is one of the true art forms in the sport. For the autocrosser, the softest compound available is usually the fastest, but will wear quickly on the street. For those racing on DOT street tires, often only one compound is available. The tire engineers have made good compromises between grip and tread wear.

The compound of the tire must be compatible with the load carried by the tire and the heat and wear characteristics for a given event. If the right choice is made, the tire will operate in its optimum temperature range without overheating, blistering or wearing out during the course of an event (or between pit stops, as the case may be).

For street driving, harder compounds are needed both for sustained highway driving and for longer tread life. For the dual-purpose vehicle, two sets of wheels and tires will save considerable funds over the long haul. One set is used only for competition, the other, harder compound set for street driving.

Tire Temperatures

All racing and high-performance street tires are designed to operate within an optimum temperature range when driving near or at the limits of the vehicle. If the tire temperature is too low, the coefficient of friction will be too low and maximum traction will not be achieved. If the tire tread is too hot, traction will again be lost, and the tire will wear more quickly, with possible blistering or chunking. Neither is an ideal situation. There are a number of factors that contribute to the operating temperature of a tire.

- Rubber compound.
- Lateral and longitudinal forces, that is, how hard the vehicle is being driven.
- Tire pressure.
- Vertical load on the tire.
- Tire slip angle.
- Contact patch size.
- Weight of the tire.
- Unsprung weight on the tire.

The best tool we have for optimizing suspension set-up, handling balance and tire performance is to measure the tire temperature. Tire temperatures give you much information about the tire and set-up of the vehicle, telling you:

- If the car is being driven to the limit by the driver.
- If the compound of the tread is overheating.
- If the handling balance (roll couple distribution) is correct, and if not, which end of the vehicle is likely to be overloaded.
- If the tire pressures are correct.
- If the static camber is correctly set for optimum dynamic camber while cornering.
- If toe-in or toe-out settings are excessive.

• If the rim width is too narrow for the tire section width and sidewall construction.

The collection of pertinent data, as well as the interpretation of this information, will be covered in detail in the tuning chapter.

One important factor concerning racing tires is that they must be designed for a specific car application. If they are not, the chances are that they will never operate within their optimum temperature range. If the correct tires are being run on a given car, and temperatures are too low all around, it is most likely that the car is not being driven to the limits of adhesion (unless the ambient air temperature is extremely low). If the temperatures are out of the optimum range at one end of the car only, the problem lies with the vertical load on the tires at that end of the car.

Most high-performance tires and race tires are designed to operate in the 180 to 230 degree Fahrenheit temperature range as measured in the pits after hot laps or runs. Every tire is slightly different, and for competition purposes, an engineer from the tire manufacturer should be consulted concerning the optimum temperature range for a given vehicle, track and ambient temperature combination. As a point of interest, the actual temperatures of a heavily loaded tire while cornering in a high-speed turn can exceed 350 degrees Fahrenheit.

Tire Slip Angle and Tire Temperature

Most anyone who has raced or attended races has heard a driver complain after the completion of an event that "My tires went off after ten laps." This statement is most often made by the driver who finished second, third or fourth. The tires probably did go off, but if the driver making this statement understood what was being said about his own driving skills by uttering such words, he would probably keep his mouth shut.

Earlier in this chapter, slip angles were discussed. As the slip angle increases, so does lateral acceleration or cornering force, until the limit of adhesion is reached. Then cornering force tapers off. Let's discuss further the slip angle versus lateral acceleration graph. The slope of the graph tells us how responsive a tire is. The steeper the slope, the quicker the response rate. If the response rate is too quick, the driver cannot "feel" the tire as lateral acceleration builds. If the response rate is too slow, the vehicle feels sluggish and slow to steering inputs.

Now let's look at the top portion of the graph, where the limit of adhesion is being approached. If the graph slope was very steep, came to a point and dropped down as quickly, the driver would find it impossible to drive this vehicle near the limits of adhesion. As soon as the limit was reached, any additional slip angle applied to the tire would cause instant loss of traction. It would

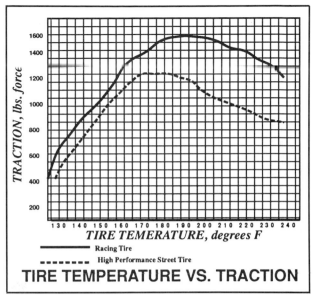

TIRE TEMPERATURE VS. TRACTION

—————— Racing Tire
- - - - - - High Performance Street Tire

As tire temperature increases, so does lateral acceleration, up to the point where the tires overheat. Then traction is reduced and so is cornering force. This chart offers clues about driving styles when compared to the lateral acceleration versus slip angle chart. Keeping the tires in the optimum temperature range is important for peak performance.

be almost impossible to keep such a car at the cornering limit. Fortunately, the characteristics of the pneumatic tire are much more subtle than this. The curve begins to flatten as peak cornering force is reached. Once peak force is reached, the curve stays relatively flat for some range of slip angle before cornering force tapers off. This tire shows forgiving handling characteristics. The limit is approached more slowly, and maximum lateral acceleration is maintained over a fairly wide range of increasing slip angle.

The basic shape of this curve is virtually the same for all tires, although the slope of the curve may vary, the slip angle range may shift to the left or right and the peak cornering force may be higher or lower.

Getting back to the hypothetical driver who cooked the tires after ten laps, look at the top portion of the graph. Maximum cornering force occurs over a range of about 5 degrees of slip. The lateral acceleration changes little over this 5 degree range. Do you think there is a difference in cornering speed between 7 and 12 degrees slip angle? Almost none! What do you think might happen to the tires of the driver who consistently drives at 12 degrees after, say, ten laps? The tires are going to overheat! Then they are going to lose grip. Then the car will drop back. Then the driver will bitch about the tires.

The rubber molecules at the tire contact patch are the ones with the real complaint. The driver in

33

victory lane, who maintained about 7 to 8 degrees of slip angle throughout the race, is smiling while he thanks the manufacturer for making such wonderful tires — even though the tire manufacturer probably made wonderful tires for everyone in the race.

What happened here? Two things. First, the larger slip angle means the tire contact patch is turned more than necessary, so that friction is increased, which causes more heat and eventually, the tire overheats. Second, and less significant, is the twist in the sidewall caused by the slip angle. The increased twist caused by the higher slip angle will also cause more heat to build up in the tire. The more skilled, sensitive driver will keep the slip angles at the lowest point where peak lateral acceleration is maintained, thus minimizing the possibility of overheating the tires. But is this always desirable?

If you autocross, the problem is different. Overheating tires in a one-minute run is not often a problem. But a lack of heat in the tire is! Remember that traction increases as tire temperature increases up to an optimum point. Since this is not a driving book, I won't offer any driving tips. But if you look at the previous two paragraphs, I bet you can find one anyway!

Handling Balance and Tires

Tires have an effect on the handling balance of a car. Let's review the definitions of oversteer and understeer. When the slip angles of the front tires exceed the slip angles of the rear tires, understeer is present. Oversteer occurs when the rear tire slip angles exceed the front tire slip angles. Our goal in tuning the car is to have the handling balance as close to neutral as possible. In other words, the front and rear slip angles should be close to equal.

Tire pressure, tire contact patch area, camber and vertical load all affect the slip angle of a tire. By altering any one of these parameters, we can alter the handling balance of the car. Since tire pressure must be correct to keep the tire contact patch flat on the road, it is not the best tuning tool. Camber is also not the ideal method of tuning for balance, since we want little dynamic negative camber while cornering. Tire contact patch area should be designed into the car properly, or modified within class rules. This is actually a good tuning tool, but rarely can be changed due to tire restrictions and rules. Manipulating vertical load, either aerodynamically or with roll couple distribution, is the most practical method for tuning handling balance. We will explore the methodology in the tuning section.

Responsiveness and Tires

Tires play a major role in vehicle responsiveness. The key tire parameter is sidewall stiffness. As sidewall stiffness increases, the tire contact patch can generate the same cornering force at a smaller slip angle. Since it takes less time for the tire to reach a smaller slip angle, the tire that can generate a given cornering force at a lower slip angle will be more responsive.

The construction of the tire sidewall, the aspect ratio and the tire pressure all contribute to sidewall stiffness. Sidewall construction is difficult to analyze, but a lower aspect ratio almost always increases sidewall stiffness. Higher tire pressures accomplish the same thing. Both will improve responsiveness. Improved responsiveness is one reason that all high-performance tires have low aspect ratios; many race tires have ratios of 35 or less.

Improved response also allows the tire to increase traction during the initial entry phase of a turn. The transition time from straight-line to turning, or from a turn in one direction to the other, is reduced, and more time is spent with the tire operating at the optimum slip angle for maximum traction. In a racing situation, reduced lap times will result.

Ride and Tires

Tires have a major effect on ride comfort. The tire works much like a spring, absorbing small bumps and road irregularities. The spring rate of a typical race tire is about ten times the rate of a coil (or leaf) spring on the same car. Passenger car tires have a somewhat softer spring rate.

Two factors in the tire affect the spring rate of the tire. The pressure in the tire raises the spring rate as it rises; increasing the sidewall stiffness will also increase the spring rate. The tradeoff is that the ride will become harsher as the spring rate of the tire increases.

One method to improve the ride of a high-performance low-profile street tire is to run at the lowest pressure recommended by the tire manufacturer when driving on city streets, or bumpy sections of road. For interstate highways or other long trips, the pressure should be increased.

Review

The most important concept concerning handling and tire traction is what happens at the tire contact patch. Nothing else really counts. Every change made to the suspension and tires ultimately has an effect at the tire contact patch. Also, there are only three ways to increase tire traction: increase the friction between the tire and the road; increase the number of rubber molecules at the tire contact patch; and increase the vertical load on the tire.

Vertical Load

The key to understanding handling is understanding how load affects tire traction. As load increases, so does traction, but the relationship is not linear. Traction does not increase as quickly as load, so if load is added to a tire contact patch as additional weight, then the tire generates more traction, but also has more work to accomplish.

The extra work is greater than the extra traction, so there is a net loss in cornering force.

Slip Angle

The slip angle is the angle between the direction the wheel is pointed and actual direction the tire contact patch is moving in. Lateral acceleration increases as the slip angle increases until the limits of adhesion are reached. The lateral acceleration ceases to increase, and finally diminishes with increasing slip angles. When front and rear slip angles are not equal in a turn, there is a handling imbalance. When the front slip angles exceed the rear, the vehicle understeers; when the rear slip angles exceed the front, the vehicle oversteers.

Handling Horsepower

Softer rubber compounds, larger tire contact patch areas, reduced vehicle weight or a combination of these factors will increase the traction potential. The trick is to make full use of the tire contact patches by tuning. Then you must establish an effective handling balance by utilizing the best tire contact patch area at each end of the car, and fine-tuning the roll couple distribution.

Set-Up

Everything done to tune the suspension attempts to keep the tire contact patch working to its fullest. Tire pressure, camber, toe-in or toe-out, rim width and so forth, all must be set to extract maximum traction for competition purposes. For the street, other compromises establish different priorities, including stability, tread wear life and ride comfort. The most useful indicator of tire set-up and performance is the tire temperature.

Since the tire is the link to the road surface, the tire has an effect on virtually all of the crucial parameters that affect handling: traction, balance, responsiveness and ride. Understanding how the tire works, and how it affects these parameters, is the key to improved handling performance. And understanding how the driver can affect the tires and, therefore, the handling of a vehicle, is also paramount to a full understanding of the high-performance handling system.

Tire Care

High-performance street tires and racing tires represent a substantial investment. By taking good care of your tires, you will receive optimum performance for longer periods of time, and tire life will increase. Here are some tips to improve tire performance and wear.

• Never drive or park a car on underinflated tires. It is dangerous, can lead to sidewall and tread damage and increased wear, and can upset handling balance if the underinflation is at only one end of the car or at one tire. Even slight underinflation will cause excessive tread wear on the shoulders of the tire.

• Overinflation will cause ride harshness and deformation of the tread, reducing traction because that tire contact patch is smaller, and leading to increased tire wear in the center of the tire tread.

• Excessive camber or toe-in or toe-out on the street can cause excessive tread wear and instability.

• Check tire pressures often on the street, constantly for competition.

• Tires must be balanced properly. Imbalance can cause vibrations and excessive tread wear in spots around the tire. If you feel a new vibration from the tires, have the balance checked immediately. A lost wheel balance weight is probably the cause. This applies to both street and competition situations.

• Routinely check the tire treads for excessive wear, in general and also in areas of the tread, such as the edges or center of the tread.

• Tires lose performance as they harden. Tires harden with age. Ultraviolet light and ozone increase the aging of rubber. If you use a set of competition tires for more than one event, it is good practice to store them off of the car, and keep them in plastic trash bags. This minimizes the effects of ultraviolet light and ozone, thereby increasing the life of the tire.

• Tires in competition get hot. The hot tread surface picks up all sorts of debris. Be careful to remove any debris that may cause a puncture if left on the tread.

• For low-pressure applications, and excessively high speed use of racing tires, consult with the manufacturer of the tire about the need for safety screws in the tire bead. These screws, when needed, are important as the bead may unseat without them. Never install safety screws without consulting with the tire and wheel manufacturers about the need for, type of screws and quantity.

• Never use a racing tire on the street. They are much too fragile for this purpose. Slicks are just plain dangerous on the highway. Always keep a check on tread wear. Never drive on DOT tires when the wear bars are exposed.

• Some DOT tires should be shaved for competition. Shaving sometimes improves traction, but often reduces heat build-up in the tread, and reduces the possibility of chunking, especially in the shoulder area.

• Some DOT street tires should not be used for driving on slippery surfaces, such as ice, snow or rain. The tread pattern was not designed for use in these conditions. This also applies to tires that have been shaved.

BFGoodrich T/A Tires

BFGoodrich has been involved in the high-performance tire business since its inception, and the T/A Radial series has been a leader in the industry for many years. BFGoodrich began racing its street tires in 1970, and has had winning programs ever since. Its involvement in racing, and the commitment to provide high-performance tires to suit every need and condition, have kept BFGoodrich at the forefront of tire technology.

BFGoodrich's twenty-year background in racing shows on the test track. Three of our project vehicles were tested on the Comp T/A, two with the R1 competition compound. The Mustang GT was tested on the Comp T/A VR4 with the stock set-up. The tires were easy to drive close to the limit, even with the poor suspension set-up and abrupt transitions of the stock Mustang. The forgiving nature of the Comp T/A made it easy to gather the wayward Mustang back in and keep it on the road.

Traction is good, but does not approach the R1 compound.

Two project vehicles used the Comp T/A R1 compound tires, both with excellent results. The first was our project Camaro. With a little tuning on the skid pad, the heavy car cornered at a 1.0 g average left and right; responsive on the racetrack was even better. Excellent turn-in, a wide range of slip angles at the top of the traction curve, and generally excellent grip, the Camaro could be driven so far sideways that the driver had to look out the side window to see where he or she was going, and still save the car. Not the fast way around, but comforting nonetheless.

The other project was a Shelby CSX running in the IMSA International Sedan series. After a computer analysis of the suspension, and a change of springs, antiroll bars and shocks, the Shelby rolled off the trailer on Comp T/A R1s and turned a 1.07 g lap on the skid pad. With a little tuning, the maximum corner force left-to-right average was 1.09 g's—great performance for a 2,700 lb. front-drive racer with sixty-one percent front weight bias. The tires had excellent grip and responded to changes predictably.

TIRE USE COMPARISON

BFGOODRICH T/A TIRES

	Traction, Dry	Traction, Wet	Snow/Mud Capable	Wear, Highway/Street	Suitable for Competition	Ride Comfort	Responsiveness	Tunability	Speed Rating
Comp T/A R1	5	2	1	2	5	3	5	5	Z
Comp T/A ZR, VR	4	3	2	3	4	3	5	4	V/Z
Comp T/A VR4	4	3	2	3	4	3	5	4	V
Comp T/A HR4	4	3	2	3	3	3	5	4	H
EURO RADIAL T/A	3	4	4	5	3	4	4	3	H
RADIAL T/A	3	4	4	4	2	4	3	3	S
TOURING T/A	3	4	3	4	2	4	3	3	S

All ratings are very subjective by the author.
Ratings: 1 = poor; 2 = moderate; 3 = good; 4 = very good; 5 = excellent

The BFGoodrich Comp T/A VR4 offers the highest treadwear rating of any V-speed-rated tire. It is made in six different 16 in. sizes for high-performance cars, such as the supercharged Thunderbird Super Coupe, Cougar XR-7, Camaros and Corvettes.

Bridgestone Tires

When it comes to creating ultra-high-performance tires, especially those used in competition events like autocross or showroom stock racing, the tire companies have a difficult series of compromises to make. Bridgestone makes one of the fastest DOT racing tires available in the Potenza RE71.

I have heard from some drivers that the Potenza is not fast, and that it wears more quickly than some other tires. Untrue on both counts! This points out an important point that is often overlooked. A tire, any tire, that is used at its, the vehicle's and the driver's, limits must be tuned to work within the system. Most competitors will tune a car to one brand or model of tire, and for whatever reason, will try another type of tire. This is fine, except for one thing. To simply replace the old type tire with a new one will rarely work. Different brands of tire, different styles of tire within one brand's line, or even different sizes of the same tire, can mean completely re-tuning the suspension to optimize the efficiency of that tire. To not do this is a complete waste of time and money. Yes, you may get lucky, but you will never know without tuning. Naturally, on the street, this is not necessary to anything approaching the same degree, but still tire pressures and camber settings need attention.

In the case of the Bridgestone tires, the design of the tire probably explains the comments from some competitors. The sidewall construction of the RE71 is very stiff for improved responsiveness and to allow the tire contact patch to stabilize more quickly in turns. Both of these characteristics cause the Potenza RE71 to turn in more quickly and take a set sooner than some other tires. This makes the tire feel like it is more difficult to drive on because the driver has less time to feel the car take a set in the turns. The feeling is similar to shocks that are set too stiffly for the experience level of the driver. The stiffer construction of the sidewall also means different pressures and camber settings are required to make this tire operate at its full potential. This may explain why some think the tire wears too quickly. Improper settings can cause premature wear. Additionally, the driver who cannot feel the car take a set often over-drives the tires and scrubs off speed, which can overheat the tire and cause excessive wear.

The real picture with the Potenza RE71 is quickness and excellent traction. The tire is sensitive, but it is responsive and can actually be quicker than most other tires, all else being equal, if it is correctly tuned and if the driver adapts to the tire. Today, the driver must adapt to the car and tire set-up. If the car and tire must adapt to the driver, the set-up is likely going to be slower. The RE71 is ultra competitive when the car is set up and driven to suit its aggressive characteristics.

TIRE USE COMPARISON

BRIDGESTONE TIRE

	Traction, Dry	Traction, Wet	Snow/Mud Capable	Wear, Highway/Street	Suitable for Competition	Ride Comfort	Responsiveness	Tunability	Speed Rating
Potenza RE71	5	3	2	2	5	3	5	5	V/Z
Potenza HP41	4	4	4	4	3	4	4	3	H
Potenza 137V	3	4	3	5	2	5	4	3	H

All ratings are very subjective by the author.
Ratings: 1 = poor; 2 = moderate; 3 = good; 4 = very good; 5 = excellent

The Bridgestone PSR RE71 tires, shown here in 245/45ZR16 size.

Firestone Firehawk Tires

The Firestone Firehawk tire line of DOT passenger car tires probably has more competition miles than any other brand of tire. These tires are used in the IMSA Firestone Firehawk Endurance Series for Street Stock cars. With everyone on the same tires, tuning becomes a crucial part of the series as no one has a tire advantage. The Firehawk tire, through the rigors of this series, has earned a reputation for reliability and wear. While not the fastest tires around, due to the relatively hard nature of the rubber compound, the tires last forever, at least by racing standards.

What this means for the high-performance enthusiast is a good, even great, all-around tire. Firestone has paid careful attention to the compromises needed for a high-performance tire. Wear, wet and dry traction, ride quality, noise, responsiveness and looks are all part of the equation for any high-performance tire designed for the street. Firestone has done well with this line, adding reasonable price to the equation to boot.

The Firehawk line is an excellent road tire, with good grip in wet or dry conditions. The tires can be driven hard and last for an exceptional number of miles. I have achieved in excess of 40,000 miles on a sports car that is often driven hard in the mountains. The tires have been used in the snow and rain, and work well in the most severe of conditions.

The Firehawk GT and SV have been raced on many Street Stock IMSA racers, and the results are commendable. Tires often last an entire event in the endurance series, which means three to four hours of driving at the limit. A softer compound may be faster, but the wear factor increases quickly. This serves to make racing more expensive, not make the competition stiffer.

The real plus for the high-performance-driving enthusiast with the race-proven Firehawk line is reliability and exceptional wear. The Firehawks require only reasonable maintenance and care, and will provide many miles of quick motoring without letting the driver down.

TIRE USE COMPARISON

FIRESTONE FIREHAWK

	Traction, Dry	Traction, Wet	Snow/Mud Capable	Wear, Highway/Street	Suitable for Competition	Ride Comfort	Responsiveness	Tunability	Speed Rating
FIREHAWK 660/670	3	4	3	5	3	4	3	3	H/V
FIREHAWK GTX	3	5	3	5	4	4	3	4	H
FIREHAWK SS	3	5	4	5	3	4	3	3	S
FIREHAWK FTX	3	5	4	5	3	4	3	3	T
FIREHAWK SV	4	4	3	4	4	4	4	4	V
FIREHAWK SVX	4	4	3	4	4	3	4	4	V
FIREHAWK SZ	4	4	3	4	4	3	4	4	Z

All ratings are very subjective by the author.
Ratings: 1 = poor; 2 = moderate; 3 = good; 4 = very good; 5 = excellent

The Firestone SV tire, which has been used on many Street Stock IMSA racers.

General Tires

General Tire has come on strong in the performance tire market over the last few years. Their racing commitment has helped them to establish an image, and more important, a tire worthy of the ultra-high-performance label. The XP 2000 range of high-performance tires covers a broad spectrum of needs, sizes and road conditions. The XP 2000 V and the XP 2000 Z have both proven themselves in serious Showroom Stock competition as a tire to not only contend with but to beat. Extensive testing and racing have brought the General name to the pinnacle of technology.

One of our project cars uses the General XP 2000 Z in competition. The Dodge Shadow ES IMSA International Sedan uses this tire in the hotly contested racing series, and the General Tires have excellent grip and are forgiving to drive on. They do require a different set-up for optimum traction than some of the other ultra-high-performance tires used in racing. The set-up is different, not better or worse. The XP 2000 Z seems to be affected more by changing track conditions, but this may mean that the tire is more sensitive and transmits feedback to the driver more effectively. It could also be that the tire is just responsive in a different manner.

General has collectively done its homework. The range of high-performance tires bears consideration for any type of highway driving or for serious competition.

TIRE USE COMPARISON
GENERAL TIRE

	Traction, Dry	Traction, Wet	Snow/Mud Capable	Wear, Highway/Street	Suitable for Competition	Ride Comfort	Responsiveness	Tunability	Speed Rating
XP 2000 V	4	2	2	3	5	4	3	3	V
XP 2000 AS	3	4	5	5	2	4	3	3	H
XP 2000 H	4	4	3	4	3	3	3	3	H
XP 2000	3	3	3	5	2	4	2	3	T
XP 2000 Z	5	1	2	3	5	2	5	4	Z

All ratings are very subjective by the author.
Ratings: 1 = poor; 2 = moderate; 3 = good; 4 = very good; 5 = excellent

General Tire's XP 2000 Z is a ZR-speed-rated tire.

Hoosier Tires

Hoosier Tire makes one range of tires for high-performance DOT applications called the DOT Sports Car. The tire is molded to a shallow tread depth so that shaving is not necessary for competition. This makes the tire less than ideal for street use, since wet traction is low and wear rates are high. However, Hoosier is in the competition tire business, and the DOT Street is a great tire for competition. With compounds available for autocrossing and for time trials and road racing, Hoosier covers the grassroots racing scene well. Both versions of the DOT Sports Car are gaining wide appeal, especially in autocrossing and SCCA Improved Touring classes, where DOT tires are required.

The DOT Sports Car is a bias-ply tire, and that has scared away a lot of competitors. A bias-ply tire requires a different set-up because it responds differently. Veteran racers who have been around awhile had nothing but bias-ply tires to work with and had to learn how to set up radials when they became popular. In reality, the bias-ply tire is as easy to set up as the radial—and in some cases easier.

The big difference is in the sidewall construction and the way the bias-plies affect the tire contact patch. The sidewall of a bias-ply tire is stiffer, all else being equal (which it is not) than a radial. A better way to state this is that the bias-ply flexes less than the radial, and here is a big clue about the set-up. First, tire pressures may be totally different than with a radial; check with a tire rep. Second, a given rim width will accept a wider-section tire with the bias carcass. On one of our project cars, we used a 205/60-14 radial on a 7 in. rim to control rollover of the tread while cornering. With the Hoosier DOT Sports Car, we can run a 225/50-14 on the same rim, allowing a larger footprint and more grip without any problem. The extra traction of the wider tire causes higher cornering force and more body roll. Stiffer antiroll bars at both ends will reduce roll and maintain reasonable camber change. Finally, the stiffer sidewalls of the DOT Sports Car require less shock damping to maintain quick response to steering input. Many racers who have tried the Hoosiers have not softened the shocks to compensate. Consequently, the vehicle responds more quickly than they are used to and the tires are hard for the driver to read. Softer shocks will keep this from occurring in the majority of cases.

TIRE USE COMPARISON
HOOSIER TIRES

	Traction, Dry	Traction, Wet	Snow/Mud Capable	Wear, Highway/Street	Suitable for Competition	Ride Comfort	Responsiveness	Tunability	Speed Rating
DOT SPORTS CAR	5	2	1	1	5	2	5	5	.

All ratings are very subjective by the author.
Ratings: 1 = poor; 2 = moderate; 3 = good; 4 = very good; 5 = excellent

Hoosier Tire's DOT Sports Car tire.

Pirelli P Zero Tires

Pirelli has been one of the world's leading tire manufacturers for many years, and innovations that are now commonplace were first developed by the Italian manufacturer in the 1970s. The concept of the P Zero is derived from the Pirelli's involvement in Formula One racing. The carcass construction came from the Formula One tire, designed to optimize lateral, vertical and torsional rigidity. The rigidity of the tire effects the stability and responsiveness. For example, if torsional rigidity is weak, the tire will lack traction and stability exiting a turn under power, making the car more difficult to control. Lateral rigidity effects the steady state cornering ability of the tire. A stiff tire will track well and keep the tire contact patch on the ground during hard cornering; a tire lacking rigidity here will squirm and wander during hard cornering. Vertical rigidity also helps keep the contact patch on the road surface during all load conditions, such as braking, acceleration and cornering. It also effects the responsiveness of the tire to steering inputs. Stiff tires are more responsive, soft tires less so. Naturally, the more rigid tire will ride more roughly, so compromise for the highway is a difficult design decision.

The belt package of the Pirelli P Zero features a Kevlar belt for increased tensile strength and puncture resistance. A cross-belted steel ply increases overall rigidity and two zero-degree nylon cap plies (hence the name) are added to control centrifugal growth as speed increases. This helps keep the contact patch consistent in size through the speed range. Rubber filler combined with Kevlar reinforcement stiffen the sidewall for improved steering response but help maintain reasonable ride comfort.

The tread design of the P Zero is unique. The pattern is asymmetrical, with the outer edge lightly grooved for maximum cornering traction and minimum chunking in hard cornering. The center of the tread uses longitudinal slick sections for increased traction in all directions in dry conditions. The inside edge of the tread features a more traditional grooved pattern for improved wet condition traction. The tread design has an inside and outside, but is not directional like some asymmetrical tread patterns.

The P Zero is a Z-rated tire, and has been tested at 217 mph on the Ferrari F40. It is the fastest street tire produced, and comes as standard equipment on the F40.

What does all of this mean? In this case, it means the tire is a hot performer. In our testing, the P Zero enhanced the suspension modifications made to our test car. In the original test, the car was difficult to control at the exit of the turn because of a quick transition to oversteer as power was applied. Part of this was due to soft spring rates and excessive body roll. The rest was caused by sidewall flex and squirm in the tire contact patch. The carcass construction, sidewall design and tread pattern of the Pirelli P Zero all help to solve the power oversteer problem. The stiffer shock valving and higher spring and antiroll bar rates also contributed to the solution. But bars, springs and shocks can only minimize the geometric causes of the problem. These components cannot cure design flaws in the tire.

A tire must be judged on a number of characteristics. Ride, traction, responsiveness and wear are important in varying degrees. In reality, a comfortable ride is not compatible with responsiveness, and high traction is not compatible with good wear. But even an ultra-high-performance tire like the P Zero can be manufactured with reasonable compromises by using the correct materials in a good design. The P Zero is an exceptional compromise. Ultimate dry traction is not as high as some of the stickier-compound DOT tires available for competition, but it offers excellent wear for the level of traction available and has superior wet weather traction.

Wear seems to be good. In our skid pad test, at full tread depth, the P Zero showed no signs of chunking, even though temperatures on the outside edges of the front tires exceeded 210 degrees Fahrenheit. Full-tread-depth tires often chunk severely under these extreme conditions. The compound and the tread design on the outside edge certainly contribute to this characteristic. It is difficult to judge ultimate mileage from the P Zero, but driving style and conditions will certainly play a factor in this anyway. It seems as though the tires will show excellent wear for the type of performance available.

TIRE USE COMPARISON

PIRELLI TIRE

	Traction, Dry	Traction, Wet	Snow/Mud Capable	Wear, Highway/Street	Suitable for Competition	Ride Comfort	Responsiveness	Tunability	Speed Rating
P ZERO	4	5	3	4	3	3	5	5	Z
P700-Z	3	5	3	5	2	4	4	4	Z
P600	3	4	3	5	2	4	4	4	V/H
P500	2	4	4	5	1	4	3	3	H
P6	3	4	3	5	2	4	4	4	V/H
P5	3	4	3	5	1	4	3	3	V/H

All ratings are very subjective by the author.
Ratings: 1 = poor; 2 = moderate; 3 = good; 4 = very good; 5 = excellent

Yokohama Tires

Yokohama Tires has labored diligently in the past few years to make an impression in the performance tire market, and the work has paid off. The firm arrived on the scene with a line of high-performance radial tires to suit many applications, uses and budgets. Some of our project cars have used Yokohama Tires, and the results have been outstanding. We have tested extensively on the tires, and have competed in autocrosses and races. Across the board they have proven reliable, tough and have provided excellent traction.

One of the important characteristics of any tire is its response to chassis changes. The Yokohama A008RTU is not only sticky and durable in the rigors of road racing, but the tires respond exactly the way they should. You never have to second guess the effect of a change, or try to trick the tire into working the way the driver would like.

Two of our project cars have used the A008RTU with fantastic results. Another project car, the light and speedy Consulier, averaged 1.10 g's left and right on the skid pad with the AVS Intermediate. That is remarkable performance for an all-weather tire.

The Yokohama line has much to offer the high-performance handling enthusiast.

TIRE USE COMPARISON
YOKOHAMA TIRES

	Traction, Dry	Traction, Wet	Snow/Mud Capable	Wear, Highway/Street	Suitable for Competition	Ride Comfort	Responsiveness	Tunability	Speed Rating
AVS A PLUS 4	3	4	5	4	2	4	3	3	V
AVS U PLUS 4	3	4	5	5	2	4	3	3	H
AVS INTERMEDIATE	4	4	3	4	3	3	4	4	V/Z
A008P	5	1	1	3	5	2	5	4	Z
A008	5	1	1	3	5	2	5	4	Z
A008RTU	5	1	1	3	5	2	5	4	Z
A403	3	4	4	4	2	4	3	2	V
A022	3	3	2	4	2	3	4	3	V
Y352	3	4	4	4	2	4	3	2	H

All ratings are very subjective by the author.
Ratings: 1 = poor; 2 = moderate; 3 = good; 4 = very good; 5 = excellent

Yokohama's A022 high-performance tire.

Chapter 3

Weight Transfer

While the tire has the most profound effect on handling, weight transfer ranks close behind. The amount of weight transfer alters the total traction of the tires. Where weight is transferred affects the handling balance of the car. How quickly weight is transferred is the primary factor relating to responsiveness.

But what is weight transfer? Anytime a force is applied to a vehicle, caused by acceleration, braking or cornering, weight transfer occurs. All forces acting on a body, in our case a vehicle, are considered to be ultimately exerted at the body's center of gravity. In other words, the forces push on the vehicle at the vehicle's center of gravity.

Center of Gravity

The center of gravity is a single point where all of the vehicle's weight is centered. If you could balance a vehicle from its center of gravity, it would hang in perfect equilibrium as long as no force acted on it. It is easier to think of the center of gravity location in the three planes in which we can measure it. The center of gravity location can be measured along the lateral axis (track width), longitudinal axis (wheelbase) and the vertical axis (height above ground).

It is easy to determine the lateral and longitudinal balance points. By weighing each of the four corners of a vehicle, we can add the front wheel

The location of the center of gravity above ground determines how much weight is transferred during cornering. The most important consideration is to keep the center of gravity as low as possible to minimize weight transfer. The vertical load on a tire influences the traction as more load means more traction, but the relationship is not linear, so the traction increases more slowly than the increase in load. Any time weight transfer occurs, there is a net reduction in traction capability. More weight transfer means less traction. The Mazda-powered Lotus autocrosser has a low center of gravity, and a small percentage of its already light weight will transfer during cornering. Bob Ryder

Even though the Toyota Corolla GT-S has been lowered, it has a much higher center of gravity. A higher percentage of its total weight will be transferred during cornering, further reducing the total traction potential of the car. It is, however, substantially better than the stock version. The center of gravity location is basically a design parameter. The only reasonable way to lower the center of gravity on a stock vehicle is to lower the car with shorter springs and/or tires, or to move components, such as the battery, to a lower location. Lowering the center of gravity reduces weight transfer and increases the potential traction. Bob Ryder

weights together, and divide by the total vehicle weight. The resulting percentage tells us where the balance point is located along the wheelbase of the vehicle. If the weight on the front wheels is 1,200 lb., and on the rear is 800 lb., the total weight of the vehicle is 2,000 lb. and the percentage of total weight on the front wheels is sixty percent. The balance point, or fulcrum point, of the vehicle lies along the wheelbase at a point sixty percent of the total distance from the center of the rear wheels. If the wheelbase is 100 in., then the location of the center of gravity in the longitudinal plane is 60 in. from the center of the rear wheels.

The lateral center of gravity location is found in the same way by comparing left-side weight to right-side weight. In our example, if the left-side weight was 1,000 lb., with the right side also being 1,000 lb., then the left-to-right weight distribution is fifty-fifty or equal. The location of the center of gravity in the lateral plane is exactly at the halfway point of the track width of the vehicle. Now we have two of the three points for the center of gravity location.

Finding the height of the center of gravity is more difficult, but can be calculated by measuring the front wheel corner weights when the front of the vehicle is elevated two to three feet above

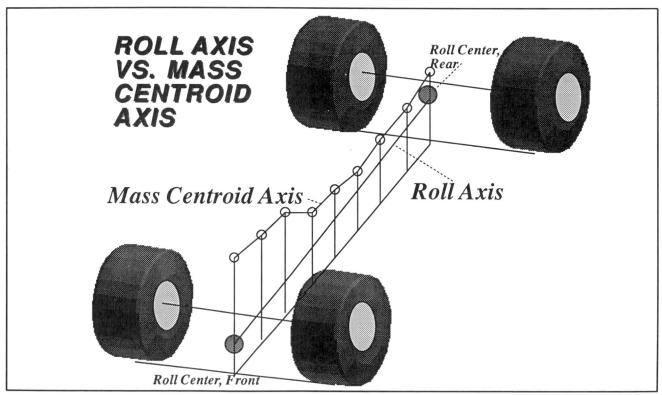

The mass centroid axis is nothing more than a series of centers of gravity for sections of a vehicle. For optimum handling balance, the roll axis should be parallel to the mass centroid axis. If it is not, more weight is transferred *at the end of the car where the mass centroid axis lies closer to the roll axis. This will change the handling balance towards the end of the car where the mass centroid axis lies closer to the roll axis.*

ground level. Once we have found the center of gravity height above ground, we have an exact location of the center of gravity. We can learn much about a vehicle with this information, and calculate some of the necessary changes for improved handling.

Weight Transfer Determinants

So what does the center of gravity have to do with weight transfer? Everything! The height of the center of gravity is one of four factors that determine the total amount of weight transfer during acceleration, braking and cornering. The lateral location of the center of gravity is one of the factors determining where weight is transferred during cornering. The longitudinal center of gravity location is one of the factors determining where weight is transferred during braking and acceleration.

Factors that determine how much weight is transferred include the following:

• Total vehicle weight. A lighter-weight vehicle will transfer less weight, all else being equal.

• Force acting at the center of gravity. This can be cornering force, braking force or acceleration force. The greater the force acting at the center of gravity, the greater the weight transfer will be, all else being equal.

• Height of the center of gravity above ground. The higher the center of gravity above ground, the more the weight transfer will occur, all else being equal.

• Track width and wheelbase. A wider track width will reduce weight transfer while cornering; a longer wheelbase will reduce weight transfer during braking and acceleration.

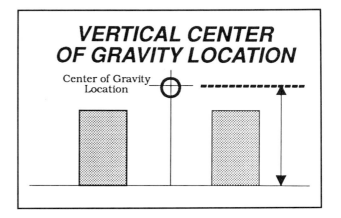

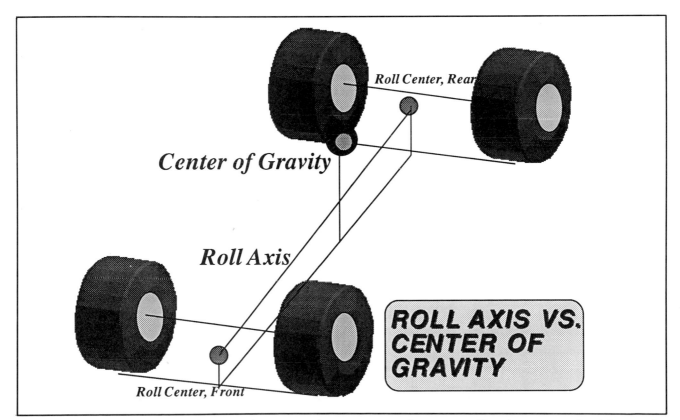

While the distance from the roll axis to the center of gravity is one factor determining the degree of body roll, it has no influence on the total amount of weight transfer. The height of the center of gravity above ground is *a major factor controlling the amount of weight transfer. The inclination of the roll axis affects where weight is transferred in a turn.*

Track width also influences weight transfer. For a given vehicle, if the track is widened, weight transfer is reduced. Additionally, if a vehicle weighs less to begin with, it will transfer less weight. The low, wide Consulier has three advantages over the Mustang GT. It weighs less (about 1,200 lb.), has a wider track width and a much lower center of gravity. What does this mean in cornering power? On similar all-season high-performance radial tires, the Mustang generates skid pad lateral acceleration in the 0.90 g range. The Consulier, on the other hand, averages about 1.10 g on the Willow Springs skid pad. Bob Ryder

The degree of body roll in a turn is not a significant factor in the total amount of weight that is transferred from the inside wheels to the outside wheels in a turn. The Consulier shows little body roll, while the Volkswagen Jetta shows considerable roll. Even if the Consulier rolled to the same angle as the Jetta, the total amount of weight transfer from the inside wheels to the outside wheels would be virtually unchanged. The opposite would also apply: if the Jetta had more roll resistance so that its roll angle was equal to that of the Consulier, the weight transfer would remain nearly the same. Only lowering the car (or center of gravity), widening the track or reducing total weight would reduce the amount of weight transfer. Reducing cornering speed would also work, but that is not the point!

Myth of Body Roll, Dive and Squat

Many people are under the impression that body roll during cornering, dive during braking and squat during acceleration cause weight transfer. None of these factors cause weight transfer.

A vehicle with no suspension will transfer weight when a force is applied at the center of gravity. Consider a go-cart. A shopping cart will undergo lateral weight transfer when you turn up an aisle in the supermarket. Have you ever had precariously placed vegetables topple to the other side of the cart while turning? Or how about the Kleenex box that slides across the dashboard of your car in a turn? That's weight transfer.

The low-slung Consulier is wide, light and low, and transfers little weight in a turn.

The stock Volkswagen Jetta shows a lot of body roll, but a look at the tires shows that the weight transfer, regardless of the roll, is substantial. The inside rear is off the ground and the inside front has little load left. Even the left rear has a relatively small load. Most of the work is being done at the outside front.

Weight transfer occurs regardless of the amount of body roll, dive or squat present. In fact, body roll, dive and squat contribute such a small amount to the total weight transfer that it is not worth taking the time to make the calculations to determine how much weight transfer occurs due to these factors. Besides, we limit body roll, dive and squat for other reasons, which we will explore later. Limiting body roll, dive and squat does not affect the amount of weight transfer by any significant amount.

Lateral Weight Transfer

We have seen that a vehicle will always transfer weight while cornering. In a vehicle without suspension, all of the weight transfer acts through the center of gravity of the vehicle. With suspension, a system of forces causes weight to be transferred in three different ways: unsprung weight transfer; sprung weight transferred through the roll centers; and sprung weight transferred through the springs and antiroll bars (roll couple distribution). Some of these terms will become clearer in the suspension chapter. For now, let's look at how these three ways to transfer weight work.

Unsprung Weight Transfer

Unsprung weight transfer occurs at the center of gravity for each corner of the vehicle that is not supported by the springs. This includes the wheel, tire, brakes, hubs and other components. The amount of weight transfer at each corner depends upon the center of gravity location (usually near the wheel centerline), the unsprung weight and the cornering force. The total amount is small.

Sprung Weight Transferred Through Roll Centers

The roll center of a suspension system is a geometric point about which each end of a vehicle rolls while cornering. The front and rear roll centers determine the roll axis location (see the

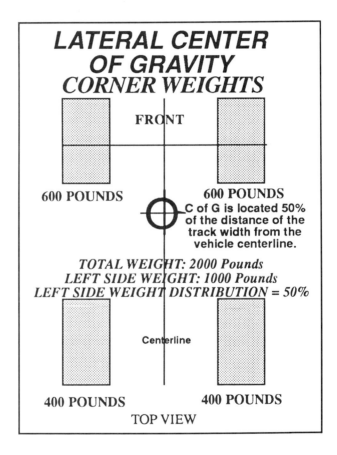

LATERAL CENTER OF GRAVITY CORNER WEIGHTS

FRONT

600 POUNDS   600 POUNDS

C of G is located 50% of the distance of the track width from the vehicle centerline.

TOTAL WEIGHT: 2000 Pounds
LEFT SIDE WEIGHT: 1000 Pounds
LEFT SIDE WEIGHT DISTRIBUTION = 50%

Centerline

400 POUNDS   400 POUNDS

TOP VIEW

suspension chapter for a detailed explanation). It is the sprung mass that rotates about the roll center. If the roll center locations are high enough to pass the center of gravity location for one end of the vehicle, then no body roll will occur. This is a very high roll center. In this case, all of the sprung weight at the end of the car is transferred through the roll center, with no body roll or no deflection of the springs occurring.

The other end of the spectrum is a roll center

The question of handling balance, oversteer versus understeer, is a matter of controlling where weight is transferred during cornering. The relative amount of roll resistance provided by the springs and antiroll bars at the front versus the rear of a vehicle will determine the handling balance. For optimum handling, you want to stay very near the neutral point on the spectrum. If the car pushes, or understeers, as can be seen in the Corolla, you need to alter the percentage of roll resistance so that the front is a less amount of the total. This can be accomplished with bars or springs or both, either softer in the front or stiffer in the rear.

at ground level. The center of gravity for that end of the car is well above the roll center, and no part of the sprung weight is transferred through the roll center. The entire sprung weight is transferred through the springs. When the roll center is above ground, part of the sprung weight transfers through the roll center, part through the springs.

Sprung Weight Transferred Through Spring and Antiroll Bars

As we can see from the previous explanation, some part of the sprung weight of a vehicle is transferred through the springs and bars. If the roll centers are at ground level, all of the sprung weight is transferred this way. The total amount of sprung weight transfer is always the same; part may be transferred via the roll centers, most will usually be transferred via the springs and bars. The relative roll stiffness of the front springs and bars compared to the total roll stiffness of the vehicle is the roll couple distribution and determines where the sprung weight transferred through the springs and bars will go.

The total amount of unsprung weight transfer at all four corners is added to the sprung weight transfer through the springs and bars and via the roll centers to arrive at the total amount of lateral weight transfer. The amount of weight transfer while cornering is exactly equal for a suspension-less vehicle and one with suspension, as long as the track width, center of gravity location and total weight are the same.

Why Limit Weight Transfer?

All of these details about weight transfer are interesting, but what's the big deal? The big deal is

The Mustang, which has been lowered, has less weight transfer than in stock trim, but the total amount is still substantial. At 1.0 g cornering force, the outside tires show some signs of strain from the additional load, but the inside tires are still doing a significant amount of work. Bob McClurg

traction! The greater the weight transfer, the less traction the tires can generate, all else being equal. If we can limit the amount of weight transfer, we can improve total traction.

We need to step back for a moment. We learned how vertical load affects tire traction. If we increase vertical load, we increase traction; if we decrease vertical load, we decrease traction. Remember, though, that the relationship is not linear. The traction increase occurs more slowly than the vertical load increase. Conversely, the traction reduction occurs more quickly than the vertical load reduction.

So what happens when weight is transferred? Let's explore what happens in a corner first. When the steering wheel is turned by the driver, the tires generate a slip angle, and cornering force is created. Remember physics class in high school? For every action there is an equal and opposite reaction. That applies here. The tires create the action. The reaction occurs at the center of gravity. Also remember that forces must be in equilibrium. For every force, there is an equal and opposite force. These forces are called centripital and centrifugal. In our example, the tires create centripital force that steers the vehicle. The centripital force acts at the tire contact patches. The equal and opposite centrifugal force acts at the center of gravity and tries to keep the vehicle going in a straight line.

Picture a weighted object attached to a string. Swing the weighted object around in a circle overhead. The weight is turning a corner. The cornering force is proportional to the weight (mass) of the object and the cornering velocity (speed) of rotation. Swing the object faster (or use a shorter string) and the force is higher. As long as the speed of the object is not increased too much, the object will follow the radius of the turn determined by the length of the string. But what happens if the speed becomes too great? The string will break and the

In the middle of the turn, the extreme load on the outside front tire can be seen.

A front-drive Honda in a hard turn, illustrating the dramatic effect that weight transfer has on traction. Here, the car is in the entry phase of the turn. The inside rear is virtually off the ground and doing no work. The outside front is handling more than fifty percent of the cornering and deceleration. The inside front is providing about thirty percent of the work capacity and the outside rear about fifteen percent.

Now the car is exiting the corner under power. Weight transfers to the rear just when the front tires need more traction. The inside front is doing a little more work, as is the outside rear, but the great majority of cornering and acceleration is happening at the outside front tire.

object will take off in a straight line. Equilibrium was lost, momentarily. In our vehicle example, the tires are the string, holding the object in the turn. The weighted object is the car, trying to go straight on. When the limit of the tire's traction is reached the vehicle will try to go straight on, or at least the circle will grow larger, in an effort to reestablish equilibrium.

When we compare the vehicle example to the string and object example, we find one major flaw. If you extend the line formed by the string through the object, the line will pass through the object's center of gravity. On the vehicle, the string is the tire contact patches which are at ground level. If the center of gravity of our vehicle is also at ground level, then everything is fine, but it is not, unless we have a very thin driver and very low tire profiles. The center of gravity must be at some point above the ground. Here we have a centripital force acting at the tire contact patches at ground level and centrifugal force acting at the vehicle's center of gravity at some point above ground. This is not a state of equilibrium, unless something else occurs. That something else is weight transfer.

When opposing forces act in different planes, as with our vehicle example, a rotational motion is created. In physics this is called a *moment*. In the case of centripital force at the tire contact patch and centrifugal force at the vehicle center of gravity, the moment is called the overturning moment. This is an appropriate name, because the centrifugal force is trying to overturn the vehicle. The result is weight transfer, and in the extreme case of 100 percent weight transfer, the inside tires lift off of the ground. If enough extra force is gener-

ated by the tires, the resulting centrifugal force at the center of gravity exceeds 100 percent weight transfer. If the center of gravity moves outside the track width of the vehicle, the vehicle will roll over. In this case, all four tire contact patches have lost all vertical load and provide zero traction. This in itself is a pretty good reason to limit weight transfer. But don't be overly concerned. Few vehicles create enough cornering force to cause the vehicle to overturn in a corner, without hitting something that will trip the vehicle. Some vehicles are, however, marginal in this respect.

But all vehicles will transfer weight, and that reduces traction. In reality, some of the work capacity of the tires is used to transfer weight, not to help the vehicle turn a corner. So how can we limit weight transfer? We could slow down in the turns. But that defeats our purpose, especially in competition. We want to increase cornering force and, therefore, cornering speed. We could reduce total vehicle weight. That helps all areas of performance.

Here the Corolla is neutral, with the front and the rear tires losing traction at nearly the same instant. This is controllable and makes for a fast car.

Here the Corolla can be seen oversteering. The rear tires have broken loose, while the front tires still have plenty of grip. The fact that one end breaks loose earlier than the other indicates that the cornering speed is not as high, which is borne out by the lap times on the skid pad. The near neutral state is the fastest because all of the tires are doing more work, and breakaway is at a higher cornering force. Bob Ryder

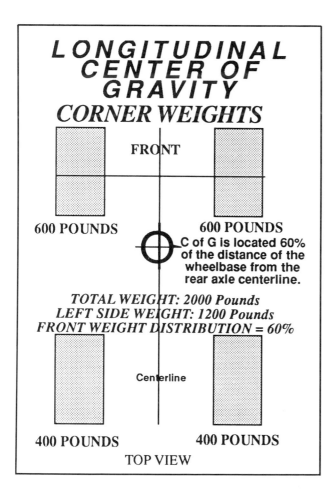

LONGITUDINAL CENTER OF GRAVITY
CORNER WEIGHTS

FRONT

600 POUNDS 600 POUNDS

C of G is located 60% of the distance of the wheelbase from the rear axle centerline.

TOTAL WEIGHT: 2000 Pounds
LEFT SIDE WEIGHT: 1200 Pounds
FRONT WEIGHT DISTRIBUTION = 60%

Centerline

400 POUNDS 400 POUNDS

TOP VIEW

We could also widen the track width. The wider track will resist weight transfer, and reduce it so that the tires have more traction available for cornering. Have you ever read a competition rule-book for virtually any racing class? All of them limit minimum vehicle weight and track width. If the rules didn't place limits on these parameters, we would have flyweight, wide cars. Most cars would probably be about as wide as the racetrack. Winning pole position would become quite important if that were the case.

Finally, we can lower the center of gravity height. While not easy, small changes here can make a big difference in performance. Lowering the ride height of your car will lower the center of gravity, reducing weight transfer and increasing traction with no other changes at all being needed. These are among the most important changes you can make to a vehicle to improve handling.

Longitudinal Weight Transfer

Longitudinal weight transfer has the same effect as lateral weight transfer. In this case, one end of the car gains weight while the other loses weight.

During acceleration, weight is transferred from the front to the rear tire contact patches. The front tires lose traction, the rears gain traction. If we have a rear-wheel-drive vehicle, this increases traction at the drive wheels. However, with a front-wheel-drive vehicle, traction is diminished at the drive wheels.

As engine horsepower increases, longitudinal weight transfer becomes more of a problem, and for two reasons. First, more horsepower means more acceleration, which causes increased weight transfer which reduces traction at the drive wheels. Second, more horsepower means more work for the front tires, which will overload them more quickly. This is especially true at the exit of a slow turn when peak torque is applied and wheel spin is easier to induce. Since front-wheel-drive cars usually are much heavier at the front, the problem becomes even worse. Front-wheel-drive vehicles are at their worst with high engine horse-

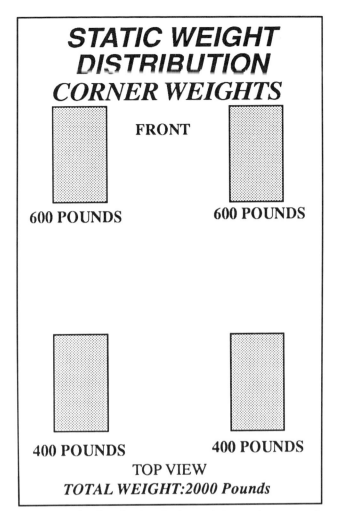

STATIC WEIGHT DISTRIBUTION
CORNER WEIGHTS

FRONT

600 POUNDS   600 POUNDS

400 POUNDS   400 POUNDS

TOP VIEW

TOTAL WEIGHT: 2000 Pounds

Static weight distribution is the weight resting on each tire contact patch at rest. The static weight distribution affects where weight is transferred. Changing of the static weight distribution will change where weight is transferred during cornering.

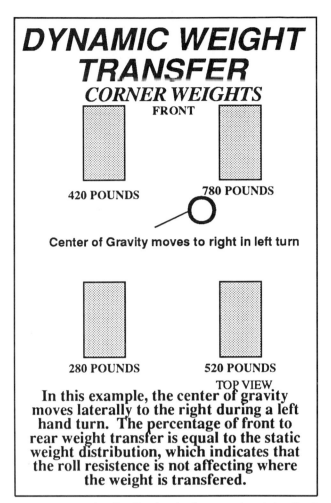

DYNAMIC WEIGHT TRANSFER
CORNER WEIGHTS
FRONT

420 POUNDS   780 POUNDS

Center of Gravity moves to right in left turn

280 POUNDS   520 POUNDS

TOP VIEW

In this example, the center of gravity moves laterally to the right during a left hand turn. The percentage of front to rear weight transfer is equal to the static weight distribution, which indicates that the roll resistance is not affecting where the weight is transfered.

Dynamic weight distribution is the actual weight distribution on each tire contact patch during cornering, braking or acceleration. The total weight on all four tire contact patches during cornering is always equal to the total weight at rest. The total vertical load on the tire contact patches in the dynamic (moving) state can be more or less than the static weight due to aerodynamic downforce or lift. Downforce increases load and traction while lift reduces both.

power output and low-speed turns where wheel spin is likely (or in a drag race situation). Front-wheel drive has many disadvantages.

During braking, weight is transferred to the front from the rear. The rear tires have less traction, the front more. The more weight being transferred, the more work the front tires have to do during braking. This makes brake pressure balance between the front and rear brake systems important. If either the front or rear brakes lock too soon, braking performance is lost. We will cover brake balance more in a later chapter.

Where Weight is Transferred

Longitudinal weight transfer is a simple matter; braking transfers weight from rear to front and acceleration from front to rear. Lateral weight transfer during cornering is another matter. Some of the weight is transferred to the outside front tire, some

to the outside rear tire. Since the front-to-rear ratio of lateral weight transfer alters the available traction at the front versus the rear, it is a crucial parameter affecting handling balance.

If we had a vehicle with a perfectly rigid chassis and no suspension, on a perfectly smooth road, the ratio of front-to-rear weight transfer would be exactly the same as the ratio of front-to-rear static weight distribution. In order to achieve handling balance (neutral handling), the ratio of front-to-rear tire contact patch area would need to match the front-to-rear static weight distribution ratio. Then, as long as the front and rear tires operated at the same slip angles while cornering, a perfect balance would be achieved.

Since we do not have perfectly rigid chassis on

The relative amount of roll resistance at the front of a vehicle versus the rear is called roll couple distribution. The amount of roll resistance at the front is divided by the total amount of roll resistance in the vehicle: the resulting percentage is the roll couple distribution. Only one figure is the neutral point for a given vehicle under given conditions. Anything higher than that single point on the scale is in the area of understeer while any number lower is in the oversteer region. The Stock class Volkswagen Jetta autocrosser shown here is lifting the inside rear tire completely off the road surface. This shows a one hundred percent weight transfer at the rear. Some of the weight that rests on the inside rear at rest has transferred to the outside front, most to the outside rear. The lifting of an inside wheel is caused by one of two factors. In the case of a stock vehicle, it is usually caused by inadequate suspension travel. In other cases, the culprit is too little roll resistance, and a roll couple distribution that is high enough for the inside front or low enough for the inside rear to cause the inside tire to lift from the ground. The point at which this will occur is calculable.

perfectly smooth roads, suspension is needed, and that will affect where the weight is transferred while cornering. There are four mechanical factors that affect where weight is transferred while cornering: static weight distribution; roll couple distribution; inclination of the roll axis from the horizontal; and height of the roll center above ground.

Static Weight Distribution

One of the easiest ways, in theory, to alter where weight is transferred is to alter where the weight is located in the beginning. This can be accomplished by physically moving components in the car, or by changing ride heights at each corner of the car. We will explore how this is done in later chapters.

Roll Couple Distribution

Roll couple distribution is the relative amount of roll resistance at the front of a vehicle compared to the amount of roll resistance at the rear of a vehicle. Roll resistance is provided by the combined rates of the springs and the antiroll bar acting at

the wheel (wheel rates).

When the body of a vehicle rolls while cornering, the springs and antiroll bars resist the body roll. Stiffer springs and bars reduce body roll, but not the total amount of weight transfer. If we increase the roll resistance at one end of a vehicle only, more weight will be transferred at that end of the vehicle and it will lose traction compared to the other end of the vehicle. Here's what happens.

If we raise the ride height of only one corner of a vehicle, that corner, plus the diagonally opposite corner, will increase in corner weights (see section on corner weights in the tuning chapter) while the other corners will lose corner weight. The laws of physics dictate that weight will transfer to the outside during cornering. If we stiffen roll resistance at, say, only the front of the car, proportionally more weight will now transfer at the front, less at the rear, because the effect has been to raise the outside front ride height compared to the rear (less spring and bar compression at the front).

We know that weight transfer while cornering reduces traction because of the way tire traction responds to vertical load. So now, if more weight is transferred at the front and less at the rear, the front tires will have slightly less traction and the rears slightly more traction. If we started with a neutral handling balance, the car will now understeer. The opposite applies if we stiffen the rear roll resistance only.

It does not matter if the increase in roll resistance comes from springs or antiroll bars. The effect is the same, although the manner in which weight transfers is different.

Springs transfer weight laterally, that is, if we stiffen the front springs only, more of the total weight transfer will be directly to the outside front. Antiroll bars work differently. Since an antiroll bar links the left- and right-side suspension together, the bar will try to lift the inside tire in a turn while it pushes the outside tire down. Pushing the outside tire down increases vertical load to that tire. Lifting the inside tire will transfer weight to the diagonally opposite tire, increasing traction there. The method is different, the result is the same.

Increasing roll resistance at only one end of a vehicle will increase the amount of weight transferred at that end and reduce the amount of weight transferred at the opposite end of the vehicle. The end with more roll resistance will have a net reduction in traction while the opposite end of the vehicle will have a net gain in traction. This will alter the handling balance of the vehicle. The traction of the tires is altered only slightly, as long as the roll couple distribution is not too far out of the ballpark.

Roll Axis Inclination

When a vehicle's body rolls in a turn, it pivots around an axis known as the roll axis. (The roll axis will be explained fully in the suspension chapter.)

If the roll axis is approximately parallel to the mass centroid axis (defined by the locations of the individual centers of gravity for sections of the vehicle in side view), then the inclination of the roll axis will not affect where weight is transferred. If the roll axis is not parallel to the mass centroid axis, then weight is forced to transfer more to the end of the car where the roll axis lies closer to the mass centroid axis. A front-heavy car with a low front roll axis will force more weight transfer to the rear, reducing traction at the rear. This will increase oversteer, or reduce understeer.

Height of Roll Center Above Ground

We have had a glimpse of how the roll axis inclination can force weight transfer to occur more or less at one end of the vehicle. We have also seen how the height of the roll center from ground level affects the amount of sprung weight transfer at each end of the vehicle. The more weight transferred through the roll centers (higher roll centers), the less weight transferred through the springs and bar and less roll couple at that end of the vehicle. This affects the roll couple distribution and, therefore, where weight is transferred. We will get back to this in the suspension chapter.

Weight Transfer and Responsiveness

So far, we have seen that the physical attributes of the car, that is, the weight distribution and center of gravity location, affect the amount of weight transfer and therefore tire traction. The handling balance is also affected by where weight is transferred. The third parameter affecting weight transfer is how quickly the weight is transferred.

The speed of weight transfer affects the responsiveness of the vehicle, or how quickly the vehicle reacts to driver and road surface inputs. The quicker weight transfer occurs, the less response time is required. Like roll couple distribution, this parameter is easily controlled by changes to suspension components, in this case the shock absorber rates. It is the shock absorber that controls the rate of weight transfer, and therefore the transient handling response; that is, the portion of handling when forces are changing in either magnitude or direction. This occurs when a vehicle is going from acceleration to braking, from a straight line to a turn or from a turn in one direction to a turn in the opposite direction and so on. The rate of the shock absorber controls many important functions, which we will also look at later.

Let's go back to the example of the perfectly rigid chassis with no suspension. This vehicle would transfer weight instantaneously as slip angles were developed at the tire contact patch. If we were to place solid shock absorbers on a vehicle, the same thing would occur. As long as the instant weight transfer occurred at both ends of the car,

The Audi 200 Quattro Trans-Am car has used every trick of modern technology and rules interpretation to build the widest car possible with the lowest center of gravity.

Its performance proves that the concepts work. Audi of America

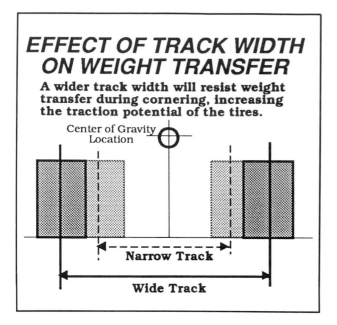

EFFECT OF TRACK WIDTH ON WEIGHT TRANSFER

A wider track width will resist weight transfer during cornering, increasing the traction potential of the tires.

Center of Gravity Location

Narrow Track

Wide Track

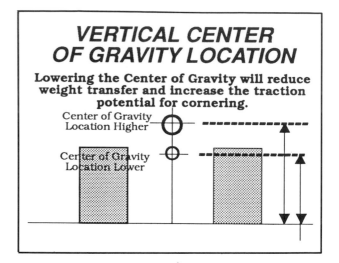

VERTICAL CENTER OF GRAVITY LOCATION

Lowering the Center of Gravity will reduce weight transfer and increase the traction potential for cornering.

Center of Gravity Location Higher

Center of Gravity Location Lower

the balance would not be affected. But it occurred at one end of the vehicle only, that end would experience instantaneous weight transfer, with a resulting sudden loss in traction at that end of the vehicle. Not a fun situation, but common when suspensions bottom, shocks bind or a chassis bottoms on the ground.

Consider the other extreme: no shocks at all. With no shocks, the body roll would occur instantaneously, but weight transfer would be very slow. Without the damping from the shocks, the body would try to roll back before the cornering forces diminished, and weight transfer would be bouncing back and forth from rear to front and back. What a mess. If you have ever attempted hard cornering with dead shocks, you have a good idea that this situation is to be avoided.

The middle ground is reality for the high-performance vehicle. The shocks designed for a given car or application will not be too stiff or too soft (the range between too stiff and too soft is actually wide). Within this wide range of acceptable shock rates, considerable tuning can be undertaken. In general, relative to weight transfer, if we increase the stiffness of the shocks, we decrease the time it takes for weight transfer to occur. If we soften the shocks, we increase the time it takes for weight transfer to occur. If we change both ends of the car equally (say fifteen percent stiffer at each end), then we change the overall responsiveness of the vehicle. If we change the shock rates at only one end of the vehicle, then we change the response time at only one end, and the transient handling balance will be altered. This can be used as a tuning tool with great success.

Weight Transfer and the Driver

The driver has a major influence on weight transfer. Steering inputs can affect both where weight is transferred and the rate of weight transfer. Cornering speed, acceleration rates and braking rates affect the total amount of weight transfer. Brake and throttle inputs affect where weight is transferred. All of these can alter handling characteristics substantially. Each factor will be fully explored in the driving chapter.

Review

Weight transfer affects handling in three ways: total amount of weight transferred; where the weight is transferred; and how quickly weight is transferred.

Weight transfers from the rear to the front during braking, from the front to the rear during acceleration and from the inside to the outside during cornering. When weight transfer occurs during cornering, there is a net loss of traction.

The factors affecting how much weight transfer occurs are: total vehicle weight; force acting at the center of gravity; height of the center of gravity above ground; and track width and wheelbase.

The handling balance (understeer and oversteer) is affected by where weight is transferred. The following parameters determine where weight is transferred: static weight distribution; roll couple distribution; inclination of the roll axis; and height of the roll center above ground.

Vehicle responsiveness is affected by how quickly weight is transferred. The shock absorber is the key element affecting the rate of weight transfer. Faster weight transfer makes the vehicle more responsive.

The driver plays a key role in vehicle handling, balance and response by the way brake, throttle and steering inputs are made.

Other factors can cause, or cure, understeer and oversteer. This Corvette is oversteering exiting a turn at an autocross. In this case the oversteer is induced by the driver applying more power to the rear wheels than they can handle. The tires lose traction and the back of the car begins to slide in what is called power oversteer. Understeer and oversteer can be caused by low tire pressure, inadequate tire contact patch size (due to the actual tire size or due to camber change causing the tire contact patch to lift from the road surface during cornering) or driver steering, brake and throttle inputs. Abrupt driver inputs cause weight transfer, which changes the vertical load on the tire and hence the traction on each tire.

Chapter 4

Suspension and Steering Systems

What function does a suspension system serve? Quite simply, its job is to keep the tire contact patch flat on the road surface, thus allowing the maximum number of rubber molecules to work as much as possible. As you can imagine, this is not an easy job.

Goal of the Suspension System

It might be best to look at what happens to the tire contact patch on a vehicle without a suspension system. Since we know that weight transfer will occur under any handling scenario, causing the inside tire contact patches to lose weight load while cornering, we can be certain that the car body will also roll while cornering. How much depends on many parameters, but we do know that the outside edges of the tire contact patches will take most of the load. As an example, if a car developed about 4 degrees of roll, the inside of a 4 in. wide tire contact patch would lift about a quarter of an inch off the road surface. A 10 in. wide tire contact patch would lift about 0.7 in. off the road surface.

It should be obvious, then, that such actions will reduce the effective size of the tire contact patch, and cause major reductions in total traction. Only tire compliance would help the situation, but as the tire size increased, and the stiffness of the tire increased, the situation would become worse. The primary job of a suspension system, for the purpose of high performance, is to minimize this lifting of the tire contact patch.

So, the job of the suspension system is to keep the tire contact patch flat on the road surface at all times. Can a suspension system be expected to do this? It depends. With wide tires and suspension travel exceeding 2 in. in bump and rebound, the answer is definitely no. With narrow tires and more than 3 or 4 in. of suspension travel at low cornering forces, there is more likelihood of success.

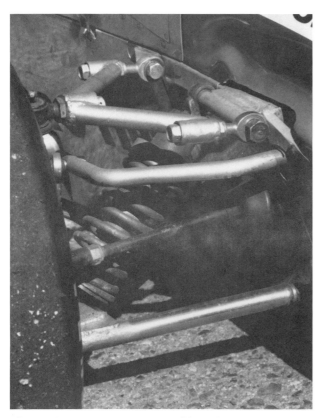

This is the time-proven unequal length arm suspension system on a Lotus 7. This simple system allows good camber control during roll and good roll center placement. It is also simple to build and is found in some form on virtually all modern purpose-built race cars.

The MacPherson strut suspension on many modern cars is cheap to manufacture, but not ideal for good camber control during body roll.

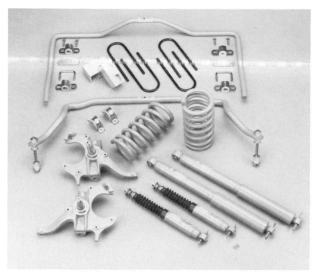

A fully coordinated suspension package offers many advantages for most street applications. Suspension Techniques designs and manufactures completely coordinated packages for many vehicles. Their expertise is at the top of the industry. Springs and shocks are designed to lower the vehicle without bottoming while maintaining a good ride, antiroll bars are stiffer to reduce body roll and camber change for better cornering performance, and urethane bushings are used to reduce compliance in the suspension and improve response to steering input. Suspension Techniques truck packages for Chevrolet S-10 and Blazer are shown here. Suspension Techniques

The only way we can create an effective suspension system, that is, one that keeps the tire contact patches on the ground through all conditions of bump, rebound and roll, is to limit body roll and suspension travel, and drive only on smooth surfaces. Optionally, we can drive well below the limit of adhesion, but we don't really care about tire traction at that point, because we have more than enough.

The suspension linkages must control the vertical movement of the wheels, which in turn controls how flat the tire contact patch rests on the road surface. How well the suspension does this is a critical design factor, and one that is even more substantial to the suspension set-up specialist. Our goal here is not the pursuit of suspension geometry design, but an understanding of the effects of suspension geometry so that we can minimize the negative effects.

Camber Angle

Let's try to visualize what occurs at the tire contact patch. If we look at the tire contact patch as a flat, rigid elliptical plate, it becomes quickly obvious that if the plate assumes any angle away from horizontal, little of the plate's surface area will remain in contact with the road surface. Even 0.1 degree of tilt would reduce the contact area to virtually nil. Only one edge of the plate would touch the surface.

Fortunately, the characteristics of the tire allow more compliance than our rigid elliptical plate. A

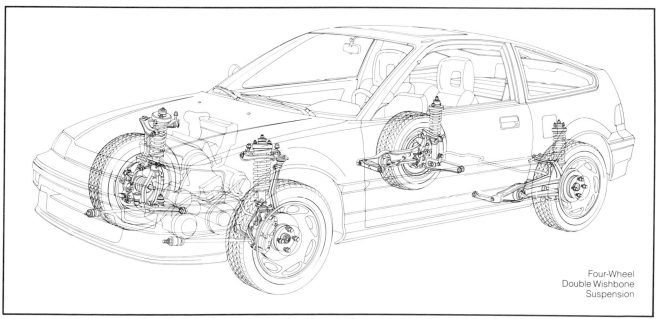

Four-Wheel
Double Wishbone
Suspension

The Honda CRX features a unique front and rear suspension design for a front-drive car. Using double wishbones increases manufacturing costs and difficulty, but offers superior geometry. The strut assembly pivots on the lower control arm, unlike the normal layout. The design allows better tire contact with the road during body roll for improved traction. This design in part accounts for the excellent success of this model in IMSA and SCCA Showroom Stock racing.

The ultra-sophisticated BMW 850i rear suspension uses a separate shock and spring activated from the lower trailing arm. As advanced as the BMW 850i is, a strut front suspension is still employed.

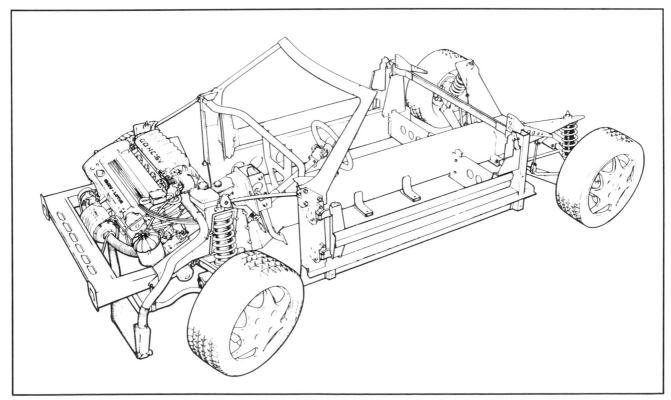

One of the most advanced front-wheel-drive front suspension systems is found on the new Lotus Elan. The geometry of this unequal length upper and lower control arm system minimizes camber change during body roll, improving traction. The rear suspension of the new Lotus Elan uses geometry similar to the front. This arrangement allows the tires to corner at optimum dynamic camber.

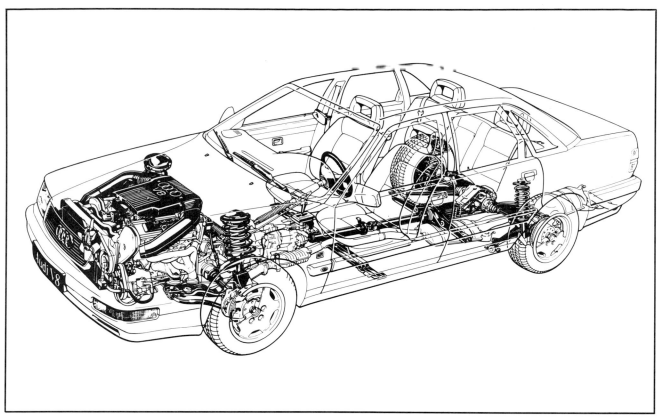

The Audi Quattro V8 uses a highly developed MacPherson strut suspension at all four corners. For a touring coupe or sedan, the MacPherson strut allows more room for passengers and luggage.

This cutaway of the Trans-Am Audi 200 Quattro shows the complexity of a modern all-wheel-drive race car. Audi of America

With the Mustang GT lowered as much as practical for comfortable street driving, and the front struts adjusted to full negative camber (without modifying the struts or towers), the outside front tire still shows some positive camber. This hurts cornering performance and contributes to the basic understeer tendency of this car. Bob McClurg

One of the fastest E Street Prepared autocrossers in the country belongs to SCCA National Champion Dan Livezy. He, and crew chief Dean Dodge, have taken the IROC Camaro to the limits of the rules. The car has been lowered and well set up. Notice that the outside front tire has a slight amount of negative camber while cornering. This is the ideal situation and partially accounts for Livezy's success.

tilt (camber angle) of 0.1 degree would have a minor effect on the tire contact patch because the tire contact patch is flexible. However, a 1 degree camber angle at the tire contact patch while cornering will have a major effect on tire traction. To illustrate this, let's get back to the rubber molecules at the tire contact patch.

We have seen how vertical load affects tire traction. For a tire to achieve maximum adhesion while cornering, every rubber molecule at the tire contact patch must carry an equal load. This occurs when the dynamic camber angle (camber angle in a turn) of the tire contact patch is about 0.25 degrees negative (top of tire tilted to center of vehicle) for a radial tire, slightly less for a bias-ply tire. This allows equal loading across the tire contact patch. Any dynamic camber angle other than the optimum will reduce traction.

Here is what happens. Assume that the dynamic camber angle is positive, so that the outside edge of the tire is more heavily loaded. The extra load on the rubber molecules at the outside third of the tire contact patch will have more load than those in the middle third. The inside third will have even less load. The resulting effect is that the outside third of the tire will have increased traction while the inside third has less traction. The relationship is exactly the same as our discussion concerning weight transfer. The rubber molecules on the outside third of the tire will gain traction at a rate slower than the inside third will lose traction. The middle third will average out.

In this situation, the outer third of molecules are overworked, the inside third are underworked

and the net outcome is that less traction is available compared to the perfect dynamic camber setting. Even increments as small as 0.2 degree can make a difference. In reality, such a difference can cost about 0.05 second in one turn. On a ten-turn track, that alone is a half second a lap that is being given away. In a ten-lap race, that's a five-second loss. What about a 500 mile race? How much extra horsepower is needed to gain a half second a lap? Suspension design and set-up, then, are crucial factors for handling performance.

We have just shown how the suspension system can affect total traction directly. Conversely, it can also affect traction indirectly. This is because weight transfer is affected by the suspension linkages. We have seen how the location of the roll centers and roll axis affect weight transfer. The suspension linkages, then, determine where the roll centers and roll axis are located.

Camber Change

Camber change at the wheel is caused by the fact that the wheel swings in an arc as it travels upward or downward through its range. This occurs during wheel travel over bumps and so forth, or through weight transfer while cornering, accelerating and braking.

All suspension systems, regardless of design, rotate about a single point called the instantaneous center of rotation, or instant center for short. This is easy to visualize on a swing-arm suspension where the wheel is attached to the chassis at one pivot point. In this case, the wheel goes into positive camber in rebound and negative camber in bump. During body roll, the outside tire will move into negative camber, while the inside tire moves into positive camber. The amount of camber

Even the fully independent, rear-drive, mid-engine Porsche 914 shows considerable camber change during roll. The inside wheels have more negative camber, while the outside have more positive camber. To keep the tire contact patch flat on the ground during cornering is the most important job of the high-performance suspension system. Optimum suspension geometry and minimum body roll help accomplish this important task.

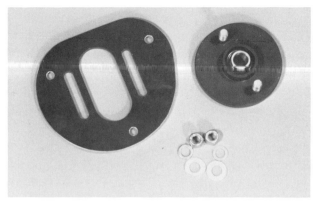

The custom camber plate for the front struts on a Toyota Corolla GT-S Twin Cam. These plates allow maximum negative camber settings with no modifications to the strut or hub assembly and improve steering rotation and eliminate suspension travel binding with the spherical bearing, which replaces the rubber bushing on the strut at the strut tower.

change depends upon the length of the swing arm (or distance from the instant center to the center of the wheel) and the amount of travel. If we start with zero camber, then any travel will cause the tire contact patch to tilt, and reduce the traction potential of the tire.

Longer instant center lengths reduce the camber change for every increment of wheel travel. Also, the vertical location of the instant center will alter the camber change characteristics at the wheel.

With independent suspension systems, the instant center location will move as the wheel travels

The camber plate assembled.

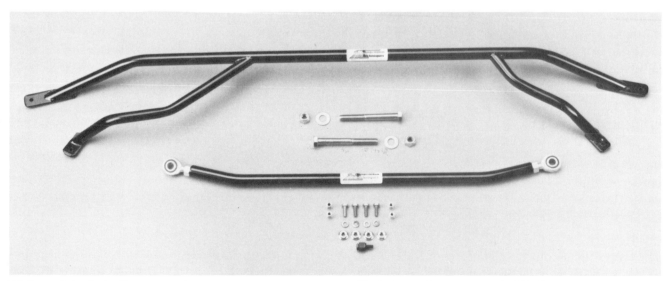

While not technically suspension components, strut tower braces and stressbars reduce chassis flex and help the suspension do its job. These are from Suspension

Techniques for water-cooled Volkswagens. Suspension Techniques

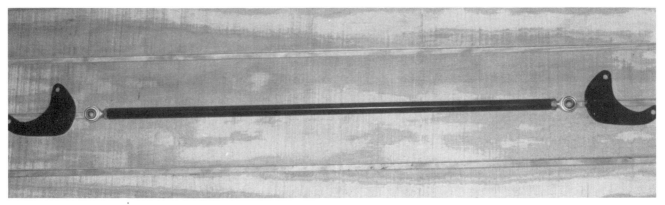

A strut tower brace is a worthwhile addition between the strut towers to reduce flex and the camber change that accompanies it. Bob Ryder

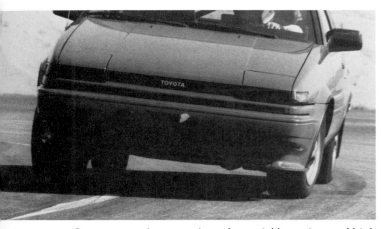

Strut suspensions require substantial lowering and high amounts of roll resistance to keep the outside front tire from moving into too much positive camber. It is virtually impossible to adjust the static camber to enough negative to overcome the camber change, as shown here.

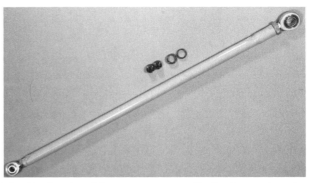

The Panhard rod for a Toyota Corolla GT-S rear-drive locates the rear axle laterally, keeping it from shifting relative to the body during cornering. The Panhard rod also determines the roll center, which is located where the Panhard rod crosses the centerline of the rear axle.

through bump and rebound maneuvers. Additionally, the instant center may be located to the inside or the outside of the wheel.

Roll Centers

Now that we have an instant center, we can find the roll center: a point in space that determines the roll characteristics of a vehicle during cornering due to weight transfer. From the instant center, we plot a line to the center of the tire contact patch on the same side of the vehicle. Where the line from the instant center to the center of the tire contact patch on the left side intersects the same line on the right side is the location of the roll center. Notice that it is not where one line crosses the centerline of the vehicle. At rest, or during vertical travel, with symmetrical suspension, the roll center will be located on the vehicle centerline,

but with asymmetrical suspension, or during body roll, the roll center may move laterally.

The roll center is also prone to vertical movement during all types of suspension travel. Roll center movement can cause force redistribution and affect the amount of body roll and degree of weight transfer. It is best if the suspension geometry limits body roll, as this will minimize roll center movement.

Different suspension geometries and systems create different roll center locations and movement patterns. As we explore different systems, we will learn about how each one affects roll center location and movement.

Roll Axis

Each suspension system has its own roll center location. The front and rear roll center heights and movement patterns will most likely be different from one another. If we connect the front and rear roll centers with a line, we will get the roll axis. The roll axis determines the pivot axis of the sprung mass (body) of a vehicle during body roll caused by weight transfer.

As we have seen earlier, the amount of body roll caused by weight transfer is determined by the location of the roll axis relative to the center of gravity. If the roll axis passes through the center of gravity of the vehicle, no body roll will take place (but weight transfer will still be present). If the roll axis is located at some distance away from the center of gravity, a torque is created and body roll will occur. The greater the distance from the center of gravity, the longer the lever arm (known as a moment arm) and the more the body will roll.

The springs and antiroll bars resist body roll. The amount of body roll is directly proportional to the cornering force and moment arm length from the center of gravity and inversely proportional to the roll resistance from the springs and antiroll bars.

The roll axis can be located just about anywhere. If the roll axis is at ground level, then the moment arm length from the roll axis to the center of gravity is equal to the height of the center of gravity above ground. This will cause substantial body roll, but not as much as is extremely possible. The roll axis can be below ground, which would cause even more roll. What happens if the roll axis is above the center of gravity? The vehicle will lean into the turn, but weight transfer still moves weight from the inside wheels to the outside wheels. This phenomenon shows that weight transfer is not caused by body roll. In fact, the opposite is true. Body roll is caused by weight transfer.

Since we know that body roll causes camber change, then why not design the suspension so that the roll axis will pass through the center of gravity? Seems like a good idea at first, but there are four important problems caused by this design. First, the camber change during bump and rebound travel is substantial, causing traction problems during braking and acceleration. Second, this geometry can cause substantial track change during bump and rebound travel, thus causing tire scrub and drag. Third, all of the weight transfer of the sprung mass will pass through the roll centers instead of the springs and bars. This causes other problems. Fourth, no roll resistance is needed, so we cannot alter where weight is transferred by changing the roll couple distribution. Most of these problems diminish as the roll axis approaches ground level.

Roll Axis Inclination

Naturally, since the roll centers can be located anywhere, the chance that both front and rear roll centers are at the same height is small. If they are not at the same height, then the roll axis will be inclined. How the roll axis is inclined can affect where weight is transferred while cornering.

If a vehicle has no suspension and if forty percent of the total vehicle weight is on the rear wheels, then forty percent of the weight transfer will occur at the rear. The same situation will occur if the roll axis passes through the center of gravity on a vehicle with suspension. Forty percent of the sprung weight transfer will occur at the rear, sixty percent at the front. In reality, the roll axis must pass through the center of gravity of the front section of the vehicle and through the center of gravity of the rear section for this to occur.

When we separate sections of a vehicle and determine the center of gravity for each (a difficult job), we have created a series of centers of gravity that can be joined by connecting line that links each point (viewed from the side). This line is called the mass centroid axis. If the mass centroid axis and the roll axis are the same, there is no body roll and the amount of weight transfer at the front versus the rear is proportional to the weight distribution at the front versus the rear.

If the roll axis is below, but parallel to, the mass centroid axis, then body roll occurs and the lateral weight transfer will still be proportional to the weight distribution of the vehicle. This is the ideal situation, and most true race car designs follow this principle. Most street vehicle designs, for myriad reasons however, do not. When the roll axis is not parallel to the mass centroid axis, then the distance of the roll center to the center of gravity at one end of the vehicle will be greater than at the other end. In this case, one end of the vehicle wants to roll more than the other end, but obviously cannot (although I've seen some designs over the years that were so flexible the chassis would twist, allowing this to occur).

If the front roll center to center of gravity moment arm is shorter than that at the rear, the front will roll less than it wants to and the rear will roll more than it wants to. This will force more of the sprung mass weight transfer to occur at the rear than the static weight distribution would dictate, and has the same effect that increasing rear roll couple distribution has, in this case causing oversteer (in a neutral vehicle). This is one of the four factors we discussed in the weight transfer chapter, which determines where weight is transferred while cornering.

Roll Center Height and Weight Transfer

The fourth factor controlling weight transfer is the height of the roll center above ground. We have seen how this affects the amount of body roll, but it also affects where the sprung weight is transferred. If the roll center is at ground level, then all of the sprung weight at that end of the vehicle is transferred through the springs and bars as vertical load. If the roll center coincides with the center of gravity at one end of the vehicle, then all of the sprung weight that is transferred does so through

While the high roll center on the live-axle, rear-drive Corolla GT-S reduces body roll, even more roll resistance is needed to keep the rear tire contact patches flat while cornering. Lowering the car another 2 in. would also help.

Struts must be shortened if the car is to be lowered significantly. Otherwise the strut cartridge will bottom out in bump and damage the valves. This strut for a Datsun 240Z has been shortened 2 in. so that the car can be lowered to the minimum ride height for SCCA Improved Touring racing. Getting the car down to the minimum ride height allowed by the rules means that the center of gravity is as low as possible and weight transfer is at a minimum.

the roll center to the wheel, part of which is a lateral load. This reduces traction. The closer the roll center is to the center of gravity, the greater this effect.

The effect is often called the jacking effect because part of the force created by the tires works vertically at the roll center and literally tries to raise that end of the vehicle. This reduces cornering force. Higher roll centers also reduce the effectiveness of using roll resistance to change the roll couple distribution. This hurts the tunability of the suspension, making a good handling balance more difficult to achieve.

It is for this reason that most modern high-performance cars and all race cars have roll centers relatively low, ranging from 2 in. below ground to about 12 in. above ground. In most cases, with independent suspension at front and rear, the rear roll center is slightly above the front, and no more than 6 in. above ground. With a beam axle, the roll center will be higher.

Moving roll centers affects all of the factors we have discussed in this chapter. Since it is difficult to move roll centers, we will not consider that here. In fact, changing roll center heights by moving suspension pick-up points causes so many other alterations to dynamic characteristics of a vehicle that it is best to start with a clean sheet of paper. That is a design problem, and a rather complex one that we will not cover here.

Keep in mind that a change in ride height by lowering the car with shorter springs lowers the suspension pick-up points on the chassis, but not

those at the wheel. This changes the geometry and moves the roll centers. This will tend to lower the roll center on most types of suspension, but will also alter the camber change curve and roll center movement. If we lower the car with a lower profile tire, all of the pick-up points are lowered an equal amount. This will lower the roll center but not change the geometry. Camber change curves and roll center movement will be the same.

What we need to know is the effect that the roll centers have on weight transfer and camber change. Then we can concentrate on limiting the effects of roll center movement and camber change, and allow the tires to create maximum traction. This is done by increasing roll resistance to limit roll while cornering. Calculating roll resistance needed to limit body roll requires some effort.

Steering Systems

Since the steering system is difficult to modify, we will spend little time on the design of the steering, but will focus instead upon the factors relating to the steering system that affect the handling's important parameters. We will not look at the mechanics of the steering system, such as the qualities of a rack and pinion system versus a recirculating ball system. The geometry of the steering system affects both traction and responsiveness, two issues we have determined play a crucial role in handling improvements.

We will look at the important factors that determine drag, feel and response caused by the

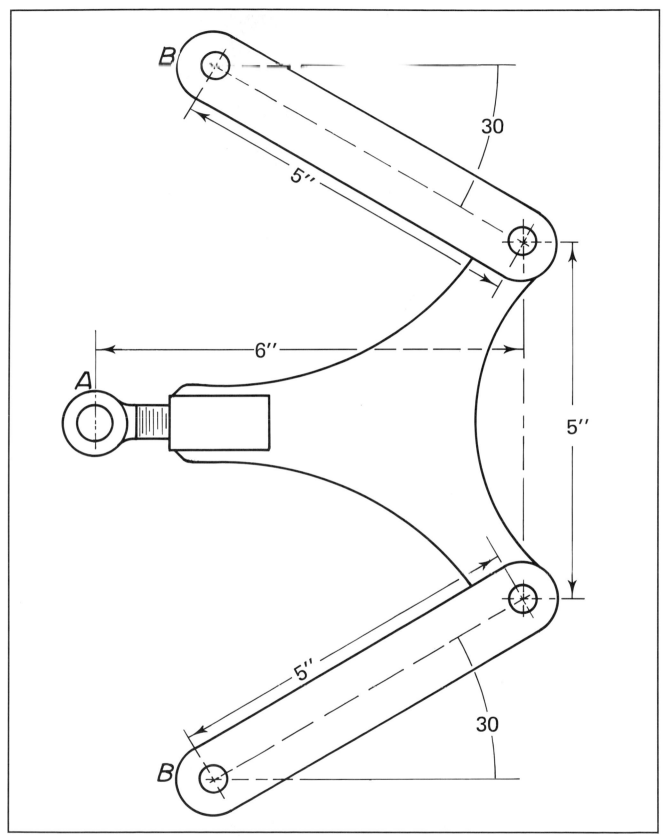

Location of the rear axle laterally is a concern with a live axle suspended by a leaf spring. The common Panhard rod locates the axle, but causes roll center movement vertically during suspension travel. The Watt's linkage accomplishes the same job without the roll center movement, and it requires less space.

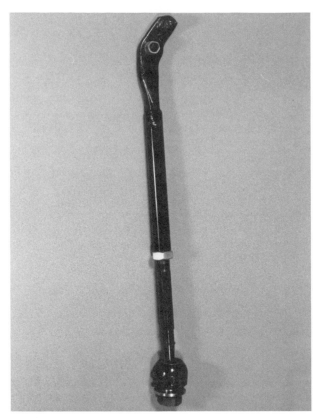

The drag strut acts as a suspension linkage on the lower control arm of many strut front suspension systems. This one has been modified to eliminate the rubber bushing by using a steel ball and socket. The ball and socket allow suspension travel vertically, but eliminate castor and other unwanted geometry changes. The threaded section allows easy, quick and accurate castor adjustment.

steering system. Most of the factors that affect drag, feel and response can be modified easily.

Castor

Castor is the angle, in side view, about which the wheel and tire pivot when steered. If we draw a line through the upper and lower ball joint centers extended to ground level, the result can be defined as the castor angle. If the line is vertical, the castor angle is zero. If the top of the line tilts to the rear, the castor angle is positive; to the front, negative.

Some amount of positive castor creates a self-centering effect in the steering. In other words, when the steering wheel is released while turning, the wheels will return to center. The primary cause of this relates to the steering axis line intersection with the tire contact patch. If the steering axis intersects with the center of the tire contact patch, there is little self-centering. If the distance is large, the self-centering effect is large (this distance is known as castor trail.)

Self-centering also occurs because of camber change during turning. The castor angle causes a change in camber angle during rotation. If you watch the spindle during steering, it will rise. The pattern from full left lock to full right lock looks like a U. This increases the weight on the wheel, and the weight helps steer the wheel back to straight when the steering input is reduced or eliminated. This effect increases as the positive castor angle increases.

It is for this reason that left- and right-side castor adjustments must be exactly the same, or the vehicle will pull to one side (the side with less positive castor) if the steering wheel is released. This is called castor stagger and requires a constant steering input to hold the vehicle in a straight line. This obviously causes tire scrub or drag.

More positive castor will increase the steering effort needed to turn the vehicle. It will also increase steering feel for the driver, the self-centering effect and tire scrub or drag while cornering. The increases in feel and self-centering are positive, the increases in steering effort and tire scrub are negative.

This clearly indicates that the castor setting must be a compromise. Too much positive castor hurts traction, too little hurts driver steering feel. The more accomplished the driver, the less castor is needed, and traction improves slightly. The improvement is small, though, and often the increased driver feel is more important than the small traction loss. Driver preference is most often the deciding factor.

Different cars use different methods to adjust castor. Use an alignment shop or consult a shop repair manual for methods to adjust castor for a specific car.

Castor Offset

If the vehicle is designed with castor offset, then a negative castor angle may be needed for correct steering feel and self-centering. Castor offset differs from castor angle. If the castor angle is zero, but the line through the upper and lower ball joints to the tire contact patch does not intersect at the center of the tire contact patch, castor offset is present. The amount of offset is the distance from the steering pivot point to the center of the tire contact patch, or castor trail. The steering pivot always leads the center point of the tire contact patch to provide stability, for the same reason a cart in a market has castor wheels with a steering pivot in front of the wheel center point.

Castor offset does not cause a camber change when the wheel is turned. For this reason, castor offset is often used to allow small (even zero or negative) castor angles. Castor offset has the same effect on steering effort, feel, scrub and self-centering as castor angle. It is difficult to change, however, requiring a major redesign of the suspension system.

Steering Offset

Steering offset is similar in description to castor. The offset measurement is the same as castor, but in front view instead of side view. A line drawn from the upper ball joint center through the lower ball joint center and intersecting the tire contact patch determines the steering axis angle; in front view, this is known as the king pin inclination. The point from where the steering axis intersects the tire contact patch to the center of the tire contact patch is the steering offset. The offset is positive if the steering axis intersects the tire contact patch to the inside of the center point of the tire contact patch. It is negative if the steering axis intersects the tire contact patch to the outside of the center point of the tire contact patch.

Much debate exists concerning the merits of positive and negative offsets. Negative offsets offer better stability, especially when uneven forces are applied to the front wheels; this is most useful on front-wheel-drive cars. Negative offset leaves less space for the hub and suspension inside the wheel.

Steering offset can be altered easily with different wheel widths and offsets. Changes to suspension geometry will also change steering offset, but require substantial effort and a complete redesign of the suspension system.

Like castor trail, steering offset will affect tire scrub, steering effort, steering feel and self-centering. Larger offsets increase the effects, while smaller offsets reduce the effects. A compromise is again necessary. If the steering axis intersects the center of the tire contact patch, the system is called center point steering.

For both castor trail and steering offset, the best compromise seems to be a small amount of each. Both are important to steering feel, but too much will cause drag and high steering efforts. It is important to be careful with wheel offsets when using wider wheels as part of a handling improvement program. Changes to offset should be kept to a minimum.

Self-Aligning Torque

Self-aligning torque is a self-centering effect caused by the tire tread twisting while cornering. This is caused by the tire slip angle, and the twist in the tire tries to turn the tire back to zero slip angle. This is an important source of feedback to the driver, and helps the steering center itself.

Self-aligning torque is not strong enough by itself to ensure self-centering, however. Stiff sidewall, low-profile tires offer more self-aligning torque at the same slip angle, and improve both feel and responsiveness.

Ackerman Steering

Ackerman steering geometry allows the inside wheel to turn to a larger angle than the outside wheel in a turn. Since the inside wheel is on a tighter turning radius, and the outside wheel on a larger turning radius, the inside wheel must be steered more than the outside wheel or one tire will scrub, reducing cornering ability and optimum tire temperatures.

Ackerman steering geometry is accomplished by the angle of the steering arms on the wheel spindles. If you draw a line through the tie-rod end and the ball joint on the spindle, 100 percent Ackerman steering geometry is present if the lines converge at the center of the rear axle. If the lines converge past the rear axle, the Ackerman effect is less than 100 percent, meaning that the inside wheel turns less than needed in a turn. If the lines converge within the wheelbase, then the effect is greater than 100 percent.

Ackerman geometry first appeared on horse-drawn wagons with a single pivot front axle. Since the entire axle rotated about its center point, the inside wheel was always turned to the correct radius relative to the outside wheel. About three decades ago, anti-Ackerman steering was developed. As the name implies, the outside wheel was turned more than the inside wheel. The reason was that the outside tire was more heavily loaded, so it needed to operate at a higher slip angle. This design was in vogue for some time.

In the last decade, Ackerman steering has returned, often exceeding 100 percent geometry. Current thinking dictates that since the inside tire is less loaded, and therefore operates at a smaller slip angle, it needs to be turned even more than 100 percent Ackerman geometry would indicate. In reality, increased Ackerman geometry seems to reduce transient corner entry understeer, especially in slow turns on cars with substantial aerodynamic downforce.

Since Ackerman steering geometry is difficult to change on most vehicles, it is considered a design exercise, not a tuning modification, and not a tool we will make use of here.

Bump Steer

When the front suspension moves through bump and rebound travel over bumps and so forth, it swings in an arc that is determined by the instant center location. The steering tie-rod also moves in an arc when the suspension moves up and down. If the arc of the tie-rod does not match the arc of the suspension, the difference will cause the wheel to be steered. In effect, there is a change in toe-in or toe-out at the wheel. This can cause an unwanted steering motion over bumps or during body roll, hence the name bump steer.

More important in competition applications is the fact that this bump steer always causes tire scrub, and the ensuing drag can hurt straight-line speed. In a turn, it causes a reduction in traction, and lower cornering speeds. If the tie-rod imitates the location and movement of one control arm, the

This aluminum knuckle riser fits between the steering arm and the strut assembly. It changes the relationship of the tie rod to the lower control arm and reduces bump steer (toe change during suspension travel).

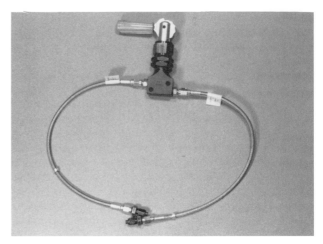

A brake proportioning valve, like this one from Tilton Engineering, allows line pressure adjustments to the rear brakes. This can balance the pressure so that the front brakes lock up just slightly before the rears, thus reducing stopping distances and improving feel and control of the car during hard braking.

bump steer is not present. Cars with Ackerman steering geometry often have some degree of bump steer because the angled steering arm moves the tie-rod away from the plane of the A-arms. Zero bump steer occurs when the tie-rod ends fall on the lines the upper and lower inner pivots and the upper and lower outer ball joints.

Most modern race cars allow easy adjustment of bump steer. Most modern street vehicles have little bump steer with stock geometry. When a stock vehicle is modified, then geometry changes can occur, often causing substantial amounts of bump steer.

For both street and competition purposes, it is a good idea to eliminate any bump steer. This will improve vehicle performance, tire wear and safety. Excessive bump steer can cause violent steering wheel movements, which make a car difficult to control, especially at high speed.

The most common modification that will introduce bump steer occurs on vehicles with Mac-Pherson strut suspension. When struts are shortened to facilitate lowering the car, the steering geometry is altered. A knuckle riser, which raises the steering arm assembly closer to its original location, will reduce or eliminate the bump steer. Another option relative to bump steer elimination requires raising or lowering outer tie-rod ends, or moving the steering rack. On production vehicles, we often use a rod end in place of the tie-rod end, modify the steering arm to accept an aircraft-quality bolt, and use spacers to raise or lower the tie-rod.

The pattern of bump steer usually indicates where the changes need to be made. By measuring toe-in or toe-out through increments of suspension travel, you can plot a simple graph that will tell you where a change needs to be made. The goal is to prevent change in toe-in or toe-out during at least the first 2 in. of bump and the first 2 in. of rebound travel. The graph should have a vertical line on the zero toe-in point.

Bump steer is easy to measure with a gauge, and easy to fix, although the process can be time consuming and tedious.

Roll Steer

Roll steer is just like bump steer only at the rear of a vehicle. Roll steer occurs during body roll when suspension linkages force a change in toe-in or toe-out at the rear wheels. Unless the design facilitates adjustment, roll steer is not easily altered and will not be covered here.

Roll steer should be measured, however, so that toe-in or toe-out changes can be measured. It is important on an independent suspension system to set the static rear toe-in to compensate for any toe-out that might be present during bump travel. Toe-out at the rear, especially in bumps, can cause serious handling problems.

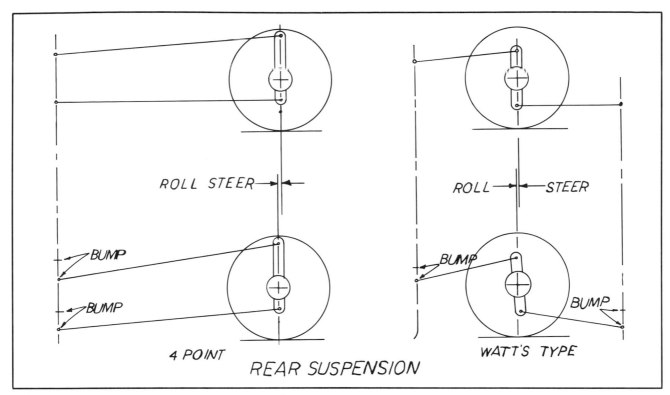

ROLL STEER

BUMP

BUMP

4 POINT

ROLL → ← STEER

BUMP

BUMP

WATT'S TYPE

REAR SUSPENSION

A four-link rear suspension system can cause roll steer
with either a live rear axle or independent suspension.
The Watt's type link system reduces this tendency.

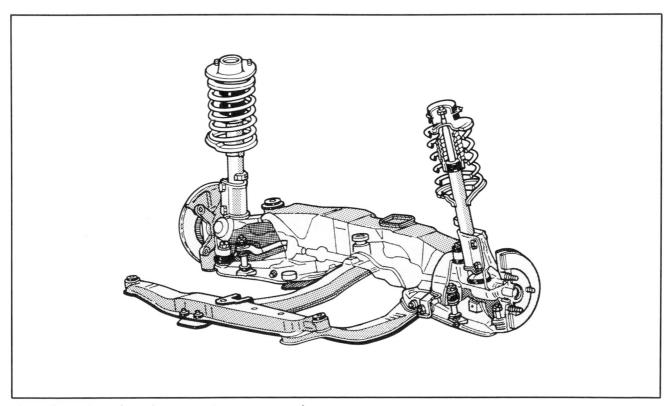

These illustrations show the suspension systems on the
Eagle Talon TSi all-wheel-drive.

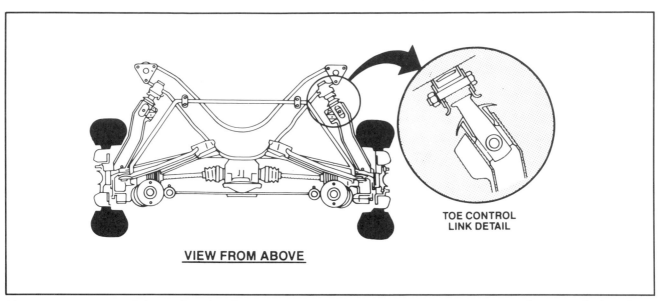

VIEW FROM ABOVE

TOE CONTROL
LINK DETAIL

The rear suspension of the Eagle Talon features a toe control link that changes the toe setting from static settings during cornering. This increases stability and allows smaller toe-in settings at the rear, which reduces straightline drag.

The strong, simple and extremely effective inboard front suspension of the Consulier uses an upper rocker arm lever to activate the inboard-mounted coil-over unit. The

threads on the shock body allow quick and precise ride height adjustment, and make setting corner weights much easier and more accurate. Bob Ryder

Chapter 5

Springs

The reason for the development of suspension systems on vehicles is twofold. First, suspension allows vehicle occupants to become more isolated from bumps, dips, ruts and surface irregularities; in other words, to make the ride more comfortable. Second, suspension allows the tire to stay in contact with the road surface over the same bumps, ruts and so on. While ride is important, our primary concern with suspension here is to improve handling. Exponently, the spring plays an important part of the suspension system.

Role of Springs

Just what does a spring do? A spring, defined in terms of physics, stores energy. When a constant force is applied to a spring, it will store the energy of that force and return to its original shape when the force is no longer applied. Many springs, when a force is applied or released quickly, will bounce back beyond their original length and oscillate until friction dampens the oscillation or vibration.

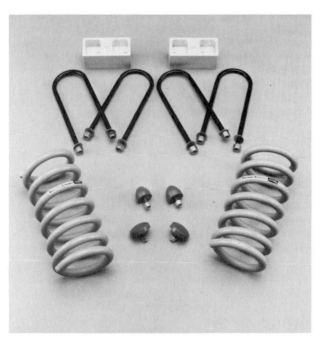

The easiest way to lower the center of gravity is to lower the vehicle. The quickest and most effective method is with shorter springs where coils are used or with lowering blocks for leaf springs. The goal is to keep the vehicle as low as possible without bottoming out on the ground or the suspension. Bottoming will ruin handling characteristics and traction. Ground clearance is crucial for the street, while suspension travel is most important for competition. For the street and many competition applications, a package like the one shown from Suspension Techniques for the Chevrolet S-10 and GMC S-15 is the most effective way to go. Suspension Techniques

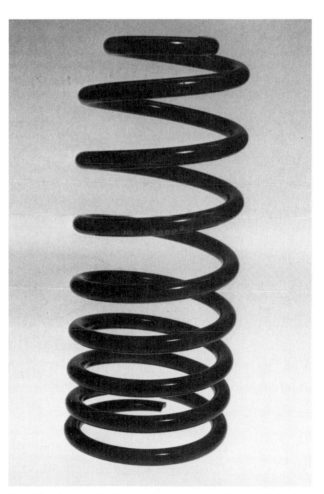

The Eibach Pro Kit Spring System is a balance kit for improved handling performance on the road. Bob Ryder

71

The Eibach ERS springs are for racing applications, but plans are in the works for a street system. The dual-element spring allows less ride height with a softer initial spring rate. The two springs work together to create a single spring rate until the smaller spring begins to bind. Then the rate increases, allowing for better response and less chance of bottoming over bumps. Bob Ryder

For our purposes, a spring absorbs shock. The shocks are caused by bumps or ruts or other forces that are fed into the tire or wheel. These forces can be caused by acceleration, braking or turning, or the terrain over which the vehicle passes. The spring absorbs these shocks or loads so that the occupants of the vehicle are less aware of them. The process of absorbing these shocks also allows the tire contact patch to maintain more contact with the surface of the road. It is the improved tire contact that is our primary concern when attempting to improve handling.

By now you may be asking what the job of a shock absorber is if the spring absorbs shock. We will get to that in the shock absorber chapter.

Let's take the definition of the spring's job one step further. In the course of absorbing shocks, the spring influences how well the tire contact patches complies with the road surface. It follows, then, that one of the jobs of the spring is to keep the tire contact patch on the ground. Take the extreme, for example. What happens with stiff springs? Look at a solid spring that cannot absorb shock, that is, where there is no suspension. When a bump is encountered the wheel will bounce off of the bump, momentarily lifting the tire contact patch from the road surface. If this occurs while the tire is attempting to brake, accelerate or corner, traction will be lost.

If the spring is soft, the suspension may bottom out, or go into full rebound, unless the car sets high in the air with considerable suspension travel. We know that a low center of gravity is critical for performance, but bottoming of the suspension also causes problems. If the suspension bottoms out, the spring rate at the corner of the vehicle rises to infinity, and instant weight transfer will occur there, causing a loss of traction.

It should be obvious then that there is a range of spring rates available that will work within these extremes. From a handling perspective, the most important concern is keeping the tire contact patch on the ground over bumps. If we had a perfectly smooth surface, we would need neither suspension nor springs. The tire contact patch would stay on the ground. As bumps are introduced we need springs to absorb shock and keep the tire contact patch on the ground. As the bumps get larger, the springs must be softer to absorb the shock and maintain tire contact with the road. Suspension travel must also increase as the bumps get larger, or we risk the suspension bottoming out or going into full rebound, which can lift the tire completely off of the ground.

The determining factor for spring stiffness is the bumpiness of the surface. The bumpier the surface, the softer the springs must be to maintain tire contact with the surface. How soft or stiff is the key question.

Suspension Frequencies

Frequency is how often something occurs over a given time span. Everyone is familiar with radio station frequencies. Electricity moves through a wire in a wave that oscillates at 60 cycles per second, also called 60 hertz. The natural frequency of a walking man is about 60 cycles per minute. Suspensions also have frequencies. Each spring working on a corner of a vehicle will oscillate at a given frequency if left undamped. We usually measure the frequencies in cycles per minute, because it is more accurate than cycles per second.

Two factors determine the frequency of a suspension. The first is the rate of the spring acting at the wheel (or actually at the tire contact patch). Leverage and movement ratios must be determined to calculate the rate of the spring at the wheel (known, conversely, as the wheel rate of the spring).

The second factor is the load resting upon the spring. In the case of a vehicle with suspension, the load on a spring at rest is called the sprung weight: it is the weight that the spring supports. The weight that is not supported by the spring is called unsprung weight. Unsprung weight is comprised of the wheel, tire, hub and brake assembly, and half the weight of the suspension arms and, usually, the spring and shock. On a solid axle, the axle weight is also unsprung.

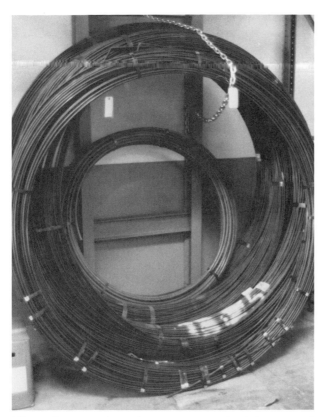

The wire is coiled over mandrels to create the proper inside diameter. Each of these mandrels used is exactly the correct amount smaller than the actual spring diameter to allow for slight recoil after the spring is wound.

The spring manufacturing process at Eibach begins with high-quality steel wire of the appropriate diameter.

If the sprung weight increases while the spring rate stays the same, the frequency is lower. If the spring rate increases while the sprung weight remains the same, the frequency rises. The suspension frequency is directly proportional to the spring rate at the wheel, and inversely proportional to the sprung weight.

The frequency of a suspension is one of the constants we can use to determine what spring rates will work for a given road smoothness situation. Our ballpark figures have been determined by much testing over a long period of time. Fine-tuning comes into play within a specific range of frequencies to allow adjustments to other factors beyond maintaining tire contact patch with the road surface, although that is the main priority.

The comfort range of frequencies for vehicles occupied by people is from about 60 to 120 cpm. For the average driver, 60 cpm is very soft while 120 cpm would be considered uncomfortable.

For improved handling, and specifically for increased traction, we want the stiffest spring possible that will allow the tire contact patch to remain on the road surface for the greatest amount of time. The stiffest possible spring will allow the lowest possible ride height without bottoming of the suspension or bottoming on the road. What frequency works for what condition?

Each mandrel has a trace that the wire is to follow to achieve the proper pitch. The bare wire is fed through this spring winder. The rollers guide the wire onto the mandrel where it is wound. The rotational speed of the mandrel determines the pitch.

On the street, if someone wants a reasonable ride, we will work for a frequency around 75 to 80 cpm. For a more sporting set-up, the frequency will go up as high as 90 cpm. Most cars can be lowered from 1 to 3 in. with this range of frequency. That would translate to a ride height (the distance from the ground to the rocker panel behind the front fender well) of 6 to 8 in. Less ground clearance would either cause bottoming or require stiffer than desirable spring rates.

In competition, three ranges and two categories are required for general consideration. The ranges include smooth, moderately bumpy and bumpy. Bumpy is smoother than the highway range. The categories include vehicles that generate little or no aerodynamic downforce and those that create substantial aerodynamic downforce.

The reason for the two categories that are influenced by aerodynamic downforce is current racing regulations. All aerodynamic downforce loads are fed through the suspension as opposed to passing directly to the tire contact patch via the hubs and wheels. All aerodynamic downforce, whether created by wings or ground effects, places additional load on the suspension, which will compress the springs. This requires stiffer springs to allow minimum ride heights — as low as 0.5 in on Indy cars and Formula One cars — without bottoming. Since we measure frequencies at rest, the frequencies must be high. Similarly, when cars run on banked tracks, the frequency must be substantially higher, because the load on the springs increases as the banking angle increases.

The frequency range for cars without significant aerodynamic downforce is as follows:

Very bumpy surface: 80 to 100 cpm
Bumpy surface: 95 to 120 cpm
Smooth surface: 120 to 150 cpm

The frequency range for cars with significant aerodynamic downforce is as follows:

Very bumpy surface: 120 to 140 cpm
Bumpy surface: 140 to 160 cpm
Smooth surface: 160 to 200 cpm

In all cases, the frequency at the front must be different from that at the rear by ten to fifteen percent to reduce the likelihood of a harmonic pitching motion between the front and rear of the vehicle. In most cases, the front is lower than the rear. In our development work, we have found in testing that with front-wheel-drive vehicles, the trend seems to reverse, with the front higher than the rear. The reason seems to be that the drive wheels are at the front, and more of the roll resistance needs to be provided by the springs at the driven end of the car. The results are promising, but the jury is still out.

The frequency for the heavily loaded car with substantial aerodynamic downforce works out to be similar to the frequency for the non-aerodynamic downforce car when we compute the aerodynamic downforce load at the average speed for a lap, then add the load to the weight of the vehicle. Lighter cars tend to run at the high end of the frequency range, usually because they have a lower ratio of sprung to unsprung weight. The higher the ratio of sprung to unsprung weight, the better the handling will be because the spring and shock absorber have an easier time forcing the tire contact patch to conform to the road surface.

As an example, a Formula Ford racer that weighs about 1,200 lb. with driver and fuel has about 240 lb. of unsprung weight total. That computes to twenty percent unsprung weight or a 5:1 ratio of sprung to unsprung weight. An International Sedan running in IMSA weighs about 2,600 lb. with driver and carries about 350 lb. of unsprung weight or 13.5 percent unsprung weight, a sprung to unsprung weight ratio of 7.5:1, which is good. The Formula Ford will have relatively higher frequencies compared to the International Sedan.

Eibach continually tests springs for rate and consistency. The Eibach ERS dual-element spring is undergoing a load test to determine the overall rate and the change in spring rate during travel for this progressive rate spring system.

The precision, computerized spring winding equipment at Eibach accounts for the high quality of their products.

Vehicles that generate aerodynamic downforce must run low ride heights for aerodynamic reasons. The airflow under the car must be minimized, especially on cars with ground effects, so that drag is minimized and lift is reduced to nil. Little suspension travel is desired to maintain the air seal under the car, even without the use of side skirts like those used in the mid 1980s on Formula One cars. In that era, it was so important to keep the air seal from breaking under the car that suspension frequencies in the 300 + cpm range were common. The ride was so horrible at that level of stiffness that many drivers suffered serious back problems, and almost every driver complained of blurred vision from the high-frequency vibrations. The ground effects of that era were banned, for good reason, and a more sane approach prevails today.

Wheel Rates

The wheel rate of a spring is the rate of a spring expressed in pounds per inch of travel acting at the tire contact patch. Unless the spring is mounted vertically at the center of the tire contact patch, acting on the ball joint of the lower control arm, the spring rate will be higher than the wheel rate for outboard suspension systems. Inboard systems, activated by a rocker arm or pushrod-pullrod set-up, can have wheel rates that exceed the spring rate.

Three factors work together to reduce the effective spring rate at the wheel. The first, and most significant, is the motion ratio of the spring on the lower control arm. The second is the motion ratio of the spring location compared to the effective swing arm length. The final factor is the mounting angle of the spring from vertical. Let's look at each factor.

Lower Control Arm Motion Ratio

If the spring is mounted so that its centerline passes through the center of the control arm ball joint, the motion ratio is 1.00. If the spring is mounted inside this point, then the motion ratio is less than 1.00.

The motion ratio is found by dividing the distance from the spring centerline to the inner A-arm pivot by the center-to-center length of the A-arm. If the spring center to the inner pivot measures 6.25 in. and the ball joint center to inner pivot measures 10 in., then the motion ratio is 0.625. The same method can be used to calculate the motion ratio for a rocker arm or pushrod-pullrod suspension system. The formula is:

$$\text{Motion ratio} = \frac{\text{Spring center to inner pivot distance}}{\text{A-arm length}}$$

Swing Arm Motion Ratio

The swing arm length is the distance from the center of the tire contact patch to the instantaneous center of rotation (instant center) found in the previous chapter. This motion ratio is found by dividing the distance from the spring center to the instant center by the swing arm length. If the spring to instant center length is 120 in. and the swing arm length is 131 in., then the motion ratio is 0.916. The formula is:

$$\text{Motion ratio} = \frac{\text{Spring center to instant center}}{\text{Swing arm length}}$$

Mounting Angle of the Spring

When a spring is not vertical, the angle causes the spring to travel less than the lower mounting point during vertical suspension travel. If the spring was mounted at a 90 degree angle, then it would not move during suspension travel at all. The larger the angle from vertical, the greater the effect. The ratio is proportional to the cosine of the mounting angle. If the angle is 15 degrees, the ratio is cosine 15, which equals 0.966. The formula is:

$$\text{Motion ratio} = \text{Cosine of angle from vertical}$$

To determine the wheel rate, all three factors must be taken into account. Each motion ratio is squared because it is affected both by the leverage and by the distance moved vertically. Each factor

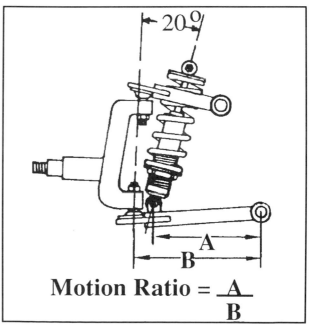

Motion Ratio = $\dfrac{A}{B}$

The motion ratio is a lever arm effect of the control arm acting on the spring. If the spring is mounted at an angle, the reduced motion of the spring must also be taken into account.

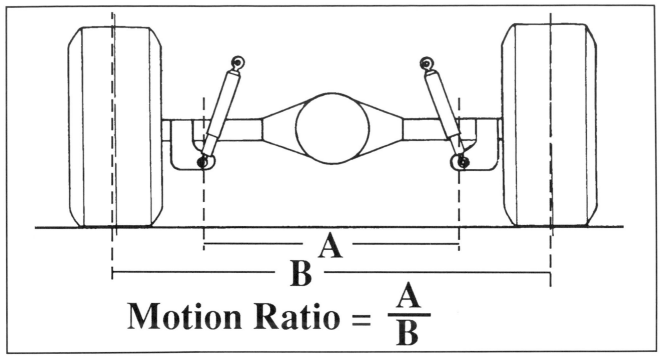

Motion Ratio = $\dfrac{A}{B}$

The motion ratio of a live axle set-up is shown here. Over two wheel bumps, the motion ratio is 1:1. Over single wheel bumps and during body roll, the motion ratio is shown. The motion ratio is only used for calculating roll resistance, but not for suspension frequencies.

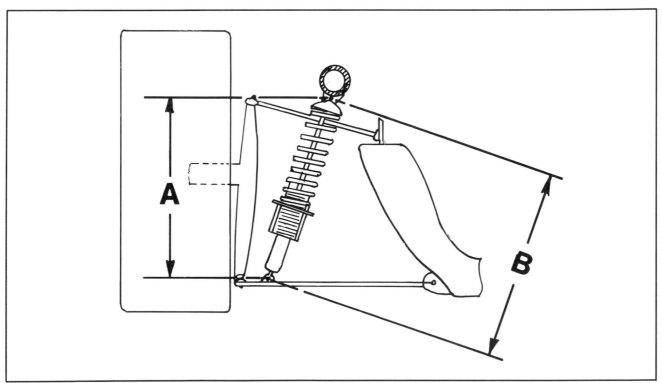

Part of the motion ratio is the mounting angle of the spring from vertical. If the spring was mounted at 90 degrees from vertical, it would have zero travel during vertical suspension movement. To find the ratio, measurement A is divided by B in the above diagram. The result is then multiplied by the motion ratio, which is the leverage applied to the spring by the control arm. An alternate method to find the spring angle is to measure the angle from vertical at rest. Use the sine of the angle in the above formula.

reduces the motion ratio by providing less leverage and less vertical movement.

Let's take a motion ratio of 0.50. If the tire contact patch travels 1.00 in., then the spring moves only 0.50 in. That would reduce the effective rate of a 100 lb.-in. spring to 50 lb.-in. The leverage acting on the spring reduces the rate of the spring by fifty percent also. The spring acting at the wheel now has only a 25 lb.-in. effective rate. The motion ratio of 0.50 squared is 0.25.

The formula to compute the effective wheel rate of a spring is:

$$\text{Wheel rate} = (MR1)^2 \times (MR2)^2 \times (MR3)^2 \times \text{Spring rate}$$

Where MR1 is the lower control arm motion ratio, MR2 is the swing arm motion ratio, and MR3 is the spring mounting angle motion ratio.

Using these examples for a spring rate of 600 lb.-in. of travel, we can conclude the following:

$$MR1 = 0.625; MR2 = 0.916; MR3 = 0.966$$
$$\text{Wheel rate} = (0.625)^2 \times (0.916)^2 \times (0.966)^2 \times 600$$
$$\text{Wheel rate} = 0.391 \times 0.839 \times 0.933 \times 600$$
$$\text{Wheel rate} = 0.3061 \times 600$$
$$\text{Wheel rate} = 183.6 \text{ lb.-in. of travel at the wheel}$$

Calculating the Suspension Frequency

To calculate the suspension frequency, we must know the wheel rate of the spring, the corner weight on that spring and the unsprung weight at that wheel. The sprung weight is equal to the corner weight minus the unsprung weight. The formula is:

$$\text{Suspension frequency in cpm} = 187.8 \times \sqrt{\left(\frac{\text{Wheel rate in lb.-in.}}{\text{Sprung wt. in lbs.}}\right)}$$

Using the above examples with a wheel rate of 183.6 lb.-in., and a corner weight of 750 lb., and an unsprung weight of 97 lb., we have the following:

$$\text{Suspension frequency in cpm} = 187.8 \times \sqrt{\left(\frac{183.6 \text{ lb.-in.}}{653 \text{ lb.}}\right)}$$

$$\text{Suspension frequency in cpm} = 187.8 \times \sqrt{0.28116}$$
$$\text{Suspension frequency in cpm} = 187.8 \times 0.53024$$
$$\text{Suspension frequency} = 99.58 \text{ cpm}$$

If we were able to reduce the sprung weight by 150 lb., the new frequency, which is substantially stiffer, would be:

$$\text{Suspension frequency} = 113.46 \text{ cpm}$$

Let's now assume, in our original example, that we choose a frequency for our International Sedan of 120 cpm. How do we calculate the spring rate needed for this frequency? The formula is:

$$\text{Wheel rate} = \left(\frac{\text{Suspension freq.}}{187.8}\right)^2 \times \text{Sprung wt.}$$

$$\text{Wheel rate} = \left(\frac{120}{187.8}\right)^2 \times 653$$

$$\text{Wheel rate} = 266.6 \text{ lb.-in.}$$

To calculate the spring rate from the known wheel rate, use the following formula:

$$\text{Spring rate} = \frac{\text{Wheel rate}}{(MR1)^2 \times (MR2)^2 \times (MR3)^2}$$

$$\text{Spring rate} = \frac{266.6}{0.3061}$$

$$\text{Spring rate} = 871 \text{ lb.-in.}$$

To achieve a suspension frequency of 120 cpm, a spring rate of 871 lb.-in. would be required.

In development testing, professional racers try out different spring rates on the left and right sides of a car when the sprung weights are different, a situation that occurs in most racing sedans. The goal is to equalize the suspension frequencies at the same end of the vehicle. The results are excellent in almost all cases.

Progressive Rate Springs

A progressive rate spring allows the spring rate to increase as it is compressed. One way to accomplish this is to create a suspension geometry that changes the motion ratio during suspension travel, especially in bumps. The other alternative is to use a progressive rate spring. Both methods are difficult to design and to manufacture.

In the first instance, a suspension system must be carefully designed to allow the correct geometric changes to increase the wheel rate of the spring. Most suspension geometry layouts cause a change in the motion ratios, but in most cases the change is in the wrong direction. The wheel rate of the springs decreases. What is wanted is a rising rate suspension geometry. Most pushrod-pullrod suspension systems are designed to allow a rising wheel rate.

For the average racer and street handling enthusiast, the second method now has more merit. Progressive rate springs are now on the market for racing, and will soon be available for the street market as well.

Progressive rate springs have been around for some time, but have been either expensive or marginally effective. Today, new designs have emerged that have made this technology available to all racers. The cost is reasonable and the results are record-beating.

Lowering Your Car

One of the most important ways to improve handling is to lower the center of gravity. This increases traction by reducing weight transfer and reduces body roll for a given cornering force. The easiest way to lower a car is with the springs. Shorter springs lower the ride height easily and quickly. But there are many pitfalls awaiting those who lower their cars. Some are obvious, others are not.

On the obvious side is reduced ground clearance. When a vehicle is lowered, it rests closer to the ground; in motion, during bump travel, especially over speed bumps and driveways, the bottom of the vehicle is more likely to contact solid ground, with possible damage to a variety of components. On the street, this is crucial, because the real world is much bumpier than the racetrack or autocross course.

There are a number of less obvious potential hazards when a car is lowered. The most important is suspension bottoming in bump travel. When a car is lowered by the springs (as opposed to lower-profile tires), less bump travel is available. When the suspension bottoms on the bump stops, the problem is minimal because the bump stops are designed to slowly stop suspension travel. In many cases, the lowering will take all of the bump travel, leaving the car resting on the bump stops. This increases the suspension rate drastically, and can cause serious problems and dangerous handling characteristics.

Even worse is the case where the bump stops are removed. The bump stop is designed to progressively limit bump travel and to keep the shock absorber from bottoming out. When the suspension bottoms out, the spring instantly rises to infinity and a sudden loss of traction can occur at that end of the vehicle if the car is cornering near the limit of adhesion. If the shock absorber bottoms first, the valving will be blown out, and little shock damping will remain. Either situation can have, at minimum, expensive consequences and, at worst, tragic results.

How to Lower Your Car

It is common practice to cut springs to lower a vehicle. From a materials standpoint, cutting springs is not a bad thing to do, assuming the proper methods are employed. But cutting springs can cause bottoming problems. The shorter spring will have a slightly stiffer spring rate, but usually not enough to limit bump travel adequately to keep the suspension from bottoming out over bumps. This often leads to the problems described above. And in many instances, vehicles with chopped springs ride horribly. The dollars savings often prove to be false.

The best way to lower a vehicle is with springs designed to lower a specific amount, with increased spring rates that will minimize the possibility of bottoming during bump travel. Even in this instance, most aftermarket spring kits include new bump stops, designed to work in the specific application. The reliable and competent suspension and spring manufacturers like Eibach, Suspension Techniques and others have engineered a package that addresses these problems and eliminates them.

Cars with MacPherson strut suspension systems cause another set of problems. Most strut cars can be lowered about 1 in. with no bottoming problems, as long as the spring rates increase accordingly. If the car is to be lowered more than 1 in., then, in most cases, the strut tubes must be shortened or relocated to allow adequate bump travel. If this is not done, the same bottoming problems will occur as previously described. A competent fabricator can accomplish such work. When struts are shortened, often a shorter strut cartridge (shock absorber) must be used to insure adequate bump travel. Good suspension shops know the scoop and find the right parts for the job. But beware! Not all vehicles have the right strut cartridges available. Check before you begin work.

Overall, the best way to lower a car for the street is with one of the aftermarket kits available for this purpose. The knowledgeable manufacturers have created packages that improve the look, lower the center of gravity and improve handling performance, while eliminating most of the hassles and possible problems.

Advantages of a Progressive Rate Spring

A progressive rate spring allows the spring rate, and therefore the wheel rate, to increase as the spring is compressed. This offers a significant advantage where a track or road is bumpy, but it is desirable to maintain a low ride or minimize suspension travel.

As the suspension moves through bump travel, the spring progressively becomes stiffer. The initial rate is softer for better tire contact over bumps. The increasingly stiffer rate will keep the chassis or suspension from bottoming. This allows a lower ride height than would be possible with a standard type of coil spring. The lower center of gravity and improved aerodynamics are important for performance. The ability to maintain excellent tire contact with the road makes the combination unbeatable, especially on a bumpy surface.

The Eibach ERS System

Eibach Springs of Germany and North America have developed the most unique spring system available to date. The ERS (Eibach Race Spring) System uses two springs, a standard coil and a tender spring, to create a truly progressive rate system. Unlike other two-spring set-ups, the Eibach ERS does not employ the second spring as a helper spring to hold the main spring in its perch. The tender spring actually works in series with the main spring to create a unique progressive system. A critical factor is the design of the tender spring, which uses flat wire instead of round wire.

The key to the system is the way that the springs work together. It is important to know the static load on the spring, and to use the proper combination of main spring and tender spring. The correct combination allows the initial compression to fall in the soft portion of the travel range, quickly building to the desired rate increase portion of travel. If the wrong combination is used, too little or too much suspension travel will occur before the rising rate will take effect. Given the necessary data, you can calculate the proper spring combination of a given application, and Eibach can test the combination on their sophisticated spring rate test plotter.

Eibach North America is currently working on an intensive development program for the ERS System. Initial results are phenomenal. In his first race in the highly competitive Formula Ford category using the Eibach ERS System, driver Shane Lewis set a new lap record at Holtville Aerodrome International Raceway in California. Lewis, in only his second race with the ERS System, dominated the competition in his Swift DB-1. Holtville is a very bumpy airport circuit. The true advantage of the ERS System was shown in the low suspension frequency used in the record run, which allowed excellent tire contact with the bumpy surface. While a low frequency can be established with any type of spring, the ERS System allowed a ride height at least 0.75 in. lower than any car in the field, without any bottoming problems on the rough cement surface. This improved traction by reducing weight transfer, while allowing excellent tire contact over the bumps.

The Eibach ERS System is now being used for all classes of formula and sports racing cars, as well as GT, Trans Am and Prototypes. The system is also being adapted for short-track stock car racing, both dirt and asphalt. By the end of 1990, the Eibach ERS System will be tested for street applications, where the largest performance improvements are to be found.

Review

Springs have two important jobs: to keep the suspension from bottoming or the chassis from bottoming on the road surface; and to keep the tire contact patch on the road surface over bumps, dips and so on.

These two criteria require opposite spring rate needs. Since maintaining tire contact with the road is crucial for good handling, we use the stiffest spring possible that allows good tire contact with the road. The bumpier the road, the softer the spring.

We use the suspension frequency as a design tool for specific types of road surface conditions. The suspension frequency is proportional to the wheel rate of the spring and inversely proportional to the sprung weight resting on the spring. The wheel rate of a spring is equal to the spring rate in pounds per inch times the motion ratios squared.

Progressive rate springs offer substantial advantages over standard springs, allowing lower suspension frequencies and lower ride heights without bottoming. The progressive rate spring comes closer to meeting the opposing needs of soft spring rates for improved tire contact over bumps and stiff spring rates to allow minimum ride heights without bottoming.

Chapter 6

Antiroll Bars

The antiroll bar, which is also called a sway bar or stabilizer bar, controls the amount of body roll while cornering. The roll resistance provided by the antiroll bar is added to the roll resistance provided by the springs. The total roll resistance determines the total amount of body roll for a given situation. The total roll resistance at the front of the vehicle, compared to the total roll resistance for the entire vehicle, tells us the roll couple distribution; in other words, the front versus rear roll resistance. This determines the handling balance of the vehicle. If we have too much rear roll resistance, the car will oversteer. If we have too much front roll resistance, the car will understeer.

For handling improvements, we use the antiroll bar for two purposes: controlling the amount of body roll, and controlling the roll couple distribution, which determines where weight is transferred.

Amount of Body Roll

For a car of given suspension geometry, center of gravity height and weight, changes in roll resistance will change the amount of body roll in cornering at the limit of adhesion. Both the antiroll bars and the springs determine the amount of roll resistance. We have seen that we must use a spring frequency that allows optimum tire contact with the road surface. This means we are pretty much stuck with a given amount of roll resistance provided by the springs. On a car with optimum suspension geometry, that is, one with low roll center locations, the roll resistance provided by the springs is rarely adequate to limit body roll to manageable amounts.

Excessive body roll causes camber change, which in turn reduces the real size of the tire contact patch. There is extreme camber change during roll: the inside wheel goes into negative camber while the outside wheel goes into positive camber. In order to keep the tire contact patch flat on the road surface while cornering, upwards of 5 degrees of negative camber would be necessary. This amount of negative camber would cause excessive tire wear in normal driving situations and would adversely affect transient handling response. At about 5 degrees of roll, the tire contact patch area is reduced as much as forty percent from the possible total—not the best way to improve cornering power. The correct antiroll bars will reduce roll and the associated camber change.

With small degrees of roll, camber change can be a significant factor. This Camaro is rolling about 2 degrees. The inside tire is at about 3 degrees positive camber, while the inside tire is at about 0 degrees camber. This is an excellent set-up, requiring about 1.5 degrees of static negative camber to key the tire contact patches flat on the road surface during cornering. This excess negative camber on the inside front tire is only a minor consideration, since the inside front has little load while cornering. The heavily loaded outside tire, however, is crucial.

This Mustang GT has considerably less roll than the stock version. Even so, this high-performance street set-up still shows positive camber change on the outside front wheel during hard cornering. The static camber setting was 1 degree negative. Any more static negative camber would cause rapid tire wear on the inside edge of the tread for everyday driving. Stiffer antiroll bars would improve the camber situation, but may cause other problems. Bob McClurg

Body roll is not inherently a bad factor. But the effects of body roll can cause handling problems, or at least reduce traction or responsiveness. If maximum body roll allows much more than 2 degrees of camber change, then more roll resistance is needed. If we have more than 2 degrees of roll, we will then need at least 2 degrees of static camber angle so that the tire is flat on the road surface during steady state cornering.

Any more than 2 degrees of camber angle will hurt transient traction, that is, the amount of traction while the vehicle is in transition from a straight line to a turn, or vice versa. With a camber angle in excess of 2 degrees, too little of the tire contact patch is touching the road surface to have maximum traction. This will negatively affect handling balance, cornering speed and responsiveness in the initial and final phases of a turn. The excessive static camber angle can also affect braking performance and acceleration when exiting a turn. Remember that our goal is to keep as many rubber molecules at the tire contact patch working to the limit as possible.

A secondary reason to limit body roll is to limit the vertical and lateral movement of the roll center. This is important on all types of suspension, but even more important on a MacPherson strut suspension. Radical movement, especially lateral movements, of the roll center can change weight transfer characteristics suddenly, which can upset the handling balance of the vehicle. Limiting body roll to 1.5 or 2 degrees seems to limit the roll center movement about as well as can be expected. On many designs, the amount of roll stiffness needed to limit roll center movement is high, and would cause other, more serious problems. Compromise is the name of the game.

Roll Couple Distribution

The ability to use the antiroll bar as a means to adjust roll couple distribution is important. If we were forced to use the springs for this purpose, then we would lose some control of the tire contact patch over bumps. Antiroll bars allow easy, quick and accurate adjustments to fine-tune the handling balance of a vehicle. For this reason, it is crucial to have some range of adjustment on both front and rear antiroll bars on competition cars. High-performance street applications should have at least one adjustable antiroll bar to allow fine-tuning of the handling balance.

How Antiroll Bars Work

The antiroll bar resists body roll while cornering by twisting. When the body begins to roll, the arms on the antiroll bar will twist the main section of the bar. This resists additional body roll. The arms are attached to a suspension arm (usually the lower control arm) on each side of the car. The

Stiff antiroll bars provide roll resistance, but have little effect on the amount of weight transferred while cornering.

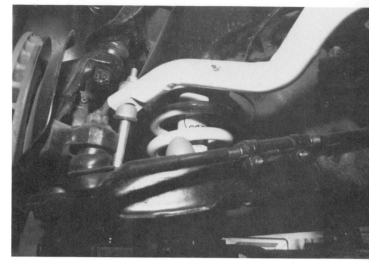

This ultra-heavy-duty antiroll bar was mounted under the front of our project GMC S-15 pickup truck to combat the truck's tendency to roll. The S-15 came stock with a front antiroll bar but more stiffness was needed after initial testing.

An antiroll bar was also added to the rear of our project GMC S-15 pickup truck. To tune the antiroll bar, holes in the bar itself offered adjustments in stiffness by mounting the rod-end bearing further from the bar's end. The slider mount on the frame gave additional adjustment.

A Speedway Engineering rear antiroll bar was used on the Shelby CSX IMSA International Sedan racer project car. The slotted rod on the frame mounting offers fine-tuning of the antiroll bar as befits a race car.

other end of the arm (the arms are usually part of the main bar) is attached to the main bar.

On independent suspension systems, the bars link the left and right sides, causing the suspension to no longer be completely independent. If the wheels encounter the same bump or dip, then the antiroll bar does not work. But when only one wheel hits a bump or dip, the antiroll bar adds to the spring rate by resisting, adding to the suspension frequency. An excessively stiff antiroll bar can cause tire contact problems over single wheel disturbances.

The stiffness of an antiroll bar is determined by the stiffness of the material the antiroll bar is made of, the diameter of the main bar, the effective working length of the main bar and the effective length of the arms.

Almost all antiroll bars are made from materials of similar stiffness. The diameter of the bar affects its stiffness to the fourth power: if you double the diameter of the bar, the stiffness will be sixteen times greater. Small changes in diameter can have a major effect on roll resistance. The effective length of the main bar is inversely propor-

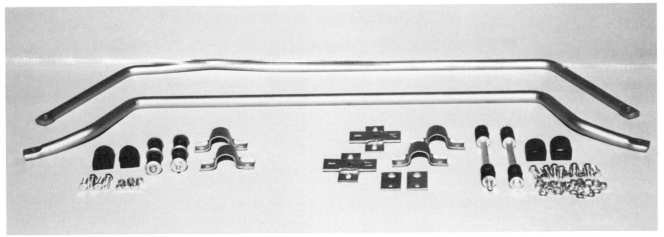

A front and rear aftermarket antiroll bar kit, complete with mounts and bushings. The front antiroll bar is a 1 in. bar. This kit is made by Addco Industries for the Pontiac Fiero.

tional to the stiffness, as is the arm length. For most applications, it is difficult to change the effective length of the bar, but the diameter of the bar can be altered, and the arm length can be easily adjusted.

Keep in mind that the leverage acting on the antiroll bar arm at the suspension mounting point has the same effect on the wheel rate of the bar as on the wheel rate of the spring. The wheel rate of a bar is the actual rate of the bar times the motion ratio squared.

Calculating the Antiroll Bar Rate

The formula for calculating the rate of a solid steel antiroll bar is:

$$\text{Rate in lbs. per inch of deflection} = \frac{315294.1 \times r^4 \times O°}{A \times L}$$

Where r is the effective radius of the main bar; 0 is the angle of arm deflection for 1 in. of bar travel (tangent of angle = 1/arm length); A is the arm length; L is effective length of the main bar.

Here's an example. With the bar diameter 1.00 in. (radius = 0.50 in.), the effective length 37 in. and the arm length 12 in.

$$\text{Rate in lbs. per inch of deflection} = \frac{315294.1 \times 0.50^4 \times \tan 1/12°}{12 \times 37}$$

$$\text{Rate in lbs. per inch of deflection} = \frac{315294.1 \times 0.0625 \times 4.763}{444}$$

$$\text{Rate in lbs. per inch of deflection} = \frac{93859.112}{444}$$

$$\text{Rate in lbs. per inch of deflection} = 211.39$$

If we change the diameter of the bar to 1.125 in. the rate equals 338.61 lb.-in. of deflection, a sixty-percent increase in rate.

If we change the effective length of the original example to 35 in. the rate equals 223.47 lb.-in. of deflection.

If we change the effective arm length of the original example to 10 in. the rate equals 304.14 lb.-in. of deflection.

From these examples, it becomes clear that the biggest effect is the diameter, while the arm length is a finer adjustment. Major changes in rate are usually made with a larger diameter bar, while fine-tuning changes are made with small adjustment in arm length.

Antiroll Bar Pros and Cons

It may seem that the antiroll bar is the answer for tuning the handling of a vehicle. It is an important factor in handling, but it is not *the* answer. It can be used to fine-tune the handling balance, and to limit body roll for improved tire contact with the road. Antiroll bars allow the springs to do their job, but there are limits. First, we can have too much roll resistance overall; second, the bars can provide too large a percentage of the total roll resistance.

Let's examine how an antiroll bar works. When a turn is initiated, the outside suspension moves into bump and the inside into rebound. The antiroll bar begins to twist, with the outside end of the bar lowering and the inside end of the bar rising. The bar pushes down on the outside suspension, while it tries to lift the inside suspension. At the inside wheel, this is the opposite of the way a spring reacts. The spring pushes the inside wheel down, and the bar lifts the inside wheel.

If the bar is too stiff, the inside wheel is unloaded too much and, if it is the drive wheel, may

Study this photo closely. The inside rear tire is off the ground during corner entry, extremely unusual for Porsche 911. The cause of this is a rear antiroll bar that is too stiff. If the antiroll bar is too stiff, it will lift the inside wheel (front or rear) off the ground during cornering. This is not a major problem at the front of a rear-drive car or at the back of a front-driver, but is serious at the drive wheels, especially at the exit of turn when power is applied. The solution is not to increase the amount of roll resistance provided by the antiroll bars, but to increase the amount provided by the springs. Stiff springs will not try to lift the inside tire off the ground as an antiroll bar will.

In cases where stock antiroll bars are used, especially on front-drive cars, the excessive amount of body roll will cause the suspension to run out of travel, thus lifting the inside wheel off the ground. This Volkswagen is on the verge of lifting the inside rear wheel. The rear antiroll bar is not too stiff, instead the suspension travel is too little to keep the tire contact patch on the ground.

cause wheel spin as power is applied at the exit of a turn. This is a serious problem if the vehicle is not equipped with a limited-slip differential, and has high horsepower. It will be worse in slow turns. The problem is unlikely in low-horsepower circumstances, and less likely with a good limited slip. This is the reason we have found it best to have the higher suspension frequency at the end of the car with the drive wheels. The optimum per-

Controlling body roll is equally important on a beam axle, because the roll causes camber change. This Corolla needs more roll resistance and a lower center of gravity to exceed the 1.0 g cornering force it is experiencing here.

centage of roll resistance provided by the bars seems to be between twenty-five and fifty percent of the total roll resistance. Springs provide the balance of the roll resistance.

If we have too much total roll resistance, we will begin to lift an inside wheel off the ground in a turn. The vehicle has reached 100 percent weight transfer at that end of the car. This often happens at the end of the vehicle opposite the drive wheels when the driven end carries a high percentage of the total vehicle weight. You often see a Porsche 911 lifting an inside front wheel in a turn, or a racing front-wheel-driver lifting an inside rear wheel. Lifting a wheel is not the optimum situation, but sometimes it is unavoidable. The problem stems from too much traction at the offending end of the vehicle. Take the front-driver as an example.

If a front-driver has sixty-two percent front weight bias and a MacPherson strut suspension system (both are common), it will also often have substantial roll center movement and significant camber change, both situations calling for lots of roll stiffness. Now, the racing regulations call for the same size tire at all wheels. Immediately, we have overabundance of traction at the rear. The rear tire contact patch area is too great compared to the front (actually the front is too small; it's all relative). So now we have high front roll stiffness to control the wandering roll center and maintain a level tire contact patch. To get some sort of decent handling balance, we use a very stiff rear bar to balance the roll couple. With the roll couple right, the inside rear launches, causing chassis flex, aerodynamic drag, even more loading on the overloaded outside front tire contact patch and, at

The optimum set-up for a modified street vehicle requires enough roll resistance from the antiroll bars and springs to reduce camber change to no more than 2 degrees during body roll. Once springs are selected for the correct suspension frequency, the amount of roll resistance needed to keep the camber change below 2 degrees must be determined. Then the antiroll bars are specified to provide this resistance. The ratio of front resistance to that of the rear will determine the handling balance of the car, and must be an important part of the equation.

least, boisterous cheers from the spectators. So what is the solution to the problem?

The best solution is a smaller tire contact patch at the offending end of the vehicle. The easiest way is a smaller tire, but that is not allowed, so we need to make the tire contact patch smaller in some other way.

Chances are that the rear tires are running cold anyway, so we have two options. The first is to overinflate the tire, making the contact patch smaller, and allowing the contact patch that is working to heat up to a decent temperature. The alternate choice is to lower the tire pressure, allowing the tire to work at a higher slip angle at a smaller load. Don't get carried away in either direction, however, or you will see where you have been very quickly! A 2 to 3 psi change in pressure will make a noticeable difference. Make a change in steps, not a quantum leap. A skid pad is the place to test tire pressures. Also keep in mind that this technique usually has different effects in low-speed turns than in high-speed turns. Opt for balance in the high-speed turns. A handling imbalance is easier to drive around in low-speed turns.

There may be times where the best compromise is to let the inside wheel fly. The operative word here is compromise. He who reaches the optimum compromise will be fastest.

Roll Resistance

How stiff should an antiroll bar be? Just stiff enough to limit camber change, which is caused by body roll, to a manageable amount, such as 2 to 3 degrees on most cars. The relative amount of front antiroll bar stiffens versus rear antiroll bar stiffness should allow for optimum roll couple distribution, with near neutral handling characteristics. Excessive bar stiffness can cause the inside wheel to lift from the road surface during cornering. This causes wheel spin when the bar is too stiff at the drive wheels. Corner exit speed is hurt, especially in low-speed turns.

Choosing the correct bar rates is a complex process, requiring a significant amount of data and plotting. To truly calculate the proper bar rates, the center of gravity height must be known, as well as the roll center locations and camber change curves. The work involved is extensive, and is best left to an experienced designer or antiroll bar manufacturer. Additionally, when complex bends are required in a bar design, the true rate cannot effectively be calculated. The actual rate of the bar must be measured on heavy-duty test equipment. The easiest approach is to purchase antiroll bars from an experienced manufacturer or to consult with a suspension design expert. The calculations are often done on suspension geometry computer software, which saves incredible amounts of design time. The final product must be tested to be truly effective.

One way to fine-tune antiroll bars is through multiple mounts, allowing rate adjustments to dial-in the roll couple distribution. Racers need ad-

Roll resistance is the key to understanding where weight is transferred in a corner. Here is the Consulier in excessive oversteer. The tail-out attitude of the car means that the rear tires have lost traction before the front tires. This is caused by too much of the total vehicle roll resistance at the rear of the car. Less roll resistance (softer antiroll bar or springs) at the rear would reduce or cure the problem. Bob Ryder

Here the car is demonstrating understeer, where the front tires are losing traction. Less front roll resistance would help. While roll resistance is the primary factor affecting handling balance, driver inputs and reduced tire traction due to compounds, wear, size, camber change and so on also can cause handling imbalance. Bob McClurg

justable bars to fine-tune for personal preferences or track conditions. On the highway, an aftermarket non-adjustable bar is usually sufficient.

Review

The antiroll bar is used to limit body roll, allow the springs to keep the tire contact patches on the ground over disturbances, and to adjust roll couple distribution.

Antiroll bar rates are easily adjusted to fine-tune roll couple distribution. The major rate changes are best accomplished with the bar di-ameter, and fine-tuning adjustments with the arm length.

The antiroll bar works by loading the outside tire, but lifting the inside. Excessive antiroll bar stiffness can hurt handling and traction, especially at the drive wheels during the exit phase of a turn. Excessive roll resistance will cause the inside wheel to lift off the ground in a turn.

Finding the best compromise can be time consuming, but usually rewards substantial dividends to those who make the effort.

Chapter 7

Shock Absorbers

If springs actually absorb shock, then just what do the shock absorbers do? The primary purpose of the shock absorber is to dampen vibrations or oscillations. In other countries, shock absorbers are called dampeners. The goal is to keep the spring from bouncing beyond one full cycle. If you have driven a car with bad shocks, you know how uncomfortable the ride is when the car bounces over every bump, dip and rut. The properly rated shock absorber stops this.

The shock absorber has two jobs. First, it must control oscillations of the unsprung mass, that is, the wheels, tires, hubs and so forth. Second, the

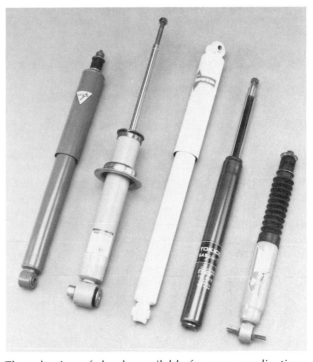

The selection of shocks available for some applications is broad. The important criteria for selection are application, cost and availability. It is important to speak with knowledgeable people when selecting the proper shock concerning the way you use your vehicle. The shock absorber should be compatible with the spring rates being used. Nearly all high-performance aftermarket shocks have adequate damping characteristics for performance driving, and will work with springs fifteen- to twenty-percent stiffer than stock. Springs and shocks any stiffer will cause a harsh ride on the street. A stiffer spring set-up will require competition shocks with custom valving to handle the additional load created by the stiffer springs. In the above photo, all of the major aftermarket shock absorber manufacturers are represented. From left: Koni, Bilstein, KYB, Tokico and Stiletto by Suspension Techniques.

One of the crucial links to improved handling is the shock absorber, more correctly called a vibration damper. The Koni double-adjustable racing shock has been the leader in application and quality for many years. These strut cartridges are for a Nissan 240/260/280 Z for competition use only.

shock absorber must control the sprung mass of the car. The spring does most of the work in bump travel, while the shock controls the return motion with rebound travel. Over dips, in rebound travel, the shock slows the downward movement of the body, allowing a more level ride. For this reason, the bump resistance is about one third the rebound resistance for street use.

For competition applications, the ratio of bump to rebound resistance is between 1:2 and 1:1.5. The higher bump rates reduce ride comfort, but improve traction over surface irregularities. The bump rate will also be relatively higher when the ratio of sprung weight to unsprung weight is lower.

The spring rates used in competition, or even on high-performance street applications, are somewhat higher than used in the typical production vehicle. The valving in the shock absorber must be stiffer to work with the stiffer spring rates. If the shock absorber rates are too soft, the vehicle will continue to bounce over bumps, dips and ruts—not a desirable situation. On the other hand, if the shocks are too stiff for the springs, the shock absorber will overpower the spring, keeping it from working. This often results in jacking up or jacking down where the ride height changes and is held by the overly stiff shock absorber. Again, this is a bad situation.

Between these two extremes is a fairly broad range of shock absorber rates that will provide adequate dampening, and considerable fine-tuning capability.

The other difference between the standard passenger car shock, and a high-performance or competition version, is the shock absorber travel over which the energy is absorbed by the shock absorber. Whereas a standard passenger car may have 10 in. of total wheel travel, the high-performance street version may have only 7 in. of travel. The same car used for competition may be limited to 4 to 5 in. of travel. Thus, the same work must be accomplished over a much smaller distance of piston travel within the shock absorber. This requires different valving within the shock.

Gas pressure shock absorbers have become popular in the last decade. The gas pressure shock absorber has some advantages over the oil-only shock absorber in certain applications. The greatest advantage of the gas pressure shock absorber is its ability to dissipate heat and keep the oil in the shock body from foaming as quickly. The gas pressure shock absorber offers the greatest advantage in applications where considerable piston travel is needed over bumpy surfaces for long periods of time. A regular shock works at its best where little travel is needed or wanted, and piston speeds are high. The gas pressure shock absorber works well in a broader range of applications, with few if any disadvantages.

When designing a suspension system, the shock absorber engineer needs the appropriate data to specify the correct shock for the application. Shock absorber design, like tire design, is a highly specialized and complex field. All of the best shock absorber manufacturers have experienced staff that will create the best possible unit for the application. For high-performance street applications, use a shock absorber designed for that application as recommended by the reputable shock absorber manufacturers.

Shock Absorber and Weight Transfer

The shock absorber, as we have already discovered, controls how quickly weight is transferred. This makes the shock absorber an important tuning tool for transient handling response.

By altering the shock absorber rates in bump and rebound, you can change the rate of weight transfer. How quickly weight transfers while turning into or exiting a corner will affect the handling balance of the vehicle until all weight transfer has occurred.

Weight transfer occurs more quickly when the shock valving is stiffer. Let's look at an extreme example to illustrate this. If we have solid shock absorbers, the weight transfers from the inside to the outside instantly, since the shock absorber cannot move. All forces pass through the solid shock with no time needed for the shock absorbers to compress or extend. With no shock absorber at all, weight transfer would be slow. As body roll takes place, the springs would begin to oscillate, forcing the weight transfer to take a considerable amount of time. By stiffening the shock absorbers, we have quicker weight transfer. By softening the shock absorbers, we have slower weight transfer. This, of course, assumes that the range of valving is correct for the application.

The overall effect of changing shock absorber rates alters the responsiveness of the vehicle. Stiffer shock absorber rates mean quicker weight transfer and faster vehicle response. Softer shock absorber rates slow weight transfer and reduce responsiveness. This has a substantial effect on the vehicle "taking a set" in a turn.

Taking a Set

Essentially, a vehicle takes a set after all weight transfer has occurred. Here is how the process works. First, the driver initiates a turn by moving the steering wheel. The tires assume a slip angle, which generates a force. That force reacts at the roll center and then the center of gravity, causing weight transfer and body roll to take place. The slip angles at the outside tires will increase as the cornering force builds and as weight transfer continues. The quicker the weight transfer occurs, the quicker the car will take a set.

The car has taken a set when maximum cornering force is reached and all weight transfer has oc-

Selecting Shock Absorbers

One of the most difficult tuning jobs to improve handling is selecting the shock absorber. Since the shock has a major affect on ride and handling, it can be tricky business walking the fine line between good handling and good ride. In some cases, specifically competition, the nod goes to handling; ride is not a consideration. But on the road, while the pleasure of blasting a few quick corners is enhanced with firm shock valving, the price is a harsh ride for many commuter miles, often with less than sympathetic passengers.

Additionally, the shock valving needs for a relatively smooth track or parking lot autocross course are different from the harsh, bump- and rut-filled real-world roads. For pure competition purposes, an all-out racing shock is the best bet, although some of the aftermarket shocks available for street applications will work. Consult with a knowledgeable tuning shop or the manufacturer specifically about your application. This is crucial if your car has been lowered more than 2 in. with the suspension (as opposed to lower-profile tire sidewalls), or if the spring rates are more than twenty-percent stiffer than stock or both. Aftermarket shocks are usually designed to work with springs which are about ten to fifteen percent stiffer than the stock units. Any stiffer in the spring rate, and damping will be inadequate for that spring rate.

If you replace your springs with stiffer units designed for highway applications as opposed to racing, it is best to replace the shocks or strut cartridges with an aftermarket set designed for a slightly stiffer spring rate.

Another question is adjustability. This is just about mandatory for dual-purpose vehicles and even for competition vehicles where the shock is used as a tuning device. Since few racers know how to tune shocks to improve handling characteristics, it is unlikely that adjustability is really an issue on the street, except for a change in ride quality. The cockpit-adjustable system on the project Mustang GT has a very different ride from soft to stiff. The car handles better on the stiff setting, at least on smooth roads, but the ride is harsh. On the softest setting, the ride is comfortable. The major drawback is the cost. Adjustable shocks cost more; electronic adjustables a lot more.

There are two important questions to ask when selecting the right shock for your car. First, do you need adjustable shocks for the kind of driving you do? Second, will you take the time to actually adjust them? Honest answers to these questions will save you time and money, and not take away from the driving pleasure you demand from your car. In most cases, especially where the vehicle is only driven on the street, nonadjustable shocks or shocks where the adjustment is easily made at the top of the shaft are the only practical solutions.

The major shock absorber manufacturers do a good job of creating a valving for each application that is a good compromise between performance handling and ride. And most of the companies make a specific racing-application shock for competition purposes. It is not truly possible to have the best of both in a single set of shocks.

---

curred. Since the shock absorber controls how quickly weight transfers, it also influences how quickly the vehicle takes a set. Since responsiveness is important for improved handling, we want the vehicle to take a set quickly; the quicker the better. Then again, maybe not.

Can a vehicle take a set too quickly? The answer is yes. It is important for the driver to feel the vehicle take a set. It allows the driver to sense the approaching limit of traction. If the vehicle takes a set too quickly, the driver does not feel the limit, and is slower. Here, the fast response hurts the overall package, in this case the driver response. It is important to establish a rate of weight transfer that allows the driver to feel the limit approaching, and to react to it.

If the shock absorbers are too stiff, then the entire process bypasses the driver's ability to sense the limit and respond. In essence, the transitional period during corner turn-in is too brief. The limit of responsiveness is more related to the driver's feel, reactions and sensitivity. What may be the fast shock absorber rates for the car may overpower the driver. This is especially true for new drivers or drivers in a new car. Experience counts here. The last word on shock absorber rates depends upon driver preference.

Rate of Weight Transfer and Handling Problems

What happens when weight is transferred more quickly at one end of the vehicle than at the other in a corner? One end of the vehicle will reach peak cornering force sooner, that is, the end with quicker weight transfer. The end of the vehicle with slower weight transfer is likely to have less traction than the end with the quicker weight transfer.

Theoretically, the rate of weight transfer should be the same front and rear. By varying bump and rebound rates, and the rates at one end versus the other, transient handling response can be affected. Before we move on, let's explore another factor that affects the rate of weight transfer: the driver.

Rate of Weight Transfer and the Driver

The driver has a major influence on where and how quickly weight is transferred. How the steering wheel, brake pedal and accelerator are used will affect weight transfer. If, for example, the steering wheel is turned abruptly, weight transfer will occur more quickly, but with less stability. If the brakes are applied heavily, and the steering input is made, weight will transfer to the outside front tire contact patch. This will likely overload the tire with a loss of traction resulting. In this situation, if the outside front tire is not overloaded, the inside rear (the weight transfer is diagonal in this case) tire contact patch will lose load and traction, causing oversteer. This often happens with a Porsche 911.

Similar situations can occur at the exit of a turn. If the accelerator is abruptly applied at the exit of a turn, the diagonal weight transfer from the outside front to the inside rear improves rear traction but reduces front traction, with understeer the result. There are many other examples, but the idea is the same.

The astute observer is probably asking an important question right now. If both the shock absorbers and the driver can affect weight transfer (rate and location), then how can we tell if it is driver error? Be patient! I'll answer that question later.

Let us pose another question here. How many drivers are sensitive enough to feel a transient handling problem? The answer is, very few. It takes considerable concentration, sensitivity and experience to focus on handling balance in the few milliseconds needed for transitions to occur. More drivers can feel corner exit problems, because at that point, the fear factor is reduced and car control is easy.

Here's another question. What is the approximate ratio of driver-induced transient handling problems versus shock-absorber-caused transient handling problems? It's about 20:1, especially for corner entry.

The best way to learn about shock absorbers is to test them. Try different combinations of settings until you have a personal data base of information. What feels best probably is best! For the highway, use quality aftermarket shock absorbers. The factory rate will be close to ideal for most applications. If rates are adjustable, start soft and go up. What rides comfortably will be close for high-performance applications. For the dual-purpose vehicle, use full, soft settings for the highway, and experiment for competition situations.

Review

The shock absorber must be compatible with the spring rates to work effectively. It controls the rate of weight transfer, and therefore the transient handling response of a vehicle.

A stiffer shock absorber means quicker weight transfer and faster vehicle response. It is best when the rate of weight transfer at the front is the same as the rear. If the rate of weight transfer is different front to rear, handling balance will likely be affected. The end with stiffer shock absorber settings will reach peak lateral acceleration first.

It can be difficult to distinguish if a transient handling problem is caused by the shock absorber rates, or by driver inputs. Trying different combinations of shock absorber settings is the key to fine-tuning transient handling response.

Chapter 8

Suspension Bushings

Control arms, struts, steering boxes, antiroll bars, springs and shock absorbers all attach to the chassis of a vehicle through bushings. The bushings allow rotational, and in some cases, angular movement of the suspension components. The material used in most production applications is rubber in one form or another. The use of rubber helps isolate noise and vibration from the passengers inside the vehicle. Rubber bushings also isolate important feedback from the driver.

Bushings can cause handling problems by allowing movements of suspension components in directions that are undesirable. For instance, the control arms of the front suspension are intended to move in a single plane only to control the vertical movement of the wheel. With soft, pliable bushings in place, when steering loads or torque loads from braking pass through the bushings, they can twist and deform, allowing changes in toe-in or toe-out settings and the camber of the wheel. This deformation is difficult to accurately predict. It also changes the wheel rate of springs and antiroll bars, always softening their effect.

Compliance, as the distortion in the bushing is called, can affect camber, castor, toe, spring rates, antiroll bar rates, shock absorber responsiveness, driver feedback and sensitivity, bump and roll steer, and overall vehicle responsiveness. In almost every case, the effect of compliance hurts handling performance. It seems that the movements in the suspension are always in the wrong direction to benefit vehicle handling. Compliance will always hurt responsiveness.

Polyurethane antiroll bar bushings and end link bushings allow quicker motion of the antiroll bar during corner entry, reducing reaction time and helping to limit body roll. The urethane bump stops increase suspension travel without allowing the suspension to bottom. The urethane bump stops are considerably more harsh when struck than the rubber equivalent. Suspension Techniques

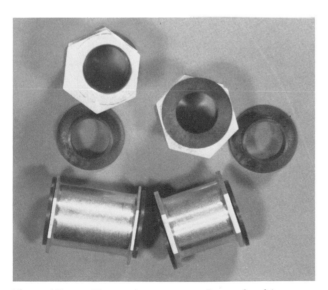

These Nissan Z rear lower control arm bushings are offset, allowing camber and toe adjustments at the rear. The plastic insert reduces friction.

Urethane control arm and steering bushings reduce suspension and steering compliance. This improves responsiveness, meaning that driver inputs reach the tire contact patch more quickly. Urethane bushings also increase noise and vibration, but not nearly as much as metal bushings will. Bob Ryder

Urethane and Hard Rubber Bushings

For high-performance and competition applications, alternate bushing materials should be used to minimize or eliminate the effects of compliance in the suspension and steering systems. If springs, antiroll bars and shocks are being upgraded, the bushings should also be changed. A choice is available. Many auto manufacturers use hard rubber bushings in high-performance applications or for aftermarket performance applications. The stiffer rubber is an improvement, and still offers desirable creature comforts, but is not stiff enough for competition applications.

The most common aftermarket bushing material is urethane. Urethane is much harder than rubber, and reduces compliance substantially, but still limits noise and vibration reaching the occupants. Not all urethane is created equal, however. Some urethane bushings, under high loads, will wear and deform with time. This can cause alignment problems and freeplay in the suspension and steering. Also, urethane is not suitable where angular misalignment is needed, such as upper strut insert mounts, or trailing arms. They will not handle any amount of misalignment since urethane is not resilient and will not retain its shape effectively after deformation.

Hard rubber and urethane are the best choices for street and some competition applications. Urethane should be used only where motion is restricted to one plane, such as control arms, antiroll bars and shock absorber eyes, and in applications where the bushing is not solidly mounted, such as antiroll bar end links and upper strut mounts.

Metal Bushings

The best method to limit compliance in suspension and steering is to use a solid metal bushing. The use of metal bushings will increase interior noise and vibration dramatically, and is not recommended for daily transportation. On the

Selecting Bushings

For the high-performance vehicle that is only driven on the highway, the selection of bushing materials is crucial for ride comfort. Metal bushings of any type will increase noise and vibration excessively. Maintenance rates will also increase. If the decision is made to replace bushing materials, the best compromise is urethane. While noise and vibration will still increase, most performance drivers will find these increases a reasonable tradeoff for the improved responsiveness.

Still, it is wise to consider what real improvements can be made by replacing stock rubber bushings. For competition, the choice is clear. Solid bushings improve performance. On the street, however, no clear choice is evident. Yes, performance will improve, but the amount is small. The tradeoff is not only the ride harshness, vibration and noise, but the cost and work. While good-quality urethane bushings are reasonably priced, the cost in time or labor for installation can be substantial. Any component where bushings are to be replaced must be removed from the car. Old bushings must be pressed out and the new ones installed. This can be time consuming and costly for a small performance gain.

There is an exception to this. Antiroll bar bushings and end links made from urethane improve responsiveness and can increase the stock bar rates by as much as twenty percent. They are easy to install, and the harshness and noise increases are minor.

For the performance street vehicle, give careful consideration to bushing changes before making the investment. If you decide to make the change, use the best-quality bushings available. You don't want to replace them routinely.

other hand, the near elimination of compliance pays major dividends in competition.

The other negatives for using metal bushings are increased wear and maintenance. The metal materials are prone to damage if not properly lubricated and cleaned regularly. In some instances, the ability to easily reach and maintain some bushings makes urethane a better choice, even in competition.

Like urethane, metal bushings should be used only where motion is restricted to one plane. Solid metal bushings are not suitable for antiroll bar end links or upper strut mounts.

Rod End or Spherical Bushings

Where any angular misalignment is needed, the best material choice is the rod end or spherical bearing. These are ideal for tie-rods, trailing arms, antiroll bar end links, upper strut mounts and so on. Only high-quality, lined rod ends and bearings should be used. Rod ends and bearings must be the proper specification for the application, or failure of the piece may result. Consult with an engineer from the bearing company or from a reputable racing suspension shop.

Never lubricate Teflon bearings, as the lube will attract grit and rapid wear will result. Rod ends and spherical bearings require constant attention and maintenance. Lack of care can result in part failures, which is not desirable on any suspension or steering component.

Review

One important aspect of suspension design for many new production cars is the use of bushings to alter handling characteristics in the dynamic state. Often, deformity is forced into the bushing, causing geometry changes that are designed to change handling characteristics. Often rubber bushings are used to supplement the spring rates. Changing these types of bushings can cause serious handling problems that can be difficult to trace. Consult with the vehicle or bushing manufacturer before changing bushings on cars of such designs.

For competition purposes, it is important to eliminate as much compliance as possible. The cost of the parts and the time needed for care and maintenance are small compared to the performance improvements. For the street, the compromise is more difficult. In the vast majority of cases, urethane will be the best choice where it is appropriate to use. For many new production car

The ultimate bushing for near zero compliance and quick response is the spherical bearing, with or without the rod end. These bearings offer close tolerance, high strength-to-weight ratios and fine adjustments. When allowed by the rulebook, these are the optimum set-up for competition purposes, but require constant maintenance and transmit considerable road noise and vibration. They are not a good choice for street applications on suspension control arms and trailing arms. Bob Ryder

applications, it is wise to check with the manufacturer as to the advisability of changing bushing materials, since the bushings are often designed to twist and rotate as part of the spring and suspension system of the vehicle.

Chapter 9

Aerodynamics and Handling

Among the most dramatic factors affecting handling performance in the last twenty years is the increase in aerodynamic understanding and products for cars. Aerodynamic downforce, generated by wings and ground effects, have increased the cornering forces of Grand Prix cars from the 1.2 g range in the early 1970s to well in excess of 4.0 g today. It is hard to comprehend how a 4.0 g cornering force actually feels. Since our purpose here is to discuss handling for road vehicles, we will limit our discussion to vehicles without wings. On the highway, aerodynamics plays only a small role, with cosmetics being the primary function of road-only aerodynamic additions. However, as speeds approach 50 mph, aerodynamics begin to play a factor in handling performance; below 50 mph, aerodynamic parts, such as air dams and spoilers, have little or no effect.

For the production-based road racer, time trial car and autocrosser, aerodynamics should not be ignored as a source of improved performance. There are basically two areas of concern for the racer. First is to increase aerodynamic downforce; second to reduce aerodynamic drag.

Many high-performance production cars such as this BMW M3 come with rear deck spoilers, which improve airflow and possibly even create some high-speed downforce.

Increasing Aerodynamic Downforce

The reason to increase aerodynamic downforce is simple: the load created by aerodynamic downforce increases the load on the tires. As we have seen, increasing the load on the tires increases traction, but the aerodynamic load does not add weight to the car, so the engine, brakes and tires do not have to work harder to accelerate, brake or corner the vehicle. This increase in cornering force is nearly free. The price for the increased downforce is more aerodynamic drag.

How do we increase downforce on a production vehicle? The basic method is to change the airflow characteristics over and under the car. This is the principle behind the wing. A wing creates lift by altering airflow over its surface. Each side of the

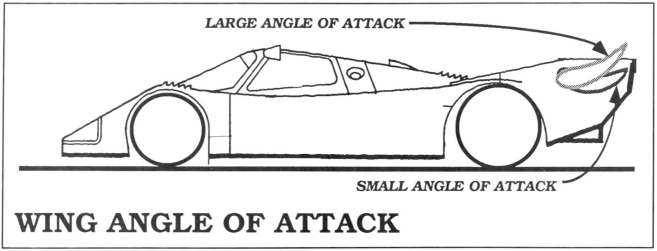

WING ANGLE OF ATTACK

A greater wing angle of attack will create more downforce than a smaller angle of attack, but will also create more aerodynamic drag. If the angle of attack is too great, the wing will stall and drag will increase while downforce decreases dramatically.

Indy cars, IMSA GTP, Group C and Formula 1 cars such as this Tyrrell have very stiff suspensions to allow minimum ride height. On a smooth oval, for instance, an Indy car has a dynamic ride height at top speed of less than 0.25 in. This reduces drag and increases downforce.

In the case of this sports racer, the body shape itself creates downforce. Minor adjustments to the Gurney lip on the rear deck and the splitter depth on the nose will alter the handling balance by changing the proportion of front versus rear downforce. This will have the greatest effect in high-speed corners. Notice the minimal ground clearance, which minimizes turbulence under the car and reduces aerodynamic drag while improving downforce.

Race cars with wings alter the wing angle of attack to change the front-to-rear downforce balance.

wing has a different surface shape, and the air must travel a greater distance across one surface. The air flowing across the longer surface must travel faster than the air flowing across the shorter surface. The faster flowing airstream creates less pressure, while the slower-flowing air is at a higher pressure. This pressure differential creates lift, or in the case of the car, with inverted wings, downforce. The wing also causes aerodynamic drag. The ratio of downforce to drag determines the efficiency of the wing shape. For a given wing profile, the larger the wing aspect ratio, the more efficient the wing will be. The aspect ratio is the comparison of the chord (the width at the widest section) of the wing to its length. The longer a wing of given width, the better the downforce-drag ratio becomes. Gliders, with their long, slender wings, have the highest efficiency of any aircraft wing.

On the production automobile, we try to simulate the effect of a wing. We want the air flowing over the top of the car to travel farther than that flowing under the car. This acts somewhat like an inverted wing, potentially increasing downforce, or at least reducing lift, which reduces traction. And the effect increases as the vehicle speed increases.

If you compare a wing profile to that of a car, it is fairly obvious, under the best of circumstances, that the car shape is not an efficient wing. The aspect ratio is low, and downforce is minimal when compared to drag. In the late 1960s the spoiler was invented to improve airflow over the back of a production race car. This improved airflow over the car, but did not address airflow under the car. While drag was reduced, and some downforce helped the rear of the car stick more, the front was not affected significantly.

Soon after the advent of the rear spoiler, the air dam was added to the front of most production-based race cars. This clever addition improved high-speed handling enormously. By reducing airflow underneath the car, and at the same time increasing air speed around the sides of the car, two factors worked together to improve downforce and reduce aerodynamic drag. Reducing airflow under the car reduces turbulence, and therefore drag. A low-pressure area is also now created under the car, which tends to place a vertical downforce on the car similar to ground effects; the effect is small but significant.

Increasing the air speed around the sides of the car also helps the car body function more like a wing, tending to increase downforce and reduce drag at the same time. The result is free cornering power, and often better straightline speed. In fact, this effect is so dramatic that in 1990, Indy cars race with a dynamic ride height (ground clearance under the chassis at top speed) of 0.25 in. on smooth oval tracks, and 0.5 in. on bumpier tracks. The range is 0.5 in. to 1 in. on road courses.

This Formula Super Vee racer has a wing at the rear only. Front downforce changes are made with an adjustable splitter along the lower leading edge of the nose section. Moving the splitter forward (making it longer) will increase front downforce but also increase drag.

This Formula Ford has no wings. Minimum drag is the goal of this design. A Gurney lip on the rear deck allows small downforce changes to alter high-speed handling balance.

The amount of aerodynamic downforce and drag depends upon the body shape, the spoiler configuration, the size of the air dam and how close it is to the ground, and many other factors. The design of aerodynamic devices requires costly research and development. In many cases, especially on today's more efficient aerodynamic body styles, it is common for aerodynamic add-ons to increase drag with little or no increase in downforce. The design process is best left to the experienced aerodynamicist.

Automobile Rake

Another way to increase downforce on a production car is to set the vehicle on a slight rake, so that the front is lower than the rear. This increases surface area and improves flow over the body, but it also increases frontal area, which causes aerodynamic drag to increase as well. Rake is usually measured by a difference between front and rear ride height. The normal amount of rake, and a good starting point for most cars, is 0.5 in., with the front lower. Rake over 1 in. is excessive. Like setting wings and spoilers, rake adjustment requires testing and trial and error to find the best compromise between downforce and drag.

Reducing Aerodynamic Drag

The reason to reduce aerodynamic drag is simple. Aerodynamic drag steals horsepower, reducing not only top speed, but also acceleration. The effect grows more substantial as speed increases. While the air dam tends to reduce drag substantially, the spoiler increases drag. How much depends upon design and the angle of attack, which is the inclination of the spoiler from vertical.

The angle of attack is crucial. At some point, the angle will be too steep, causing the airflow to separate. This increases drag and reduces downforce. If the angle is too flat, little effect will take place and downforce will be virtually nil. Within the range of efficient operation, the best angle is the one that gives the most downforce for the least drag. Testing is required to determine that point.

The spoiler is not the only item affecting aerodynamic drag. While the shape of the body certainly affects drag, other factors can also increase aerodynamic drag. When body panels, windshield seams and grilles do not fit correctly, drag increases. By carefully fitting these items, drag can be reduced significantly. Other factors to pay attention to include mirror shapes, air ducting, headlights, body molding and any item on the car that can hinder the flow of air. The higher the top speed potential, the more crucial these details become. Keep in mind, however, that even at 50 mph the effect is pronounced.

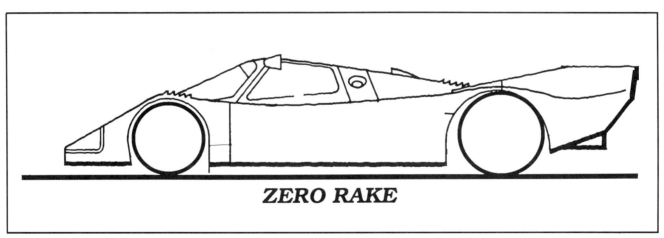

Rake is the tilt of the chassis from level in side view.

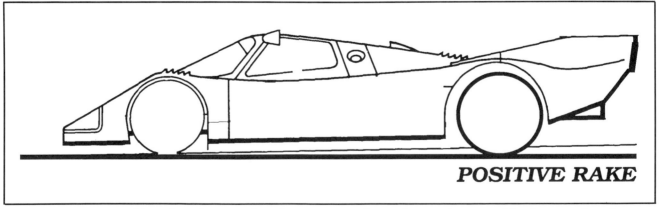

Most cars use some positive rake to increase downforce and minimize airflow underneath the vehicle. Positive rake can be overdone, resulting in more drag due to an increase in effective frontal area.

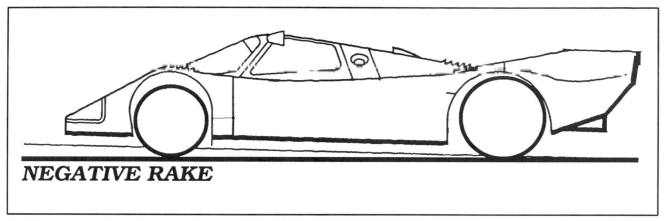

NEGATIVE RAKE

In all cases, negative rake causes front-end lift and drag increases. Negative rake should always be avoided.

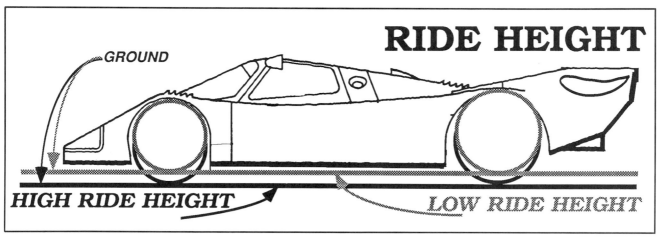

GROUND

RIDE HEIGHT

HIGH RIDE HEIGHT

LOW RIDE HEIGHT

Ride height has an effect on aerodynamic drag. All cars generate the least drag when the ride height is as low as possible. This reduces the effective frontal area to the minimum, and reduces turbulence underneath the vehi-cle. Unless dictated by rules, the ride height should be as low as possible, taking suspension travel into account. If the car bottoms, either stiffer springs or higher ride height is needed.

The air dam under the front of this GT car reduces airflow under the body. This keeps the front end from lifting and reduces turbulence. If the air dam is close enough to the ground, it can even create downforce and reduce aerodynamic drag.

Front air dams reduce aerodynamic drag by reducing turbulence under the car. This can create downforce by creating a partial vacuum under the front of the car. While many production cars use air dams, the ground clearance needed for highway and city driving reduces the effectiveness.

The best air dam is the one closest to the ground. In most competition classes, the level of the air dam is set by rules. If not, run the lowest one possible.

Airflow Through the Car

Airflow around the car is only half the picture. One of the most substantial sources of aerodynamic drag is airflow through the car. Any place air enters the car is a source of aerodynamic drag. Careful ducting of airflow to radiators, brakes and so on can reduce drag. The exiting of

Ride height is crucial. Not only does it lower the center of gravity, but the lowest possible ride height also reduces aerodynamic drag by reducing turbulence under the car and the effective frontal area.

Any competition car should be set at the lowest ride height the rules allow, or as low as possible without the suspension or chassis bottoming.

the air from the car is also worthy of attention. The worst place to exit air is under the car, but that is exactly where most air exits. We have already seen that air flowing under the car causes increased aerodynamic drag. The goal should always be to exit airflow through the sides or top of the body structure. Fenderwells are often accessible and easy places to vent airflow. Forcing airflow under the car will increase drag and reduce any downforce.

Aerodynamics and Rules

Naturally, racing rules will determine what can and cannot be added or modified aerodynamically. But even in a class where no aerodynamic modification are allowed, body panel fit and other minor modifications that fall within the confines of body blueprinting can offer a major advantage. Attention to aerodynamic detail is just as important as the engine, drivetrain or suspension.

It is crucial to pay close attention to all rules, but rules concerning aerodynamics are often vague, allowing liberal interpretation. Even simple rules that are clearly written are often overlooked by most competitors. Those who notice and take advantage of the rules can gain valuable speed and traction.

One of the more interesting examples of this is in the SCCA Improved Touring class. This class is for outdated Showroom Stock and various other production cars. Rules severely limit modifications: no aerodynamic modifications or devices are allowed except for a front air dam. Since an air dam virtually eliminates front-end lift at speed, this can be considered a safety rule as well as a performance enhancement. The rule clearly states that

Aftermarket aero kits can improve performance and the looks of a car, but in most forms of competition in stock classes, aerodynamic add-ons are not legal. In some classes, aerodynamic modifications are allowed, and can enhance performance.

the air dam can protrude no lower than the lowest point on the front wheel rim. Few cars have air dams that close to the ground. The lower the air dam, the more effective it is. Since this is a simple modification, no one has an excuse for missing the importance of this.

Let's go one step further. Rim diameters must remain stock, and rim widths are limited, but any DOT legal tire is allowed. In many cases, both 60 series and 50 series tires are available in the same cross-section width and diameter. Running the 50 series tire could lower the lowest point of the wheel rim by 0.5 in. That has a considerable aerodynamic effect. Paying attention to the rules can provide real advantages in the simplest areas.

Aerodynamics on the Street

If you never exceeded the legal speed limit, a discussion of aerodynamics on the street would be unnecessary. Since that is not too likely, we needed to address the topic. In terms of pure performance, stability and even safety, all of the above applies on the road. As speed increases, keeping airflow from under the car is important. Aerodynamic lift can be dangerous, causing high-speed instability and a reduction of front tire traction. Air dams reduce this. At the rear, spoilers improve high-speed stability and traction at the rear of the car. Both are worthwhile additions to the performance vehicle. Ground effect kits offer little in the way of improved performance and probably add a little to total aerodynamic drag.

Possibly the best reason to add an aero kit to your vehicle is looks. Some of the kits available today not only improve performance, but enhance the look of the car as well. If you are in the market for an aero kit, make sure the design will actually enhance high-speed handling and stability. Also check the fit and finish of the parts. Installation can be difficult, so check into the availability of factory or dealer installations.

For the road, clearance over bumps, ruts and driveways becomes an important factor when determining ride height.

Chapter 10

Suspension Alignment and Set-Up

Suspension alignment and set-up serve only one real purpose: to allow the tire contact patches to work effectively during all phases of motion. If this sounds like compromise is needed, you are correct. Many compromises are necessary to find the optimum set-up for a given car or condition. For performance highway applications, the set-up is nearly as important, but the parameters are vastly different.

There are four areas of alignment that are important for performance and stability both while cornering and in a straight line. Note, however, that these adjustments vary greatly from one car to another; refer to a shop manual or consult with an alignment expert to make these adjustments safely and correctly for your car.

Camber

Camber is the angle of the wheel from vertical in front view. The goal with camber is to achieve a small amount of negative camber (top of tire tilts towards centerline of car) during cornering. For any competition set-up, camber must be set according to tire temperatures. The maximum useful negative camber is about 3 degrees. Any more will cause poor transient handling because it takes too long for the tire to flatten out once the turn is started.

For highway driving, any amount of negative camber over 1 degree will cause rapid wear to the inside edge of the tire. More camber will also cause a slight reduction in straightline stability. For dual-purpose cars, it is handy if camber can be easily adjusted for competition and returned to a sensible setting for highway driving.

Castor

Castor is the inclination of the steering axis from vertical in side view. Positive castor is the most often used setting. Castor causes castor trail, which is force imbalance at the tire contact patch. This force twists the tire tread and creates a torque around the point where the steering axis intersects the tire contact patch. The greater the castor, the

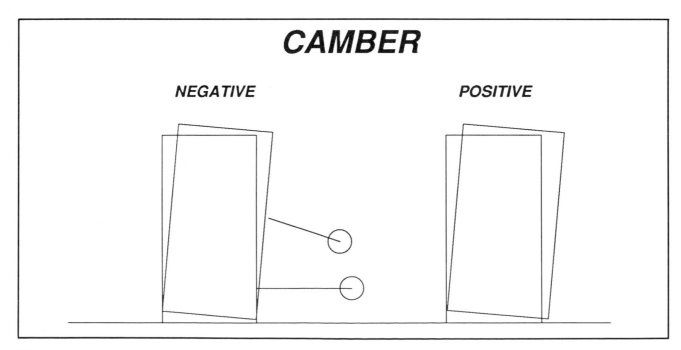

An electronic angle finder is the easiest way to measure camber. This instrument can compensate for the ground plane angle, giving an accurate reading without being on level ground. Bob Ryder

The Dunlop castor gauge is ideal for most applications, since it adapts to a variety of hubs.

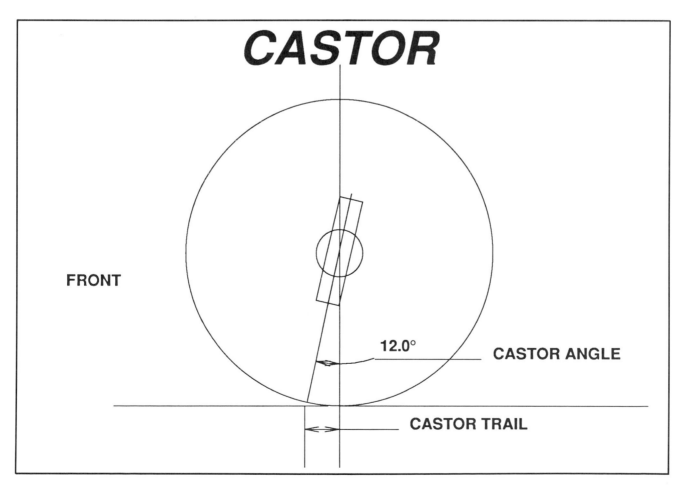

CASTOR

FRONT

12.0° ——— CASTOR ANGLE

CASTOR TRAIL

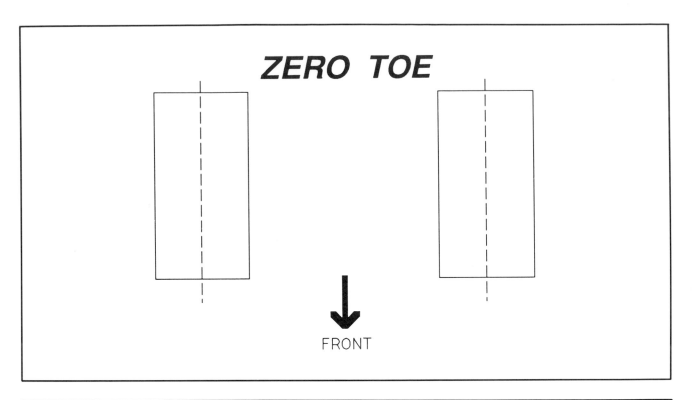

ZERO TOE

FRONT

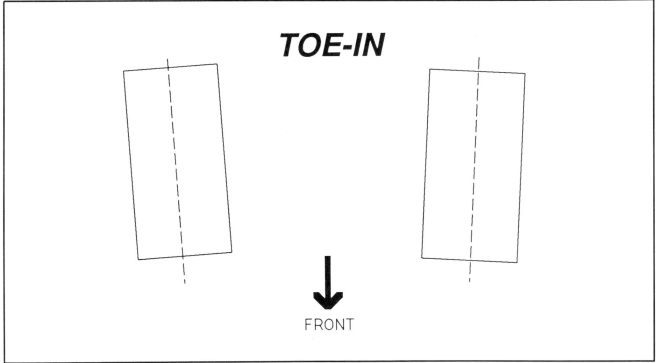

TOE-IN

FRONT

more castor trail is present. The torque increases with castor and so does the steering effort. The self-centering effect of the tires caused by this torque also increases, which improves straightline stability and driver feel of the tires. Less castor reduces tire scrub while cornering, but reduces stability and feel.

For competition applications, castor should remain within 2 degrees of stock if wheel size has not increased by more than 1 in. Major changes to wheel size and offset or suspension geometry may necessitate larger changes to castor. This is a design problem.

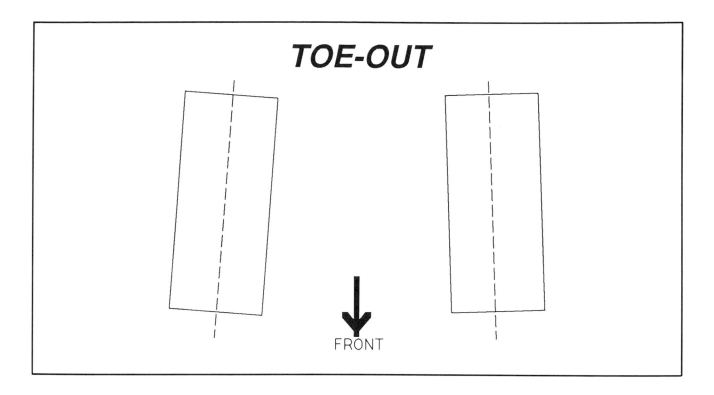

For the street, stock castor settings usually work adequately, unless major changes are made to wheel offsets or suspension geometry.

Toe

Toe-in or toe-out is the static alignment of the front wheels (or rear wheels on cars with independent rear suspension) in top view relative to the centerline of the vehicle. Zero toe is when all wheels are parallel to the vehicle centerline, allowing minimum tire drag. Toe-in occurs when the front (leading) edge of a tire points towards the center of the vehicle; toe-out is the opposite. Any toe-in or toe-out will increase tire drag, so small amounts are usually specified. At the front tires, toe-in improves straightline stability, while toe-out will help steer a car into a turn by reducing corner entry understeer slightly. Toe-out causes a car to wander in a straight line, and is not recommended for street driving, since it is difficult to deal with in most cases. At the rear, with independent suspension, toe-in is mandatory, since it promotes stability in a straight line, but also when turning into a corner. Rear toe-out is not safe for any condition.

A quick, easy and reasonably accurate toe measure can be taken by scribing a line around each front (or rear) tire and measuring the distance between the lines at the front of the tires versus the rear of the tires. If the front measurement is greater, toe-out is present; smaller measurements indicate toe-in. This gives a total measurement for both sides. Most specifications are per side and are measured at the edge of the wheel rim. Using this method, the per side specifications should be doubled for the total amount of toe.

The range of front toe setting is from 0.125 in. per side in or out to zero. At the rear, the toe-in should be set to 0.125 in. or more per side, but not over 0.25 in. Any toe setting over 0.125 in. will cause excessive tire wear, toe-in wearing the outside edge of the tread, toe-out wearing the inside edge.

Corner Weight Balance

One of the most important phases of set-up is the balancing of the corner weights. Adjusting corner weights is a great tuning tool for the street and is a necessity for any type of competition. This requires corner weight scales, patience and a means of adjusting ride heights at each corner of the vehicle. Unless care is taken here, the outcome will be worse than the original set-up.

The first step in balancing corner weight is to properly weigh the car on a set of scales. Knowing each corner weight is crucial for this process. Ideally, you would like the left side total weight to equal the right side total weight, and the diagonal totals to be equal. In most cases, weight is offset in the car, especially in models for two or more passengers. Always weigh the car as it will be driven, with some fuel load and the driver, plus a passenger if one will be along for a ride or event.

By recording the four corner weights, some quick calculations can be done. First, you want total weight of the car, then left side, right side, front and rear totals. Finally, you need the diagonal to-

Setting Toe Alignment

Here is a quick and easy method to align toe using a plumb bob, four jack stands, string and a machinist's ruler. Place the car on jack stands so that the underside is easily accessible. Using a plumb bob (carpenter's style with a rubber tip), drop the plumb from an inner suspension pick-up point on the chassis at each corner of the car and mark these points on the floor. Measure the mid-point between the two front marks and the two rear marks; this is the centerline of the car. Tape a length of string under the car so that it passes over the front and rear centerline marks. Use the plumb bob from the body to the string to mark the centerline on the chassis of the car for future reference. The car can now be placed on the floor. Drop the plumb bob to the floor and make a mark on the floor at the centerline at both front and rear.

Now set up two jack stands on each side of the car with a string taut between them. The string should be within 6 in. of the rims and set at axle height. Measure from each string to the centerline mark at the front and rear and move one jack stand on each side until the front and rear measurements are equal, meaning that the strings are parallel to the centerline of the car and to each other. Now toe can be measured.

With the machinist's ruler parallel to the floor, measure the distance from the string to the wheel rim at the front edge of the wheel, then at the rear edge of the wheel. If the measurements are equal, zero toe exists. If the rear measurement is smaller, toe-in is present. If the rear measurement is larger, toe-out is present. Adjust the toe until the desired results are obtained.

As a final check, measure the distance from the left front suspension pick-up point mark on the floor to the right rear suspension pick-up point mark on the floor. This distance should equal the same measurement on the right front to left rear diagonal. Any difference indicates a chassis out of square. Anything with 0.125 in. is excellent; more than 0.5 in. is a problem. If you are setting toe on a solid-axle car, take measurements as well. Toe-in or toe-out indicates that the housing or axle is not square in the chassis or is bent.

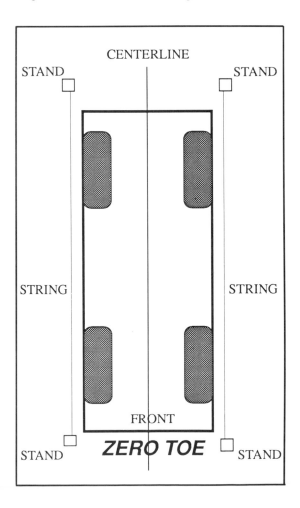

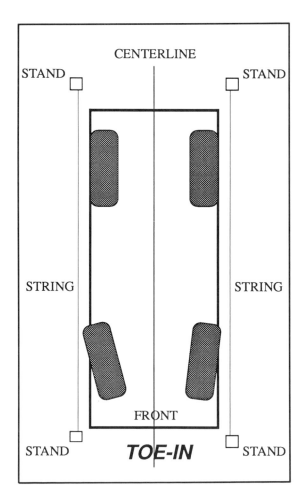

Front-Drive Versus Rear-drive Suspension Set-Up

One question that inevitably pops up is the set-up differences between front- and rear-drive cars. They certainly handle differently. Driving techniques vary somewhat also. But does the set-up and tuning require different approaches for the different drive arrangements? Simply stated, there is little difference in tuning or set-up. The exact settings will vary, but the trends are the same.

Let's look at different settings and tuning points. Castor is usually set to factory specifications. With front-drive cars, castor is often reduced to ease steering effort, but, as with rear-drive cars, castor is kept to a minimum to reduce tire scrub, but enough is used to give the driver good feel and some self-centering in the steering system.

Camber is set by tire temperature readings on any type of vehicle. The rubber molecules at the tire contact patch only know if they are working hard, not if they are on a front-drive or a rear-drive vehicle. The same holds true for tire pressures: temperatures tell the tale.

Toe-in or toe-out have more differences than any other settings, but even here the trend is the same. Both front- and rear-drivers like front toe-out for better turn-in. The front-driver likes more toe-out than the rear, as much as 0.5 in. total on tight autocross courses. That amount is even common on tighter road courses. The toe-out limit is tire drag in a straight line: too much toe will cause tire scrub and reduce top speed, and the faster the track is, the more important this becomes.

The big fight with front-drive cars is overcoming the compliance caused by all of the soft rubber bushings used to reduce the feel of torque steer to the driver. Some front-drive cars require excessive amounts of toe-out to combat this compliance. At the rear, toe-in is still the stable set-up, front- or rear-drive.

Corner weights are set the same for front- or rear-drive: equal cross weights are equal cross weights. The scales do not know if the car is a front-driver.

Every car is a little different and different cars require different suspension setting, as do different tracks and drivers. While a front-drive car may require a different set-up, it is based upon the design of the specific vehicle, not whether it is front- or rear-drive. Based on this premise, try different settings. You may find one that works better.

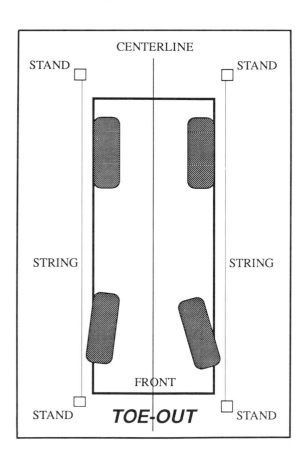

The RuggleS'cales use bathroom scales and lever arms to measure corner weights. The four-scale set-up is easy to use, durable and accurate. Measuring and adjusting corner weights is a crucial part of the set-up procedure. The RuggleS'cales are the most efficient and cost-effective means of measuring corner weights.

tals, left front and right rear total and right front and left rear total. These diagonals are crucial for good handling balance. The goal for most cases is to have both diagonals equal to each other, or at fifty percent of the total vehicle weight. When this occurs, the vehicle will have equal handling balance in both left- and right-hand turns. Cornering speeds will not necessarily be equal left to right, but the feel of the car will be the same.

For oval tracks, or even road race courses, the diagonal percentage can be more or less than the ideal fifty percent. The improved cornering in one direction will be lost in the opposite direction. In fact, the loss to the other direction will be greater than the gain in the first place, so this practice is limited to ovals or courses with most of the turns running in one direction. For the street or autocross, even diagonal weights are the goal.

After weighing the corners of a car, and computing the diagonal weights, the next step requires changing ride heights to transfer weight around the car. To do this, you must raise the light corner, or lower the heavy corner or both. This can be done with spacers, different-diameter tires or with adjustable spring perches as seen on formula cars. Keep in mind that one change will affect all four corners. Raising one corner will put more weight on that corner *and* the diagonally opposite corner. It will also remove weight from the two remaining corners. It is best to make small changes at each corner rather than one big change at one corner. The process can be time consuming, but the payoff is often large.

STATIC WEIGHT DISTRIBUTION
SETTING CORNER WEIGHTS

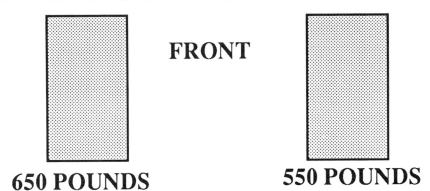

FRONT

650 POUNDS   **550 POUNDS**

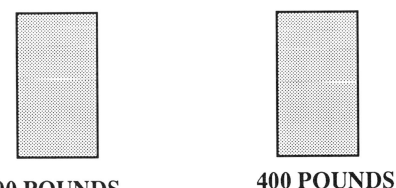

400 POUNDS   **400 POUNDS**

TOP VIEW

TOTAL WEIGHT:2000 Pounds
LEFT FRONT/RIGHT REAR DIAGONAL: 1050 POUNDS
RIGHT FRONT/LEFTREAR DIAGONAL: 950 POUNDS
LEFT FRONT/RIGHT REAR DIAGONAL PERCENTAGE: 52.5%

STATIC WEIGHT DISTRIBUTION
SETTING CORNER WEIGHTS

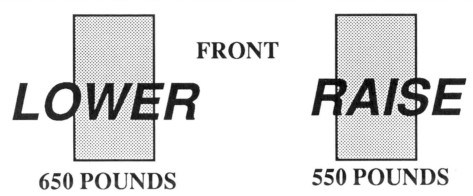

FRONT

LOWER

650 POUNDS

RAISE

550 POUNDS

To change the corner weights, the heavy corners must be lowered and the light corners raised. The biggest changes come from the heaviest corners, and at the end of the vehicle with the largest discrepency.

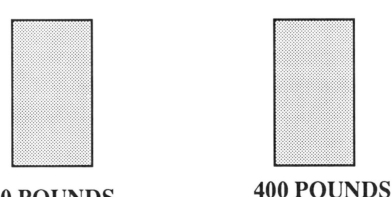

400 POUNDS   **400 POUNDS**

TOP VIEW

TOTAL WEIGHT:2000 Pounds
LEFT FRONT/RIGHT REAR DIAGONAL: 1050 POUNDS
RIGHT FRONT/LEFTREAR DIAGONAL: 950 POUNDS
LEFT FRONT/RIGHT REAR DIAGONAL PERCENTAGE: 52.5%

STATIC WEIGHT DISTRIBUTION
SETTING CORNER WEIGHTS

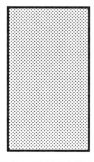

FRONT

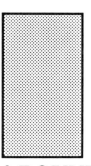

615 POUNDS

590 POUNDS

ADJUSTED CORNER WEIGHTS

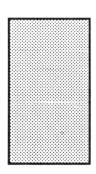

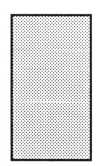

410 POUNDS

385 POUNDS

TOP VIEW

TOTAL WEIGHT:2000 Pounds
LEFT FRONT/RIGHT REAR DIAGONAL: 1000 POUNDS
RIGHT FRONT/LEFTREAR DIAGONAL: 1000 POUNDS
LEFT FRONT/RIGHT REAR DIAGONAL PERCENTAGE: 50.0%

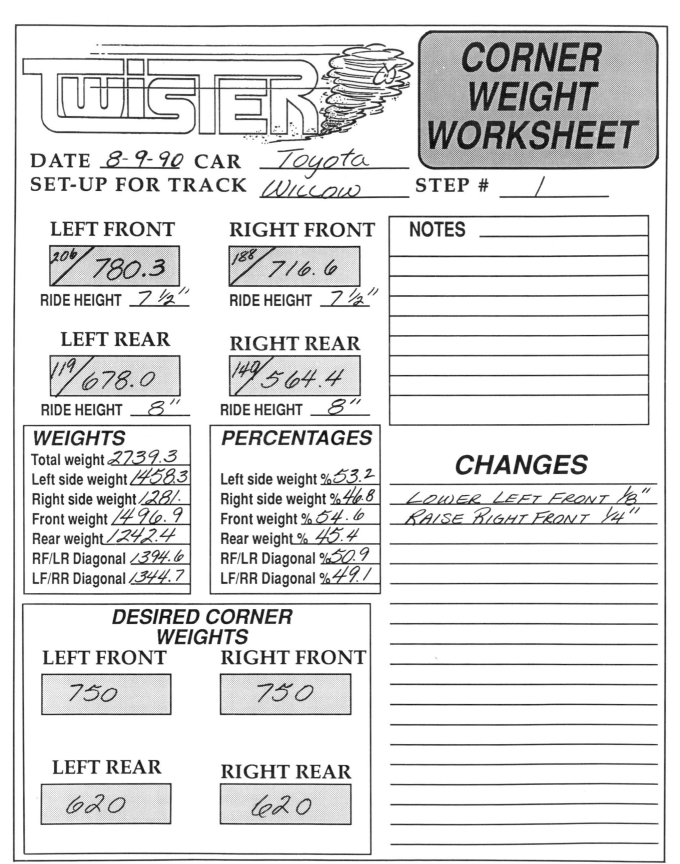

CORNER WEIGHT WORKSHEET

DATE _8-9-90_ CAR _Toyota_

SET-UP FOR TRACK _Willow_ STEP # _1_

LEFT FRONT

206 / 780.3

RIDE HEIGHT _7 ½"_

RIGHT FRONT

188 / 716.6

RIDE HEIGHT _7 ½"_

LEFT REAR

119 / 678.0

RIDE HEIGHT _8"_

RIGHT REAR

149 / 564.4

RIDE HEIGHT _8"_

NOTES ____

WEIGHTS
Total weight _2739.3_
Left side weight _1458.3_
Right side weight _1281._
Front weight _1496.9_
Rear weight _1242.4_
RF/LR Diagonal _1394.6_
LF/RR Diagonal _1344.7_

PERCENTAGES
Left side weight % _53.2_
Right side weight % _46.8_
Front weight % _54.6_
Rear weight % _45.4_
RF/LR Diagonal % _50.9_
LF/RR Diagonal % _49.1_

CHANGES

LOWER LEFT FRONT ⅛"
RAISE RIGHT FRONT ¼"

DESIRED CORNER WEIGHTS

LEFT FRONT

750

RIGHT FRONT

750

LEFT REAR

620

RIGHT REAR

620

Test sheet number 1 for the Toyota Corolla GT-S Twin Cam at Willow Springs. Note the changes in ride heights at the left front and right front to balance out the handling.

CORNER WEIGHT WORKSHEET

DATE _8.9.90_ CAR _Toyota_

SET-UP FOR TRACK _Willow_ STEP # _2_

LEFT FRONT
761
RIDE HEIGHT _7 3/8"_

RIGHT FRONT
716
RIDE HEIGHT _7 1/2"_

LEFT REAR
654
RIDE HEIGHT _7 7/8_

RIGHT REAR
609
RIDE HEIGHT _8 1/8"_

WEIGHTS
Total weight _2740_
Left side weight _1415_
Right side weight _1325_
Front weight _1477_
Rear weight _1263_
RF/LR Diagonal _1370_
LF/RR Diagonal _1370_

PERCENTAGES
Left side weight % _51.6_
Right side weight % _48.4_
Front weight % _53.9_
Rear weight % _46.1_
RF/LR Diagonal % _50_
LF/RR Diagonal % _50_

DESIRED CORNER WEIGHTS

LEFT FRONT

RIGHT FRONT

LEFT REAR

RIGHT REAR

NOTES

CHANGES

Test sheet number 2. With the changes in ride height, the handling is balanced out.

113

Chapter 11

Tuning for Improved Handling

While the right pieces are important to obtain improved handling performance, tuning those parts is even more critical.

Here's an example. I was tuning a car for a magazine article. The correct springs, bars, shocks and bushings were installed on the car by the manufacturer. The larger, stickier tires should have made an instant improvement in lateral acceleration. But the car did not drive well, and the first stint on the skid pad indicated that the lateral acceleration was 0.90 g, only 0.01 g better than the showroom version of the car. Within four hours, we altered tire pressures, camber angles, toe and rear antiroll bar settings, but never changed one part on the car. Our final session on the skid pad that day showed an improvement to 1.0 g. And on the track the car was delightful to drive at the limit, with excellent responsiveness and forgiving handling characteristics. All of the magazine test drivers were pleased with both total grip and the handling balance of the car. One driver, a competitor in a pro racing series in the identical type of car, was all grins when he stepped from the vehicle. His own car had experienced handling problems all year.

The point here is that tuning makes all the difference in the world. You would not expect an engine builder to extract maximum power, or the most effective torque curve from an engine, without spending time on the dynamometer. The same holds true with suspension tuning. The real tuning comes on the handling "dyno," the skid pad.

When developing a suspension set-up, you will spend considerable time fine-tuning settings

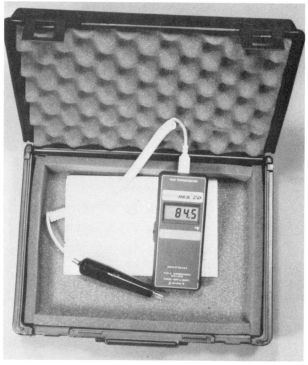

Certain data is crucial to tune a suspension system properly and among the most important data is the tire temperature. Tire pyrometers measure the temperature of the tire tread and offer considerable information about the set-up of the car. The standard Reb-Co tire pyrometer responds quickly and accurately to readings taken with the probe.

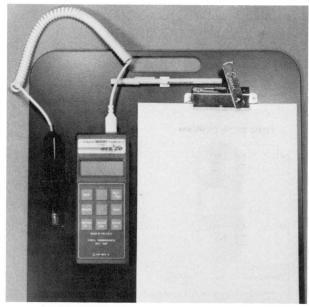

The Reb-Co Memory Pyrometer has a record button and stores up to fifteen temperatures. This makes taking tire temperatures easy for one person.

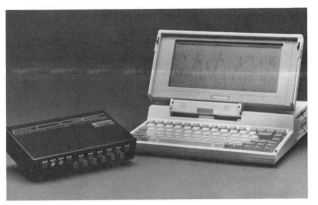

The EDGE Performance Monitor is an on-board data acquisition system that can tell the suspension and tire engineer a great deal concerning specifics of performance. The data, when analyzed carefully, can offer insights into settings and even design parameters that will improve cornering traction and tire contact patch compliance with the road surface. Peerless Electronics

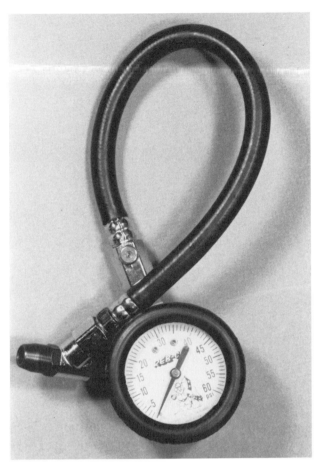

Another important tool for tuning is the tire pressure gauge. Tire pressures alter the shape of the tire contact patch and must be monitored for correct settings.

and parts. Begin on the 200 ft. diameter skid pad, running in both clockwise and counterclockwise directions and taking tire temperatures on the outside tires. The tire temperatures allow you to fine-tune camber angles and tire pressures. You can also use tire temperatures and driver input to establish a handling balance. If the car understeers, for example, look at the temperatures and alter the roll resistance with the antiroll bars accordingly. The lateral acceleration improvements are sub-

---

Tools for Testing

Following is a list of tools needed for track testing:
- Multi-function stopwatch
- Tire pyrometer
- Wheel scales
- Suspension alignment equipment
- Tire pressure gauge
- Optional equipment: video camera, g.Analyst, laptop computer

---

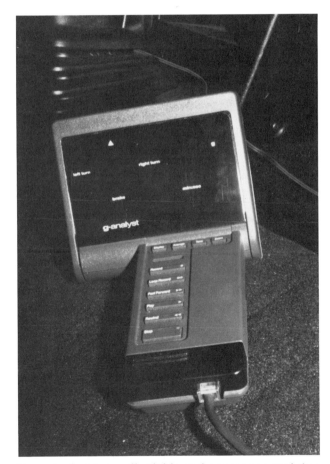

The g.Analyst is an affordable and easy-to-use tool that measures acceleration, both lateral and longitudinal. Much important data can be gathered from the g.Analyst to improve set-up and even driving technique. A few years ago, the equivalent data acquisition system would cost $10,000 to purchase. The g.Analyst is under $400. Bob Ryder

How to Use a Tire Pyrometer

The tire pyrometer is the single most valuable tool you can use to set up a race car or high-performance street car. Following is a list of techniques to obtain the most accurate and consistent data. The same criteria apply for any type of test, street or race set-up. All initial testing should be undertaken on a skid pad with limited access and an adequate runoff area. Taking tire temperatures is a rule of suspension tuning!

- Take tire temperatures every time the car comes into the pits.
- Take tire temperature readings in three spots across the tread of the tire—near each edge and in the middle.
- Always start at the same tire for a given track. Start with the most heavily loaded tire first, usually the front on the outside of the last turn before the pits.
- Always start at the same point on the tire (inside or outside).
- One person should take readings, another should record them.
- The pyrometer probe should penetrate the tire tread surface slightly.
- Let the tire temperature reading stabilize, but don't hesitate at one place too long.
- Always move around the car in the same direction.
- Take tire temperature readings as quickly as possible.
- Always recheck the first tire's temperature readings. Tires cool quickly and the heat in the tire tends to balance across the tread.
- Taking readings a second time on the first tire checked will allow you to determine how accurate the readings on the fourth tire were.
- Always check hot tire pressures as soon as possible when coming in. Tire temperatures are the first priority, pressures are second.
- Save time and date your records for future reference.

stantial during this process. Once you reach a plateau, move to the 300 ft. diameter skid pad to confirm the settings at higher speeds.

Lateral acceleration is only half the story. Next, test the vehicle in low- and moderate-speed turns for traction, balance and responsiveness. Antiroll bar adjustments and shock adjustments cause the biggest improvements. From there, test in high-speed turns for aerodynamic balance.

The Importance of Tire Temperatures

In the course of testing the handling of a car, use tire temperatures and driver feel to make adjustments. This should be done for street set-ups as well as competition set-ups. It is critical to moni-

tor tire temperatures often. They offer valuable clues to the set-up of the car. The final criteria for improvements is always the stopwatch; improvements on the skidpad and test track will always show up on the stopwatch. The areas of adjustment that we use tire temperatures for include: tire pressure, camber, body roll, roll couple distribution, shock settings, wheel width and transient handling response.

Reading Tire Temperatures

It is best to check with a tire engineer from the manufacturer of the tires being used to obtain tire temperature operating ranges. For most tires, the optimum range is between 165 and 250 degrees

Troubleshooting Tire Temperatures

Reading	Handling problem	Reason
All tires too hot		Compound too soft for track and ambient temperature conditions
Front tires too hot	Understeer	Front tire pressures too low
Rear tires too hot	Oversteer	Rear tire pressures too low
Inside edges too hot	Too much body roll	Too much negative camber or too much toe-out
Outside edges too hot	Too much body roll	Too little negative camber, too little toe-out or too much toe-in or wheel width too narrow for tire width
Center of tread too hot		Tire pressure too high
Edges only too hot		Tire pressure too low
All tires too cold		Compound too hard for track and ambient temperature conditions or car not being driven to limit
Front tires too cold		Inadequate load on front tires
Rear tires too cold		Inadequate load on rear tires

Skid pad testing plays an important part in development work. It isolates parameters and allows you to quickly reach baseline settings for steady state situations. Camber, tire pressure, tire loading characteristics, total trac- *tion, and front and rear handling balance (roll couple distribution) are quickly determined on the skid pad. Here the Ground Zero Mustang GT is at an average cornering force of 0.90 g. Bob McClurg*

Fahrenheit. Generally, the hotter the tire, the more friction the tire is creating. The friction increases with load. If all tires are running too hot, then a harder compound is needed.

Suspension Testing on the Racetrack

It is extremely difficult to maintain a competitive race car or a well-tuned street car without a test program. For competition, the more testing conducted, the more competitive the car will become. Every racing budget should include a test program. It is not practical to test at events, but it may be the only possibility.

The type of test program many race teams and factories conduct for a new race car would include the following:

• Two days minimum on a skid pad for testing roll rates, camber settings, tire pressures and compounds, and to familiarize the driver with the car.

• One day minimum of aerodynamic testing (for any type of car—two days for cars with adjustable aerodynamic devices) to determine downforce versus drag.

• Two days of track testing at a track that is familiar to the driver. Segment times and accelerations (all directions) as well as vehicle speed are all worthwhile inputs to help reduce lap times.

Track testing is the only reasonable way to balance the transitional handling of a vehicle, and determine the true performance of a project car like the Ground Zero Mustang, here testing at Willow Springs. Bob McClurg

• Additional testing should be undertaken anytime a change is made to the car, or when the effects of changes to bars, springs, shocks, aerodynamics and power output need to be evaluated.

Testing Procedures

The following is a list of suggested testing procedures:

Timing a test lap on a skid pad at Willow Springs. Bob Ryder

After a test lap, quickly bring your car in for a tire temperature reading.

• Have a game plan before you undertake a test session.

• Have the car fully prepared before arriving at the track for a test day. Testing is expensive. Preparing the car at the track wastes time and money.

• Keep detailed records of the car set-up as it was when it arrived at the track. This data will allow you to return to a baseline setting.

• Start the test day with a test at the baseline setting.

• Record everything about the car, driver, track conditions and ambient weather.

• Make only one change at a time, and make it big enough to have a noticeable effect.

Skid Pad Testing

Most racers never consider testing on a skid pad. It's not very exciting. Even fewer street set-ups are skid pad tested. But more can be learned about car set-up in a day or two than a whole season of racing. It is also inexpensive and low risk.

Skid Circle Test

The skid circle test determines lateral acceleration and can be used to optimize roll resistance, tire pressures and camber settings. This type of testing helps the driver to learn car balance, throt-

Measure both front and rear temperatures as quickly as possible. Tires cool quickly, and the temperatures rapidly balance across the tread of the tire. Bob Ryder

tle control and the effects of throttle steer, and requires that the driver be smooth and consistent.

It is important to lap times to calculate g force, tire temperatures and changes. The formula for lateral acceleration on a skid pad is:

$$\text{lateral acceleration in g} = \frac{1.225 \times (\text{radius of skid pad circle})}{\text{time in seconds, squared}}$$

Offset Lane-Change Test and Pylon Slalom

The offset, left-right-left lane-change test and pylon slalom helps the driver evaluate transient handling and helps to determine optimum shock absorber bump rates. This test improves driver feel of car.

It is important to record segment times, tire temperatures and changes.

Ninety-Degree Turn Test

The 90 degree turn test allows the driver to evaluate turn-in characteristics of a car and aids in setting shock rates and toe-in or toe-out. This test also helps the driver to judge trail braking effectiveness and technique as well as steering inputs.

It is important to record segment times, g force with a g analyst if possible, vehicle speed, tire temperatures and changes.

The needle on the probe of the tire pyrometer must be inserted into the tread of the tire for an accurate reading. Temperatures are read at three points on each tire. The temperatures at each point indicate how hard the rubber molecules are working in that portion of the tire tread. Bob Ryder

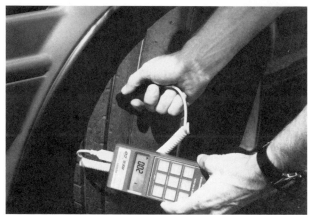

Actual temperature readings at three points on a front tire after a skid pad test. At the top, the inside temperature is 152 degrees. The middle temperature is 200 degrees, which shows that the tire is working hard. The outside temperature is 191 degrees. The cooler inside temperature indicates that the inside portion of the tire contact patch is not working enough, and could be generating more grip. Too little negative camber is the cause, or the rim width is too narrow for the tire size. The fact that the hottest temperature is in the middle shows that the tire is slightly over-inflated about 1 psi. This data is invaluable for quick and accurate suspension tuning. With a couple of minor changes, the car will have more grip and easily exceed 1.0 g average cornering force on the skid pad. Bob Ryder

Brake Bias Test

The brake bias test allows you to adjust brake balance so that the front brakes lock just before the rears. It is best to use two visual spotters, one for the front and one for the rear wheels.

It is important to record settings of balance bar or proportioning valve and track conditions.

Suspension Tuning on the Road

Not all drivers have access to racetracks and skid pads, especially those who do not compete. For those who want to improve the handling of their street machine it is possible to tune your suspension on the road.

Certain suspension settings require actual data to make good setting decisions; others relate more to seat-of-the-pants feel and driver preference. Let's separate these two distinct segments of feedback into individual testing programs.

Getting the Tire Contact Patch Flat on the Road

The most important factor effecting handling is the tire contact patch interface with the road. The tire contact patch should be nearly flat on the road surface during maximum cornering. You can use tire temperatures as the quickest, easiest method to tell you if the tire contact patch is actually flat on the road surface while cornering, and also to tell if the camber angle is correct and if the tire pressure is in the proper range. A skid pad is the safest, quickest and easiest place to undertake this type of test, but only if you have access to a skid pad. Most people do not.

To test on the road, you need a tire pyrometer and a tire pressure gauge, and to take notes. You should never drive the car to its cornering limits on the street, but you can drive to about seventy-five percent of the maximum cornering speed. This is best done on a deserted windy road. After about four or five turns, at a convenient turnout, stop to measure tire temperatures. The readings are recorded, then analyzed. Changing pressures is easy, and can be tried as soon as the adjustments are made. On some cars, camber settings are also easy to alter. Again, when possible, camber changes can be quickly checked. Keep testing until tire pressure and camber settings are adjusted so that tire temperatures read nearly even across the tire contact patch.

Seat-of-the-Pants Settings

Virtually all other settings require driver feel and often are adjusted to the preferences of the individual; all of these settings are easily tested on the road. Castor, toe-in or toe-out, antiroll bar adjustments, shock absorber settings and even corner weights can be set in the garage or driveway,

Tire pressures play a key roll in contact patch contour. The pressure can distort the contact patch, reducing maximum tire adhesion. Reading temperatures, then checking pressures is important. Knowing the optimum hot tire pressure allows the tire contact patch to do its job. Once the optimum hot pressure is found, let the tire cool completely to determine the optimum cold pressure. Be aware that the ambient air temperature will affect the cold pressure and could significantly alter the hot pressure. The type of event also influences the cold starting pressure. At an autocross, where little heat builds up in the tire while running, a higher cold starting pressure will be needed. Bob Ryder

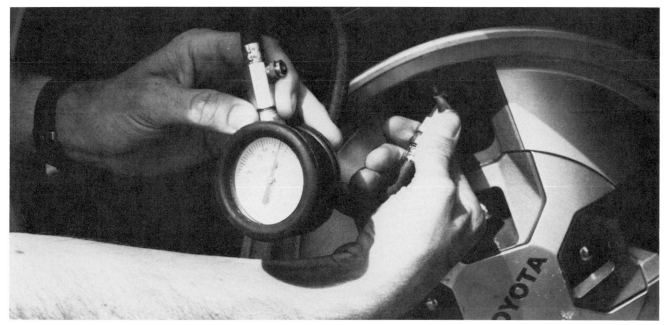

If the tire temperatures show hotter in the center of the tire tread, the tire is overinflated for the conditions and load on the tire, the tire contact patch area is reduced and traction is lost. Temperatures as little as 3 degrees more require adjustments. If the outside edges are running hotter than the middle, the pressure is too low. This also reduces the tire contact patch area, but the sidewall stiffness is reduced, causing the tire to operate at higher slip angles and further reducing corner power at that tire. Handling problems can occur due to under- and over-inflation. The realistic range of adjustment in tire pressure to affect handling balance is about ten percent of the optimum pressure, or 4 psi for a DOT tire running 40 psi at its optimum. Bob Ryder

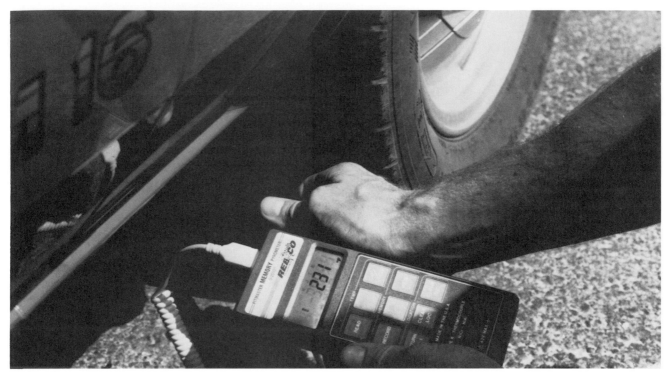

Tire temperatures as high as this indicate excessive loading on a portion of the tire. In this case, the 231 degree reading is about 10 degrees hotter than the maximum temperature for good traction. This tire would begin to chunk at the outer edge of it ran for long at this temperature. The problem at the rear of this car appears to be too little negative camber. With a solid rear axle, camber is *not adjustable. The real problem here is a rim that is too narrow. This 6 in. rim with a 205/60-14 is too narrow to keep the tire contact patch flat on the road surface. A 7 in. rim would work much better. A 195/60-14 tire on the 6 in. rim would actually corner better because the tire contact patch actually working is larger with the smaller tire. Bob Ryder*

then tested on the road. When it feels right, run it. Use the information throughout this book to make baseline setting decisions, and then, changes. While the process can take some time and energy, it is great fun and very challenging. Just be cautious on the road. Meaningful data does not require driving like a maniac.

Effect of Suspension Changes

Before making changes to suspension components and settings, it is good to know how the changes will effect performance and ride. The following chart will help give you a general idea of the effect a specific change will make to handling and ride.

Spring Rate Changes

Modification	Effect on Suspension
Increase front and rear rate	Ride harshness increases; tires may not follow bumps causing reduced traction. Roll resistance increases
Increase front rate only	Front ride rate increases. Front roll resistance increases, increasing understeer or reducing oversteer
Increase rear rate only	Rear ride rate increases. Rear roll resistance increases, increasing oversteer or reducing understeer
Decrease front and rear rate	Ride harshness decreases; tires follow bumps more effectively, possibly improving traction. Roll resistance decreases
Decrease front rate only	Front ride rate decreases. Front roll resistance decreases, decreasing understeer or increasing oversteer
Decrease rear rate only	Rear ride rate decreases. Rear roll resistance decreases, decreasing oversteer or increasing understeer

Antiroll Bar Changes

Modification	Effect on Suspension
Increase front rate	Front roll resistance increases, increasing understeer or decreasing oversteer. May also reduce camber change, allowing better tire contact patch compliance with road surface, reducing understeer
Increase rear rate	Rear roll resistance increases, increasing oversteer or decreasing understeer. On independent rear suspensions, may also reduce camber change, allowing better tire contact patch compliance with road surface, reducing oversteer
Decrease front rate	Front roll resistance decreases, decreasing understeer or increasing oversteer. More body roll could reduce tire contact patch area, causing understeer
Decrease rear rate	Rear roll resistance decreases, decreasing oversteer or increasing understeer. On vehicles with independent rear suspension, more body roll could reduce tire contact patch area, causing oversteer

Shock Absorber Changes

Modification	Effect on Suspension
Increase rebound and bump rates	Ride harshness increases
Increase rebound rates only	On bumps, tires may leave track surface
Increase bump rates only	Body roll resisted; outside tire loaded too quickly; car won't stabilize into a turn
Decrease rebound and bump rates	Ride harshness decreases; car may float over bumps
Decrease rebound rates only	On bumps, tires follow track surface more effectively; car may continue to oscillate after bumps
Decrease bump rates only	Body rolls quickly; car is slower to respond to turn-in

Solving Handling Problems

The key to setting up your suspension is in diagnosing what the handling problems are and resolving how to fix them. While car enthusiasts often baulk at the "black art" of suspension tuning, there's no reason to. As with working on the mechanical aspects of an engine, the trick to suspension tuning is in the troubleshooting; there is always a cause and an effect.

Solving Handling Problems

Problem	Manifestation	Solutions
Steady state understeer	All turns or low-speed turns only	If front tire temperatures are optimum and rears are low, stiffen rear antiroll bar; if front temperatures are too hot, soften front (most likely) If front tire pressures are optimum, decrease rear tire pressure. Increase if chunking occurs Improper front camber Too much body roll at front, causing excessive camber change
Steady state understeer	High-speed turns only	If front tire temperatures are OK, increase front downforce If front tire temperatures are too hot, reduce rear downforce
Steady state oversteer	All turns or low-speed turns only	If rear tire temperatures are optimum, with fronts too low, stiffen front antiroll bar; if rear temperatures are too hot, soften rear antiroll bar (most likely) If rear tire pressures are optimum, decrease front tire pressure. Increase if chunking occurs. Improper rear camber
Steady state oversteer	High-speed turns only	If rear tire temperatures are OK, increase rear downforce If rear tire temperatures are too hot, reduce front downforce
Corner entry understeer		Front shocks are too soft in bump resistance Too much front toe-in; use a small amount of front toe-out Ride height is too high in front
Corner exit understeer		Rear shocks are too soft in bump Front shocks are too stiff in rebound
Corner entry oversteer		Rear shocks are too soft in rebound Rear ride height is too high (too much rake) compared to front
Corner exit oversteer		Rear shocks are too soft in rebound Too much rear toe-in or any rear toe-out
Straightline instability		Tire pressure is too low in one or more tires Too little positive front castor Too much front toe-in or any toe-out in rear Shock rate is too stiff for bumpy surfaces
Straightline speed too slow		Too much overall downforce Too much toe-in or toe-out Ride height is too high Too much chassis rake
Excessive steering effort	All turns	Too much positive castor Front tire pressures are too low
Chassis or suspension bottoms		Spring rates are too soft Shock absorber bump rates are too soft Inadequate suspension travel Inadequate ride height

TWiSTER

TIRE TEMPERATURE EVALUATION

DATE _8·8·90_

CAR _Toyota_ DRIVER _SHANE_ SESSION _#1_

LEFT FRONT

157	172	147

PRESSURE _____

RIGHT FRONT

153	152	154

PRESSURE _____

LEFT REAR

181	174	155

PRESSURE _____

RIGHT REAR

148	147	146

PRESSURE _____

LEFT FRONT
Camber OK? _NEED MORE NEG._

Pressure OK? _HIGH_

Toe OK? _OK_

RIGHT FRONT
Camber OK? _OK_

Pressure OK? _OK_

Toe OK? _OK_

LEFT REAR
Camber OK? _—_

Pressure OK? _OK_

Toe OK? _—_

RIGHT REAR
Camber OK? _—_

Pressure OK? _OK_

Toe OK? _—_

COMMENTS: _RIMS TOO NARROW FOR TIRES. NEEDS 7"_
RIMS FOR GOOD FRONT TIRE PRINT. LOWER LEFT PRESS.

HANDLING BALANCE: _GOOD_

These charts were used to evaluate tire temperatures and make changes. The five charts are from a series of tests on a Toyota Corolla GT-S Twin Cam rear-drive. On test 1, the predominance of right-hand turns on the test track at Willow Springs means that the left-side tires work harder than the right side. This is apparent in the hotter left tire temperatures. The left front tire is overinflated and the higher outside temperatures on the heavily loaded left side indicate too little negative camber. The real problem is wheel rims that are too narrow for the tires.

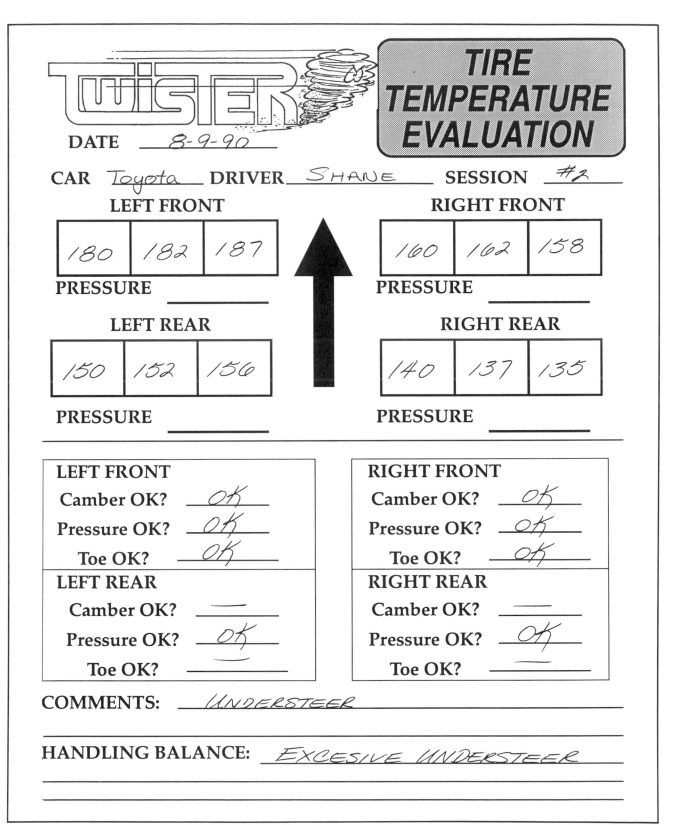

TIRE TEMPERATURE EVALUATION

TWISTER

DATE 8-9-90

CAR Toyota   **DRIVER** Shane   **SESSION** #2

LEFT FRONT

180	182	187

PRESSURE _____

RIGHT FRONT

160	162	158

PRESSURE _____

LEFT REAR

150	152	156

PRESSURE _____

RIGHT REAR

140	137	135

PRESSURE _____

LEFT FRONT
Camber OK? _OK_
Pressure OK? _OK_
Toe OK? _OK_

RIGHT FRONT
Camber OK? _OK_
Pressure OK? _OK_
Toe OK? _OK_

LEFT REAR
Camber OK? ___
Pressure OK? _OK_
Toe OK? ___

RIGHT REAR
Camber OK? ___
Pressure OK? _OK_
Toe OK? ___

COMMENTS: _Understeer_

HANDLING BALANCE: _Excesive Understeer_

Test 2 shows an improvement, but the front tires are much hotter indicating that excessive understeer is present. This is mostly a problem relating to where weight is being transferred, so a change in roll couple distribution is called for. Since the front antiroll bar is not adjustable, we need to make our adjustment to the rear. Since there is too much weight transfer at the front, we must increase the weight transfer to the rear by stiffening the rear antiroll bar.

126

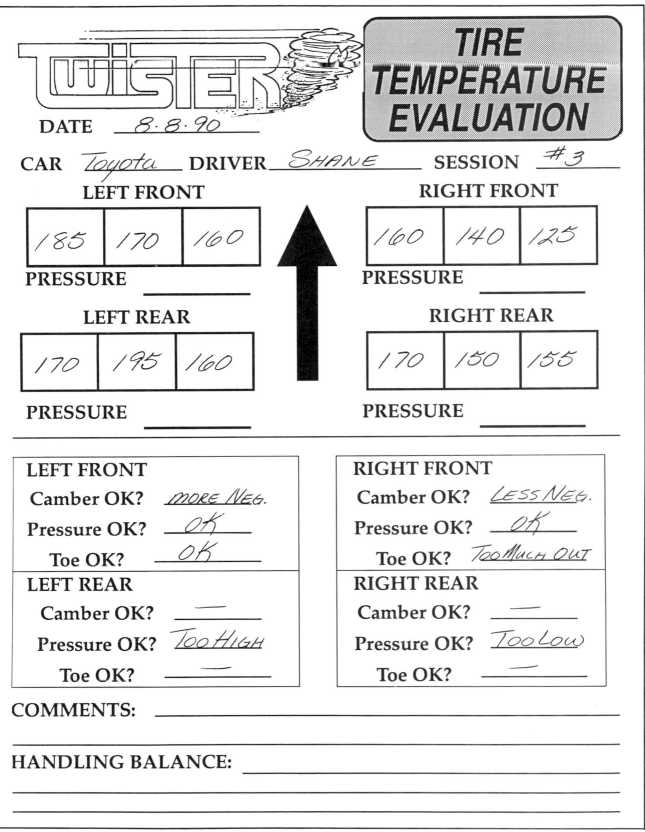

TIRE TEMPERATURE EVALUATION

DATE _8·8·90_

CAR _Toyota_ DRIVER _Shane_ SESSION _#3_

LEFT FRONT

185	170	160

PRESSURE _____

RIGHT FRONT

160	140	125

PRESSURE _____

LEFT REAR

170	195	160

PRESSURE _____

RIGHT REAR

170	150	155

PRESSURE _____

LEFT FRONT
Camber OK? _MORE NEG._

Pressure OK? _OK_

Toe OK? _OK_

RIGHT FRONT
Camber OK? _LESS NEG._

Pressure OK? _OK_

Toe OK? _Too Much Out_

LEFT REAR
Camber OK? _____

Pressure OK? _Too High_

Toe OK? _____

RIGHT REAR
Camber OK? _____

Pressure OK? _Too Low_

Toe OK? _____

COMMENTS: _____

_____

HANDLING BALANCE: _____

_____

Here the increased roll resistance has put more load on the rear tires, as shown by the higher rear tire temperatures. The extra load has raised the left rear pressure too much. The right rear tire has lost some pressure from a slow leak. The front tires are rolling over too much on the narrow rims.

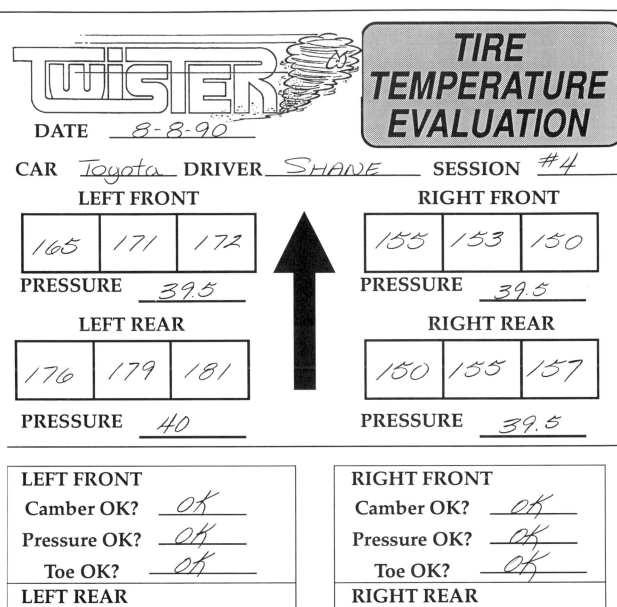

TIRE TEMPERATURE EVALUATION

DATE 8-8-90

CAR Toyota **DRIVER** SHANE **SESSION** #4

LEFT FRONT		
165	171	172

PRESSURE 39.5

RIGHT FRONT		
155	153	150

PRESSURE 39.5

LEFT REAR		
176	179	181

PRESSURE 40

RIGHT REAR		
150	155	157

PRESSURE 39.5

LEFT FRONT
Camber OK? _OK_
Pressure OK? _OK_
Toe OK? _OK_

LEFT REAR
Camber OK? ———
Pressure OK? _OK_
Toe OK? ———

RIGHT FRONT
Camber OK? _OK_
Pressure OK? _OK_
Toe OK? _OK_

RIGHT REAR
Camber OK? ———
Pressure OK? _OK_
Toe OK? ———

COMMENTS: TEMPS ON 7" Rims

HANDLING BALANCE: GOOD BALANCE

By going to a 7 in. rim, the tire temperatures have come in nicely, but the extra traction at the front has caused some oversteer at the rear. This requires softening the rear antiroll bar to reduce rear roll couple.

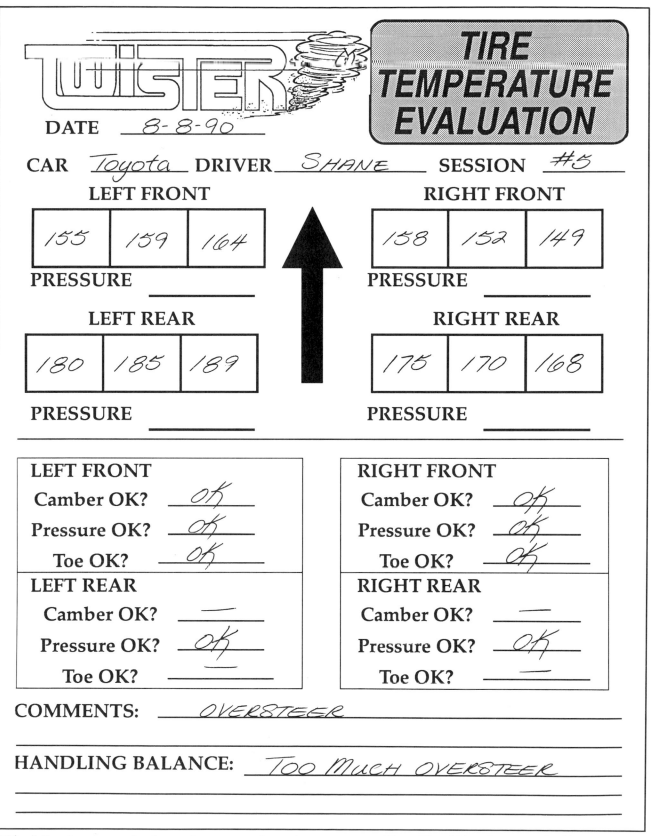

TIRE TEMPERATURE EVALUATION

DATE 8-8-90

CAR Toyota **DRIVER** Shane **SESSION** #5

LEFT FRONT

155	159	164

PRESSURE _____

RIGHT FRONT

158	152	149

PRESSURE _____

LEFT REAR

180	185	189

PRESSURE _____

RIGHT REAR

175	170	168

PRESSURE _____

LEFT FRONT
Camber OK? _OK_
Pressure OK? _OK_
Toe OK? _OK_

RIGHT FRONT
Camber OK? _OK_
Pressure OK? _OK_
Toe OK? _OK_

LEFT REAR
Camber OK? ____
Pressure OK? _OK_
Toe OK? ____

RIGHT REAR
Camber OK? ____
Pressure OK? _OK_
Toe OK? ____

COMMENTS: _OVERSTEER_

HANDLING BALANCE: _TOO MUCH OVERSTEER_

With all the changes made, the car is now transformed from good to excellent. The tire temperatures show near perfect balance front to rear and good camber and pressure settings. The skid pad test resulted in a cornering force in excess of 1.06 g average.

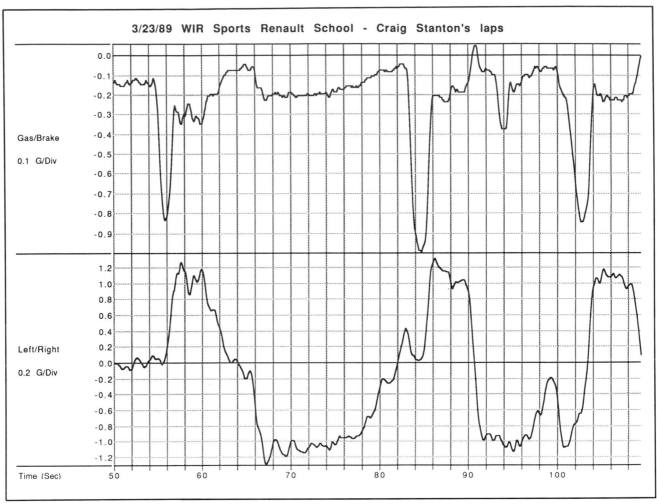

3/23/89 WIR Sports Renault School - Craig Stanton's laps

One valuable tool used for development work is the g.Analyst. The above charts show a lap driven in a Sports Renault at the 2.5 mile course at Willow Springs. The cornering and acceleration force plots allow interpretations about the set-up of the car, especially during transitions and over bumpy sections. The smooth driving style is apparent here, and makes the charts much easier to use for suspension tuning purposes.

Chapter 12

Handling and the Driver

The goal of suspension tuning is to be able to drive quickly and safely on the racetrack, autocross course or the street. The skills needed to get around a track quickly are exactly the same ones needed to drive effectively and safely on the road. The speed you choose to drive your car is only a minor factor, but those who leave little or no safety margin on the highway are asking for trouble. Not developing the skills of the true high-performance driver is even worse. Let's look at some of the skills needed to become a true high-performance driver.

There are three basic functions that the driver controls. First is the car speed at any point. Second is the path of the car around a turn. Third is the method—smoothness—of the driver when using the controls. All of these factors have a dramatic effect on vehicle speed and safety. And these factors apply to any form of driving, on the road or the track.

Cornering and Corner Entry

The most common place for driver error to occur is at the entry to a turn. Two mistakes usually happen at the same time here. There is one point in a turn where a driver makes a choice affecting two of the parameters mentioned above. The turn-in point is the most crucial point of a turn. At that point, the driver chooses the path of the car through the turn and also the entry speed of the car into the turn. Both factors play a major role in safety and speed.

Most drivers have a tendency to drive deep into the turn and then hang on for dear life, fighting the car and the corner. The fast entry speed into the turn usually upsets the balance of the car, and forces it to take a less than ideal path through the turn. The car will slide and speed is scrubbed off, causing lower cornering speeds. This is also dangerous.

Even more crucial is the loss in corner exit speed. That means a loss in speed at every point along the next straightaway. And you thought that the driver who rockets past you down the straightaway had a trick motor. Not so! All he or she really had is corner exit speed. The driver had the patience and discipline to enter the turn at slightly reduced speed so that he or she could maintain control, increase cornering speed and get on the power sooner. This technique also increases the safety margin when driving on the road, and thus is even more important on unfamiliar roads. In competition situations, the driver on the power early has made the straightaway 10 ft. longer than the driver sliding into the turn. If one driver can get on the power 10 ft. sooner then the next driver, who will get to the end of the straightaway first?

Of course getting into a turn fast is important on the track, but most drivers get into turns *too* fast. The line between fast and too fast is small. The driver who best finds that limit will be the fastest.

Consider this: how much time do you spend on the power versus slowing down. On the racetrack, less than ten percent of the lap time is used for slowing. Spending a little more time slowing will not cost a significant amount of added time to a lap, and will allow the driver the opportunity to work on reducing the time spent on the ninety-percent portion of the lap. The real gains will be found in cornering speed and corner exit speed because that's where you spend most of your time. And on the highway, using this technique allows driving quickly over your favorite windy road with a higher level of safety and more control; unexpected encounters are also easier to avoid when these techniques are used.

The key to fast driving is the exit of the corner. The earlier power is applied, the faster the straightaway speed will be. If too much power is applied too soon, the driver may induce understeer which will slow the car at the corner exit—not the fast way around. Shane Lewis

131

The extreme understeer with the Toyota is caused by too much body roll and subsequent camber change. Smooth, balanced driving will reduce the understeer while excessive power application will make it worse.

Try a few exercises the next time you practice:
• Slow down early coming into a turn,
• Try a variety of lines through the turn until you find the one that allows you to get on the power the earliest.
• When you find the trick line, practice it.
• After you practice the correct line, replay it through your mind a few times so that you have a strong mental image of the path through the turn.
• On the racetrack, slowly increase the car's entry speed into the turn. Take small steps until you can no longer hold the car on the correct line. If you have to ease off the power or turn the steering more to negotiate the turn, the car speed is too fast or the line is not correct. Back off and get back on track.
• Practice smooth steering motions. Abrupt steering inputs upset the balance of the car, and scrub off speed. Remember patience and discipline.
• On a continuous circuit, work on one turn at a time, starting with the most important turn—the one leading onto the longest straightaway.
• Once you're dialed in on a turn, practice alternate lines that will still allow early power application. When you are in race traffic, you will seldom have the best line available to you. Be prepared.
By practicing these techniques, you will be able to carry more speed through the turns, get on the power sooner, blast down the straights and increase the safety margin when driving quickly on the road.

Weight Transfer and the Driver

Weight transfer, as we have seen, plays a crucial role in the handling picture. Since the driver can affect both the rate and location of weight transfer, the driver is a key factor in the handling equation.

Driving a car to its limit is what competition is all about. To do so, the driver must manipulate weight transfer while driving at the limits of adhesion. Not an easy task, and for this reason driving will always be an art, not a science. Feel, precision and control are some of the key elements of a talented driver. Often, the competition driver walks a tightrope. Driving fast is not paramount; driving fast smoothly and precisely is.

A driver in competition must push the tires to their limits, use the line through the turn that allows maximum cornering speed, apply the power early on to maximize corner exit speed, not upset the balance of the car with excessive steering inputs, and adjust to changing conditions. If the job is done without a soft touch, or lacking precision, the driver will be slow, or go off the track. Small inputs can cause, or cure, major problems.

As we have seen, weight transfer is caused any time a force acts upon the vehicle in motion. The force can be a change in speed, such as acceleration or deceleration, or a change in direction. All of these factors are controlled by the driver and how he or she uses the controls.

Weight Transfer and Steering

Let's start with steering. When the driver moves the steering wheel, the vehicle changes direction. The amount of force (weight transfer) is determined by the speed of the vehicle and how far the wheel is turned (turn radius). The rate of weight transfer (how quickly the weight is transferred) is determined by how fast the driver turns the steering wheel. Turn the wheel faster and weight transfer occurs more quickly. Turn the wheel slowly, the weight will transfer more slowly. Does this affect the handling of the car? You bet it does!

The more weight that transfers when the car is at the limit, the less total traction is available for cornering. Only track width, center of gravity height and cornering force affect the total amount of weight transfer while cornering. Cornering force is a combination of turn radius and vehicle speed, and this is where the speed of steering motions can influence handling.

If a driver turns the wheel slowly, perhaps taking one full second to turn the wheel 90 degrees, the weight transfers slowly. This allows the tires to easily build up to the optimum slip angle for peak cornering. Additionally, the inside tires can do more work over that period of time, increasing the total amount of traction available to get the car into the corner.

If a driver abruptly turns into the corner, taking only 0.10 sec. to complete the 90 degree turn of the wheel, the tires reach their peak slip angle more quickly, and it is easy to overshoot the optimum slip angle, which will reduce cornering force and cause tire scrub. The abrupt loading of the outside tires due to the rapid weight transfer can also cause reduced traction during the critical turn-in phase of a corner. If the car is not very close to neutral handling, a severe push or extreme slide can result.

The same principle applies at the exit of a turn, when the steering wheel is turned straight. The ideal exit line is an increasing radius, allowing a slow, smooth decrease in steering lock while, at the same time, more power is fed on, increasing corner exit speed and reducing the time spent on the following straightaway. If the wheel is abruptly returned to center, the quick unloading of the outside tires can cause the same loss of traction caused by the abrupt turn-in movement. Also, the lack of a slow, smooth turn-out indicates that the line through the turn is not ideal. The line is likely slower, costing even more time.

In short, the smoother the movements of the steering wheel, the better the car will behave at the limit. The speed that the steering wheel should be turned depends upon a number of variables, including the radius of the turn and how long the turn is. If the steering motion is too slow, the car may not make the turn at all. If it is too fast, all of the factors we have discussed will likely occur.

Like most compromises, the optimum rate of steering wheel movement is learned from experience. It is easy to practice this at low speeds well below the limit. How does the car feel if the wheel is turned quickly? What occurs when the wheel is turned slowly and smoothly? What happens if the wheel is turned too slowly?

Weight Transfer, Deceleration and Acceleration

The other controls used by the driver, the brake and throttle, control speed. Changes to speed cause weight transfer. Deceleration is slowing—not just braking—and causes weight to transfer from the rear to the front. Acceleration causes weight to transfer from the front to the rear. During deceleration, the front tires gain in traction while the rears loose traction. During acceleration, the opposite is true.

How quickly these controls are used affects how quickly weight is transferred from one end of the vehicle to the other. As with steering inputs, abrupt brake and throttle inputs can upset the balance of the car. It is easy to overshoot the limits of traction, causing wheel lock-up or spin under power application. Quick, but smooth—very smooth—brake applications allow the tires to develop peak traction quickly, but without overload.

The Nissan Z has spun from excessive oversteer, in this case due to lifting off the throttle in a turn and taking needed load off the rear tires. The sudden loss of traction at the rear causes the car to spin.

Smooth applications of the throttle exiting a turn allow the power to accelerate the car, not spin the tires.

This is especially important with front-drive cars, especially exiting slow corners. The weight is transferring away from the drive wheels, reducing traction. Smooth power applications will optimize traction. Again, practice will allow the feel to be developed.

Combining Cornering, Deceleration and Acceleration

When both cornering and acceleration or deceleration occur simultaneously, new problems arise. Abrupt turn-in while the brakes are applied for maximum deceleration can overload the front tires, causing understeer, or a push. With a rear-engine or mid-engine car, the same maneuver can cause the rear tires to lose traction because more weight is transferred to the front tires. The result can be a spin.

In the same way, once power is applied in a turn, if the driver abruptly lifts off the throttle, the forward weight transfer can cause the front tires to bite and the rears to lose traction. Oversteer results, again often causing the vehicle to spin.

If power is applied too abruptly in a turn, the weight transfer to the rear can cause the front tires to lose traction and understeer will result. Conversely, if enough throttle is applied at the exit to cause wheelspin, oversteer can result.

There are many combinations of steering and throttle or brake movements that can cause problems. Sometimes they can be used to solve problems. The consistent truth is that smooth inputs of all controls will maximize traction in all conditions. Abrupt movement will result in less traction, possi-

Excessive trail braking (braking and turning at the same time) entering a turn can cause an overloading of the outside front tire and understeer will result. Shane Lewis

bly unbalancing the car, and often a loss of control. Learn to drive smoothly if you want to be really quick.

Handling Problems: Car or Driver?

Many handling problems can be attributed to driver input errors. This is especially true for new, inexperienced drivers. It can be quite difficult to determine if a handling problem is set-up related or driver induced. Following is a list of clues to help determine where to look first to correct handling problems:

• If the problem is inconsistent, then the problem is likely driver-induced.

• If a problem occurs at every similar type of turn, it is likely set-up related.

• If a problem occurs on either left or right turns only, it is likely set-up related.

• If a problem occurs at one turn only, it is likely driver-induced.

Troubleshooting Driver Input Problems

Look for these situations to determine if driver inputs are causing handling problems:

Excessive Braking

Excessive braking can mean that speed is reduced too much, but usually refers to wheel lock-up or too much pedal pressure when steering input begins in a corner. In all cases traction is reduced and the path through the turn is altered from the ideal. Excessive braking entering a turn can cause either understeer or oversteer depending upon the balance of the car.

Excessive Throttle Application

Excessive throttle application can cause wheelspin and a power oversteer condition. It also reduces acceleration and speed down the straightaway. Understeer at the exit of the turn is another possible effect of excessive throttle application. Here, weight is transferred to the rear, taking load from the front tires and reducing traction.

Excessive Trail Braking

Trail braking occurs when both braking and steering inputs are undertaken together. The tires can accomplish only so much work: if too much braking or too much steering occurs, the tires are overloaded and understeer will occur in most cases.

Abrupt Steering Input

Jerky, tentative or abrupt steering input can cause weight transfer to occur too quickly, resulting in overloaded tires and traction reduction at one end of the car.

Late Steering Correction

Steering corrections made after initial corner entry steering input—either more or less steering lock—means that the driver has made an original input mistake of either too little or too much initial steering input, chosen an improper turn-in point or incorrect speed for the condition.

Improper line

The path through a turn determines cornering speed and the crucial corner exit speed. An early turn-in causes an early apex and requires a speed reduction at the exit of the turn. A late turn-in causes reduced cornering speed and too much track width left at the exit of the turn. Not using the entire track width will reduce cornering speed. An improper line through the first turn in a series will cause subsequent turns to be taken on the improper line.

Driver Handling Problems and Cures

Problem: Corner Entry and Steady State Understeer

Corner entry understeer is often driver-induced. The most common causes are braking too late and too hard, excessive corner entry speed, too much trail braking, turn-in too late, and abrupt, excessive steering input.

All of these driver inputs create the same situation. The front tires are highly loaded, causing them to operate at higher slip angles than desired. This causes understeer. Once understeer begins, it is likely to continue through the turn or until speed is reduced. With time, heat builds up, overheating the tires and causing the understeer to become progressively worse.

Cures

Assuming that set-up problems have been eliminated as causes, the best way to cure driver-related corner entry and steady state understeer problems is to alter driving style. Try the following:

134

- Reduce entry speed; drive on precise line.
- Use minimum steering input with a very smooth turn-in.
- Reduce or eliminate trail braking; this is more important for front-heavy cars, especially front-drivers.

Problem: Corner Exit Understeer

If a driver is causing corner exit understeer, it is most likely a continuation of the corner entry and steady state understeer problem. If, however, the car is working properly in the entry portion of the turn, and begins to understeer at the exit of the turn, the driver may be applying too much throttle too soon and too abruptly.

Cures

The cure is a smooth, well-timed throttle application.

Problem: Corner Entry and Steady State Oversteer

Corner entry and steady state oversteer are not usually driver-induced. However, corner entry oversteer can be driver-caused under specific conditions. The first situation is when a driver tries to pitch the car into a turn. This occurs when the driver turns in too abruptly, combined with a sudden release of the throttle. A second and more obvious situation occurs when excessive trail braking is used in conjunction with an abrupt turn-in. If rear wheel lock-up occurs, the oversteer will be instantaneous and difficult to control.

Cures

The cures are obvious: smooth turn-in and reduced trail braking. You should note, however, that pitching a car into a very slow turn, such as a hairpin or on a Solo II autocross course, can be an effective technique to reduce times. Segment times comparing both methods will determine the best technique to use. This method does not work on faster turns, though. Too much speed is scrubbed off and the chance of a spin increases tremendously.

Mid-corner oversteer can occur due to throttle steer. This is caused by a reduction in throttle pressure, usually an abrupt release of the throttle, in mid-corner. Weight is transferred forward, reducing rear tire contact patch area. The resulting loss of traction will induce oversteer. Oversteer is reduced as speed decreases or as power is again applied, rebalancing weight distribution and contact patch size.

Throttle steer, used judiciously, can be a helpful tool in certain types of low- to medium-speed corners where turn-in is troublesome. On the other hand, throttle steer can cause excessive oversteer resulting in a spin, especially in high-speed turns. When driving near the limit of adhesion, under full power, a sudden release of the throttle can induce sudden oversteer, sometimes so much that applying opposite steering lock and throttle application is not enough to correct the sit-

The author wheels the Ground Zero Mustang into and out of a fast sweeper on the Willow Springs test track. Note the late turn-in in the first photo. By the time the car reaches the apex in the second photo, power is being applied. Note the small steering angle in each photo and

the level attitude of the car. Smooth steering, brake and throttle inputs reduce tire scrub and loss of traction at one end of the car or the other. Smoothness results in good balance and fast cornering speeds, but it looks boring. It's not!

uation. If you encounter a situation in a high-speed turn where speed must be reduced, a gradual reduction in throttle pressure combined with reduced steering lock is the most effective solution to the problem.

Problem: Corner Exit Oversteer

The most common driver-induced cause of corner exit oversteer is early throttle application or excessive throttle application. This is especially true for high-horsepower cars.

Another possible driver-related cause of corner exit oversteer is an improper entry line into a turn. If the driver turns into a corner too early (early apex approach), a steering correction requiring more steering lock at the exit of the turn will be necessary to keep the car on the racing surface. If this is combined with a sudden release of the throttle, oversteer is likely to occur.

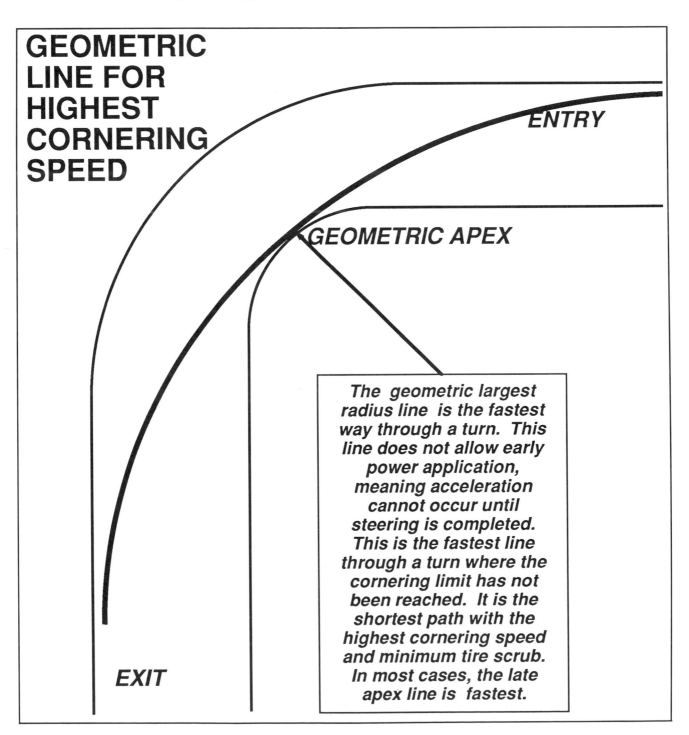

GEOMETRIC LINE FOR HIGHEST CORNERING SPEED

ENTRY

GEOMETRIC APEX

EXIT

The geometric largest radius line is the fastest way through a turn. This line does not allow early power application, meaning acceleration cannot occur until steering is completed. This is the fastest line through a turn where the cornering limit has not been reached. It is the shortest path with the highest cornering speed and minimum tire scrub. In most cases, the late apex line is fastest.

Cures

The cure is more gradual and better-timed throttle application at the exit portion of a turn.

The most effective cure for this problem is the correct line into and through the turn. The dynamics of this situation are exactly like pitching a car.

Cornering Paths: The Fast Line

There are many ways to get around a racetrack, but only one is the fastest. Finding that ideal path can take many laps of practice, but a little advance planning can minimize the time needed to find the fast line.

Let's start with a single, 90 degree turn, and analyze different paths around the turn. The fastest way around any constant-radius turn is a path that follows the largest radius around the corner. The larger the radius, the faster the car is traveling at the limit of tire traction. The relationship is squared, meaning that if you double the radius of the turn (while keeping cornering force constant), the speed potential is four times greater. Even though the distance traveled is greater the time spent in the turn is less. This is an important point. Using the entire width of the track is important for maximum cornering speed. Even driving a foot away from the outside edge of the track on entry and exit can cause a significant speed loss, as can missing the apex (midpoint) of a turn.

This constant line through the turn utilizing all of the available track is the fastest way through the turn. Less time will be spent from the point of turn-in to the point where the vehicle is again traveling in a straight line. The trick here is that speed must be kept constant throughout the turn. Power cannot be applied without upsetting the traction of the car until the front wheels are pointing down the straight.

Let's look at an example. The top speed before the end of the straight is 90 mph. The corner can be taken at 60 mph. The speed of the car must be reduced by 30 mph at the end of the straight. The turn is taken at a constant speed of 60 mph and once the straight is reached, the car can accelerate to top speed on the next straight. There is not a faster way around the turn. However, there is a faster way down the following straightaway.

If the line through the turn is altered, car speed at different points in the turn will change. The portions with a smaller radius will be slower, and the portions with a larger radius will be larger. Working from the exit, if we can have a larger radius at the end of the turn, we can go faster at the exit of the turn. If we are traveling faster at the exit of a turn, then at every point along the following straightaway, car speed will be greater. If the radius is continually getting larger at the exit of the corner, then more and more power can be applied without losing traction, and even more vehicle speed can be carried down the straightaway. So how can we increase the turn radius at the exit of the corner?

Late Apex Line

The only way to do this is to *decrease* the radius of the turn at the entry. The whole track width is still used, but the car is turned in later, and the apex is later, beyond the geometric center of the turn. The tighter turn going in allows a wider turn coming out. The wider turn allows more power application and an increase in speed. In essence, we are making the straightaway longer. Nice trick!

To do this however, we must pay the piper, and he charges a toll at the entry to the corner. The price is slowing down more entering the turn, and taking a path through the first third of the turn that is slower than the perfect geometric line we discussed earlier. How much slower depends on how late the turn-in occurred. If we must slow more to enter the turn, we should need to reduce speed earlier, right? No! We can slow at approximately the same point as before. We must slow more, but we also turn-in later, giving us the extra distance we need to further reduce entry speed.

So far we have broken even. But for the first third of the turn, speed is slower, so we have lost time. Not a good deal so far. We can actually increase speed during the second third of the corner, as we pass the late apex point on the inside of the track. This segment is a break-even proposition. We better make out in the last segment.

In the final third of the corner we are on full power (at least some amount more than before), increasing speed as the turning radius is decreased. Speed increases quickly, and at each point in this segment, and on the following straightaway, vehicle speed is higher than before. If the straight is long enough, we have saved more time than we lost in the first third of the turn. The straightaway does not need to be very long for the gain to be worthwhile. The longer the straightaway, however, the greater will be the gains.

Returning to our previous example, let's assume we have to slow to 56 mph at the entry. In the second third of the turn, we can accelerate to an average speed of 60 mph. During the last third of the turn, speed increases to 64 mph at the exit point, the same point where the speed was only 60 mph on the constant-radius geometric line. At each point along the following straightaway, car speed will be about 4 mph faster than before. At the end of the straight, the speed will be 4 mph faster, and this will require earlier slowing—but so what! The time needed to travel the straightaway is seven percent less. The time lost at the entrance to the corner is much less, so the net gain is substantial. Be warned, however, that if the straightaway is very short, or the corner leads into another corner, or the cornering limit cannot be reached, a differ-

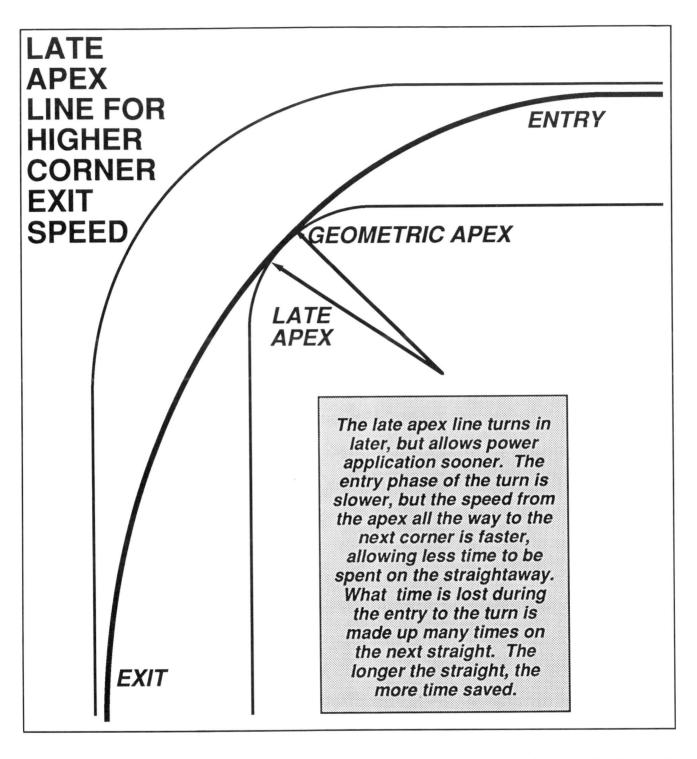

LATE APEX LINE FOR HIGHER CORNER EXIT SPEED

ENTRY

GEOMETRIC APEX

LATE APEX

EXIT

The late apex line turns in later, but allows power application sooner. The entry phase of the turn is slower, but the speed from the apex all the way to the next corner is faster, allowing less time to be spent on the straightaway. What time is lost during the entry to the turn is made up many times on the next straight. The longer the straight, the more time saved.

ent line may be called for. And in traffic, the fastest line is the one that gets and keeps you in front of the competition.

Early Apex Line

If a late apex line is good, is an early apex line bad? Yes—and no! Early apex lines work in some cases, especially when trying to pass entering a corner. In this case, the apex should be held tight until the exit line matches the late apex line. This requires a great reduction in speed, but if a pass is made, nothing else really matters. Another exception is on oval tracks. An early apex off the straightaway allows late braking, but the line must be adjusted for a late apex on the exit.

Tire Drag and Lap Times

The fastest way around any racetrack is the path that allows the least amount of turning (steer-

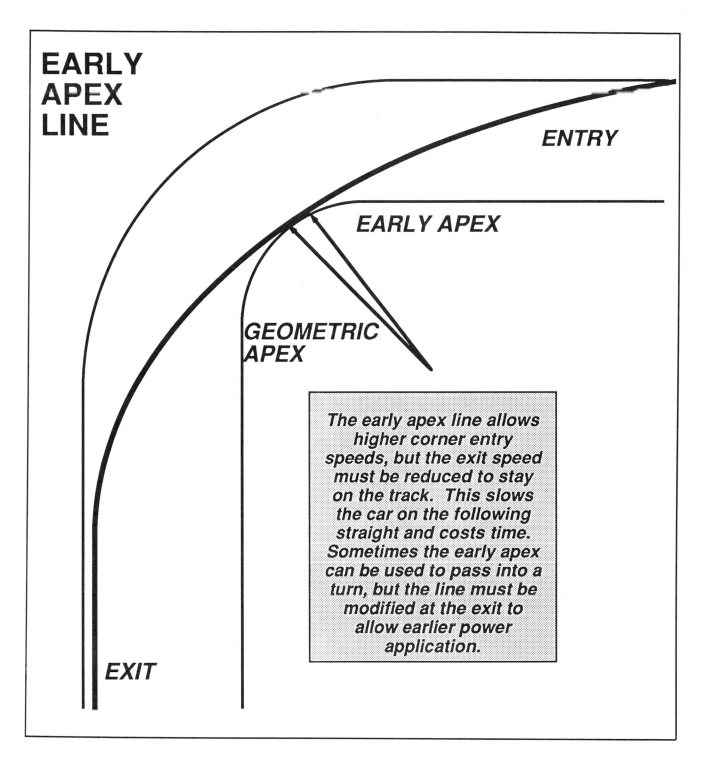

EARLY APEX LINE

ENTRY

EARLY APEX

GEOMETRIC APEX

The early apex line allows higher corner entry speeds, but the exit speed must be reduced to stay on the track. This slows the car on the following straight and costs time. Sometimes the early apex can be used to pass into a turn, but the line must be modified at the exit to allow earlier power application.

EXIT

ing input) and the most amount of full throttle operation. In other words, the driver who is on the power the most and who turns the steering the least, will be fastest. Simple! Now try to do this. Not so simple! Which is what makes any form of motorsport the challenge that it is.

It should be obvious that any time when less than full power is applied will require more time to complete a lap of a track. Less obvious is the effect of steering input. Anytime a tire is turned, drag results. Increased drag reduces speed, and more time is needed to complete a lap. If the total amount of time spent steering could be measured for a given lap for all cars, the one with the least time spent steering would be the fastest car around the course. In the same way, if power application could be measured, the car with the most consistent full power application would be the fastest. In fact, the two criteria work hand in hand. The driver who accomplishes one, and usually accomplishes both, and is the driver with the fastest lap times.

So how does one do this? The fastest line through a turn is the one allowing the largest radius through the turn. While this line may allow the minimum amount of steering input, it does not allow the maximum amount of power application. Speed cannot be increased until the car is going straight, with no steering input. We want full power to accelerate down the straightaway, and we want it as early as possible. The late apex line allows this to occur. But how late should the apex be?

If the turn is flat out with no speed reduction needed to make it through the corner, then the largest-radius geometric line is the best. A late apex will offer no gain since the car is already at full power. If, however, the turn requires any reduction in speed, the late apex line is faster overall. How late should the apex be? The slower the corner and the longer the following straightaway are, the later the apex should be. Trial and error is the only real way to tell what is best.

If you run out of track at the exit of the turn and must slow down, or if more steering input is needed past the apex of the turn, the turn-in was too soon and the apex too early. If track width is left over at the exit of the turn with full power applied, the apex is too late. Start with a slow entry speed and a very late apex. Increase speed and make the apex earlier and earlier until you must slow at the exit because you are running out of room.

Series of Turns

When the straightaway after a turn is very short, or when two turns in the same direction follow each other with little or no straightaway, such as on an oval, the first turn requires a different strategy. In order to make both ends of the straightaway longer, an early apex is needed into the first turn and a late apex is needed for the second turn. This is an unusual circumstance for road courses, but is common on ovals.

Entering the first turn with an early apex allows for very late braking, and the car carries speed for a longer distance. Minimum steering input is used until the car is near the middle of the two turns. Then a late apex, tight-radius turn is made, allowing for early power application. Late off the power going in and early on the power coming out essentially makes the straightaway longer at both ends. More total power application, less total steering input equals the fast way around these types of turns.

In a series of turns, with left-right combinations, another approach is needed. The goals are first to accelerate from the last turn of a series as early as possible. A late apex is called for on the final turn that cannot be taken flat out. Each prior turn in the series has an even later apex than the next. The first turn of the series has the latest apex. The path through the series allows for the perfect line in the last turn of the series.

The second goal is to carry the maximum speed through the series without deviation from the optimum path. Again, trial and error will be needed to accomplish this. Use the same tips mentioned previously, starting with a very late apex and work to earlier and earlier apexes. When you get it right, you will know!

The whole key is minimum steering input, and maximum power application. Too much steering will scrub off speed. Too little power application is plain slow. It is like walking a tightrope: finding the balance means maximum speed, without falling off the track. Too much steering and too little power is slow. Too much power and too little steering is slower. Focus on minimum steering inputs and smooth power application, especially at the exit of a turn.

High-Performance Highway Driving

While the sanity of driving at the limit in competition is debatable, even on closed circuits with safety precautions, the sanity of driving on the streets at the limit is not. It is plain stupid! The infinite number of variables that occur on public roads make such driving dangerous to the extreme. The high-performance vehicle with enhanced handling and maximum traction is potentially much safer with improved braking and cornering capabilities. The same vehicle also has the potential to become a more lethal weapon if misused. With improved handling performance comes a responsibility to use the performance prudently—in other words, on the racetrack or autocross course, or in emergency evasive maneuvers.

It is not necessary to drive a vehicle at the limit to enjoy enhanced handling performance. Nor is it necessary to drive at the limit to practice the techniques that allow one to become a high-performance driver. Smoothness, precise steering, vehicle placement, accurate braking, concentration and broad vision fields can be used in everyday driving.

Three basic differences present themselves when comparing performance driving on a race course, or other controlled environment, and on the highway. First is the environment. Second is the skill level of other drivers. Third is the other traffic.

On a race course, the environment of track conditions and visibility are easily determined; on the road, they are not. The skill level of the drivers participating in a speed event in a controlled situation is much higher than on the highway. In a com-

LINE THROUGH A SERIES OF TURNS IN SAME DIRECTION OR THROUGH AN OVAL TURN

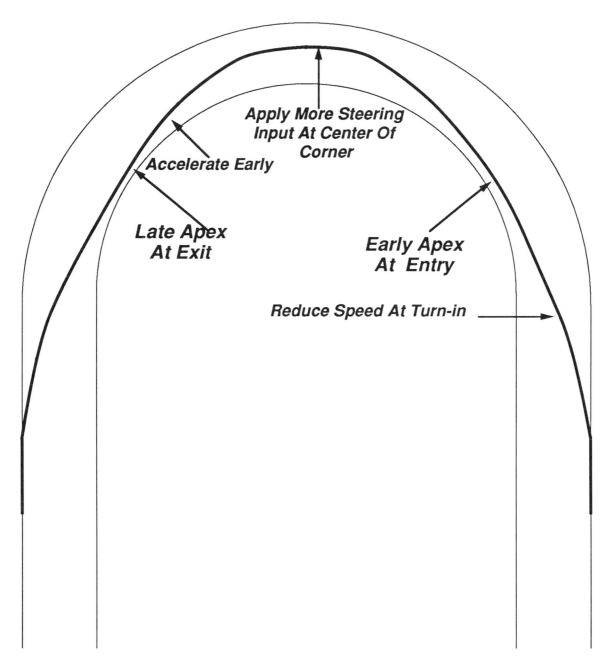

Apply More Steering Input At Center Of Corner

Accelerate Early

Late Apex At Exit

Early Apex At Entry

Reduce Speed At Turn-in

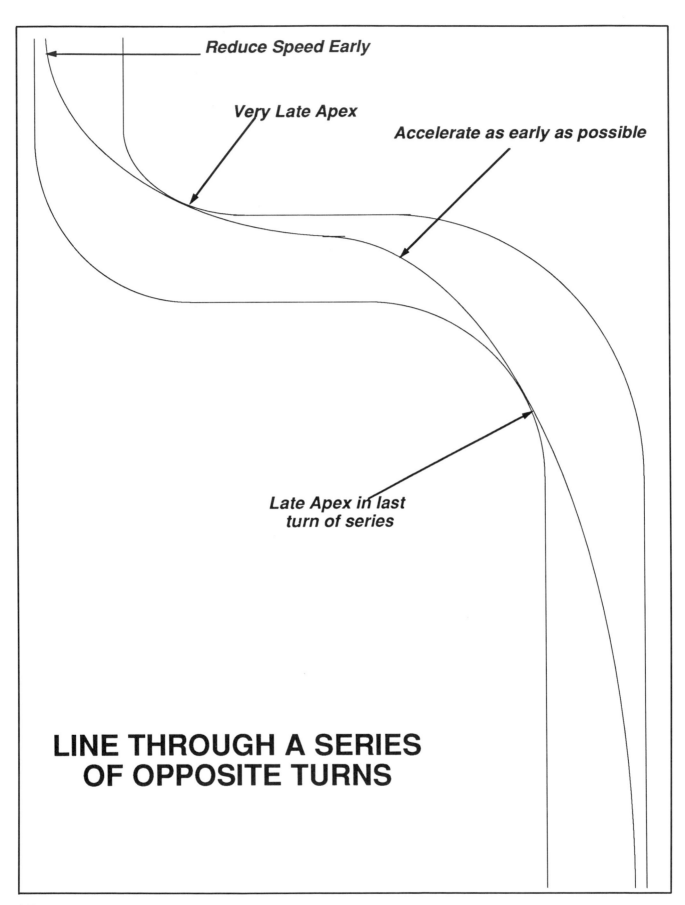

Reduce Speed Early

Very Late Apex

Accelerate as early as possible

Late Apex in last turn of series

LINE THROUGH A SERIES OF OPPOSITE TURNS

petition event, traffic, if present, is controlled and moving in the same direction. Little control of traffic is found on the highway. These factors work together to make highway driving much more dangerous.

There is good news, however. The skills needed to drive quickly on the race course are the same needed to be a safe, competent high-performance highway driver. In reality, the only true difference between the two situations is in how close you drive to the limit. For competition, reaching the limit is the point; on the highway, reaching the limit, except in extreme emergency situations, is foolhardy. The risks are too high, with virtually no potential rewards.

Here are three important tips for driving quickly on the highway.

• Always leave at least twenty-five percent of the cornering speed in reserve for emergency situations.

• Drive the proper line within your lane. Never cross the centerline of the road, unless passing on a straight section so designated.

• Exercise courtesy to all drivers. The fact that you are reading this book indicates that your driving skills far exceed those of the average driver. Use those skills on the highway to reduce your level of risk, enjoy the drive and set a good example for the less skilled.

Every time you get behind the wheel, you have the opportunity to practice the skills that make a high-performance driver. It's fun and challenging to have the driving skills to match the capability of your performance vehicle.

Getting in Touch, Safely

One element of improved handling is improved vehicle responsiveness. This allows the driver to receive more input more quickly through the suspension system. But the driver must also be in touch with the vehicle, physically. The more nerve endings linked directly to the car, the more input the driver has from the car. This improves the driver's "feel" for the limit and for vehicle response, from both outside forces as well as the driver's own inputs. If a driver is sliding about in the car, most of the input is overlooked by the driver as he or she hangs on for dear life.

A good seat and harness system will improve the situation.

Competition harnesses

A good competition harness allows the driver to more fully feel input from the car, and will help keep the driver stationary in the car. While not required in some classes of autocrossing, a competition harness can enhance performance and safety. The best system uses a 3 in. wide lap belt and two individual 3 in. wide shoulder harnesses. An anti-submarine belt should also be used to stabilize the system.

The type of latch is not crucial, with the old stand-by latch and link system the simplest and least expensive. The new style cam-lock systems are more convenient, but offer no additional safety margin.

Mounting belts are crucial for safety and comfort. Follow the manufacturer's instructions carefully, or read the section in the Sports Car Club of America's General Competition Rules covering belt installation. Improper mounting can cause reduced levels of protection.

Seats

A competition-style seat offers the driver improved lateral support and comfort. The additional support improves the driver's feel for the vehicle, and eliminates sliding on the seat. Improved feel is a combination of less movement and more nerve endings actually contacting the seat.

For competition purposes, when allowed, a seat should offer maximum lateral support, even if ingress and egress are inhibited. For the street, or limited competition, more of a compromise is sensible, especially if the driver is often entering or exiting the car. Few stock seats offer good lateral support.

When shopping for an aftermarket seat, look

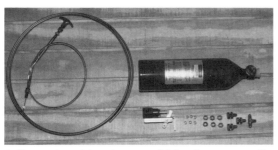

A fire extinguisher is a good idea in any car. For any car competing in high-speed events, a Halon-based fire system offers excellent protection for the driver and reduces the chance of fire damage to the car. Bob Ryder

Fuel cells, like this one from Fuel Safe, have virtually eliminated the threat of fire from autosports. All cars should have one. Bob Ryder

A racing seat gives the driver two important advantages. First, it provides improved comfort and positioning, allowing the driver to better feel what the car is doing. The improved control and sensitivity is worth about a half second a lap in most cases. Second, a racing seat offers improved protection in crashes by holding the driver firmly in place. When used with 3 in. competition belts and harnesses, the most benefit is gained. Bob Ryder

for a reasonably rigid shell, a seat design that offers the characteristics for your application, one that fits in your vehicle and one that is comfortable. An uncomfortable seat in competition is distracting; on the street it is intolerable.

Roll cage or rollover bar

In competition, some form of rollover protection is required in most classes. The safety benefits are obvious, but there are performance benefits as well. Even a bolt-in roll cage will add rigidity to the chassis structure of most cars. This reduces chassis flex, and allows the suspension to do its job more effectively. Be sure that off-the-shelf bolt-in roll cages and rollover bars meet the regulations of the sanctioning body controlling the events you plan to run.

Rollover bars and cages offer excellent protection and are a good idea for street vehicles as well. The improved structural integrity makes the vehicle more crashworthy and reduces chassis stress and fatigue.

Ironically, some insurance companies will not insure cars with aftermarket rollover protection.

Fire extinguisher or fire system

Fire is a serious problem in any automotive ap-

All autosport-sanctioning bodies require adequate head protection, like this helmet from Shoei. For any auto sport application, be sure to use only a Snell Foundation or SFI approved helmet which meets the Snell SA-85 protection standard. The SA-85 standard is for auto racing and uses a denser EBS liner to absorb the energy from the type of impacts encountered in auto racing. Motorcycle helmets use a different style of liner and offer less protection in the auto environment.

plication. Most competition groups require some sort of fire protection, usually a 5 lb. B:C fire extinguisher. Halon fire systems can contain a fire for substantial time spans. When plumbed into the passenger compartment, the fuel tank area and the engine compartment, fire risks are greatly reduced. All vehicles in high-speed events should use a fire suppression system. The increase in occupant safety is important, but do not overlook the potential protection for your vehicle. It's cheap insurance.

Fuel cell

A fuel cell also reduces fire risk by containing fuel in a crash. Again, the fuel cell is an excellent idea for high-speed competition, but also has merit for street applications.

Helmet

All forms of motorsports require participants to wear helmets. Not all helmets are created equal. For any form of auto competition, it is best to use a helmet that meets the Snell Foundation SA 85 testing standards. Such helmets are designed specifically for automobiles, and offer superior head protection in auto crashes. The slightly more expensive Snell Standard SA 85 helmet is worth its weight in gold if head protection is needed in a crash.

Driver's suit and gear

Personal fire protection for the driver is required in many forms of competition. Driving suits, underwear, and gloves offer considerable fire protection. The key elements are the material and the number of layers of protection. The best protection is afforded by Nomex and PBI materials. Two- and three-layer suits, along with Nomex or PBI underwear, offer the most protection. A number of companies manufacture driving gear.

Driving gear offers improved protection with good comfort for the competition environment. Nomex materials provide amazing protection in fires and such gear must be used in many forms of motorsport. Bob Ryder

Chapter 13

Project Cars

Toyota Corolla GT-s Twin Cam

The front-engine, rear-drive Toyota Corolla GT-S Twin Cam project car started life as a Toyota Racing Development car. The initial goal was to create a street package that would perform well in autocrossing. In addition to the antiroll bars, springs and shocks in the specifications sheet, we also fitted adjustable camber plates on the front MacPherson struts to allow easy camber adjustment, and a strut tower brace to reduce the flex at the front struts caused by high cornering loads. Knuckle risers were used to reduce bump steer,

---

Toyota Corolla GT-S Twin Cam Specifications
Springs: Toyota Racing Development (TRD) Sport
Antiroll bars: Suspension Techniques front and rear, adjustable at rear
Shocks: Tokico Illumina gas shocks front and rear
Bushings: TRD hard rubber
Tires: Yokohama A008RTU 205/60-14 front and rear
Wheels: Revolution 15x7 front and rear
Camber: 2.5 degrees negative front
Castor: Stock
Toe: 1/16 in. out front

---

and mono ball drag struts were used to assist in castor adjustment and to reduce compliance in the front lower control arms. Finally, a TRD Panhard bar replaced the stock, rubber-bushed unit.

The TRD springs lowered the car about 1.5 in., and raised the suspension frequencies to about 95 cycles per minute. This created a stiff ride, but one that was totally comfortable on the street. The removal of some components with rubber bushings, and replacement with solid or urethane bushings, increased the level of noise and vibration. But the improvement in handling performance was worth the tradeoff.

We tested the stock version of the Corolla, and the handling at the limit was erratic, requiring quick reactions to maintain control. Heavy corner entry understeer would be followed by excessive corner exit oversteer if the throttle was not applied with great care. Skid pad numbers were in the 0.8 g vicinity.

Our first test with all of the suspension modification was on Yokohama A008R tires on the stock 6 in. wide rims. We were able to get the handling

In stock configuration, the Corolla GT-S exhibits excessive roll and understeer with abrupt transitions.

With suspension modifications in place, and the Yokohama A008R tires, the Corolla was transformed into a top-handling performer on the autocross course. It still presents a comfortable ride for the street, although the noise level has increased due to all of the solid suspension mounts now in place.

dialed in quickly, with a best skid pad average of 1.0 g. The balance on the road course was good, with about a 2 sec. improvement in lap times over stock.

The basic problem with this set up was the 6 in. rims on 200/60 series tires. The 6 in. rims were replaced with 7 in. Revolution wheels, and the tire temperatures looked much better. Ultimately, we needed less negative camber at the front, and skid pad numbers improved to 1.03 g average. The car was still at a high 8 in. ride height (measured at the rocker panel behind the front fenderwell), higher than necessary even on the street. If this car was lowered to the 5 in. ride height allowed in SCCA Improved Touring rules, the lateral acceleration would improve even more to about 1.06 g cornering force.

Geo Storm GSI

Off of the showroom floor, the front-engine, front-drive Geo Storm GSI is amazingly well balanced, unusual for a front-driver. Its only real problems are body roll, the associated camber change and weight transfer. Fortunately, the cure is simple.

To reduce the weight transfer, we need to lower the Geo. The lower, stiffer springs will also increase roll resistance and help cut down on body roll, but not enough. The next step is to increase the antiroll bar size, a little at the front so that the inside wheel stays planted during hand cornering, and a lot at the rear. Then the lower-profile, wider tires on wider rims can do their job more effectively.

Suspension Techniques jumped on the Geo, and created a trick set of springs and bars, and we went testing. The 2 in. drop made the car look purposeful—it appears to be cornering at 1.0 g sitting still. But looks don't turn corners fast; good suspension and tires do.

The combination of wider, stickier rubber from Bridgestone, a lower center of gravity and less camber change due to body roll made the Geo Storm worthy of the name. The cornering power increased drastically from 0.81 g up to 0.91 g.

> **Geo Storm GSI Specifications**
> **Springs:** Suspension Techniques Sport, lowering
> **Antiroll bars:** Suspension Techniques front and rear
> **Shocks:** Stock front and rear
> **Bushings:** Stock
> **Tires:** Bridgestone Potenza RE-71 195/50ZR15 front and rear
> **Wheels:** American Racing 15x7 front and rear
> **Camber:** 1.0 degree negative front
> **Castor:** Stock
> **Toe:** 1/16 in. out front

In these photos, the excessive body roll of the stock Geo Storm GSI is apparent. Dan Sanchez

In stock trim, the handling balance is close to neutral. Dan Sanchez

The tire temperatures indicate how much the body roll is caused camber change. The outside edge of the tire overheats in a turn due to the loading. In this case, the outside temperature was about 50 degrees Fahrenheit hotter than the inside edge. The ideal reading is about 5 degrees less! Dan Sanchez

This is the stock GMC S-15 before the suspension modifications. Excessive body roll and understeer caused slow skid pad times.

Afterward, the S-15 screamed for more corners. Less body roll and camber change, great grip from the wide, sticky Yokohama A-008R tires and many skeptics-turned-believers. Dan Sanchez

The surprise was the balance of the car after the changes. The near neutral handling of the stock set-up disappeared, replaced by understeer in small, manageable quantities. On a low horsepower, front-driver a little oversteer is the quick way around a turn, so the push detracted from the potential of the Geo.

The rear antiroll bar is not adjustable, so we couldn't try a change, but we did learn an interesting piece of information from the computer. With the stock set-up, the excessive body roll was more predominate at the rear of the car, causing more camber change at the rear. This reduced the tire contact patch area at the rear, and therefore the traction at the rear. The amount was perfect to balance the car effectively. With the stiffer set-up, roll was reduced. The camber change was not made at the rear to reduce traction more than the front, so a small push set in.

To reduce the understeer, we tried the only option when there are no easy adjustments. We lo-

The rear antiroll bar installation on the GMC S-15. The bar created enough roll resistance to perfectly balance the roll couple (handling), even allowing some oversteer. However, the bar was too stiff and caused the inside rear tire to lift from the ground during hard cornering, not good for corner exit speed. Smoother driving minimizes the problem, but the true cure is to increase the rear spring rate by about ten percent and soften the rear bar slightly. That allows the springs to provide a higher portion of the rear roll resistance, and will reduce the tendency for the inside wheel to lift during hard cornering.

The holes on the antiroll bar and the slider on the frame allow adjustments to the bar rate without the link binding or going over center during travel.

wered the rear tire pressures until the car had slight oversteer, and responsiveness and cornering power improved slightly. The fun level improved much more. The reduction in tire pressure was too much, however, for good responsiveness at the rear. Over bumps, the rear of the car would oscillate. The stock strut cartridges were still in place (and will be since no one makes an aftermarket unit yet) and provided little damping.

The final cure is a slightly stiffer rear antiroll bar. Then, the car will become a little pocket rocket, especially with another 40 horsepower. The Geo Storm GSI, for a minimal outlay of funds, can easily reach skid pad numbers in the Corvette ZR-1 range, for less than the annual interest on the ZR-1 loan.

Lowering blocks were used to drop the rear of the S-15 3 in. One leaf was removed from each rear spring as well.

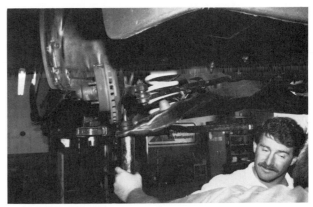

The Suspension Techniques front springs lower the S-15 3 in. Note the urethane bump stop on the lower control arm.

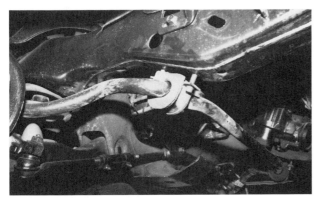

The stock GMC front antiroll bar.

GMC S-15 Sport Truck

The front-engine, rear-drive GMC S-15 Sport Truck really comes to life with minimum modifications. This project was intended to improve the handling of the S-15 without creating a ride like a truck. By lowering the truck 3 in. on Suspension Techniques springs, and increasing roll resistance with stiffer bars, weight transfer and body roll are both reduced. With Bilstein shocks and the wider, stiffer tires, response improved dramatically.

As with most stock pickups, the ride of the S-15 is harsh without a load in the bed. The compromise design is centered around hauling, but our goal was to haul something else, especially around corners. On the freeway, the springs of the stock S-15 caused a slightly uncomfortable pitching at cruising speeds. Hard cornering caused excessive body roll and camber changes. The OEM tires were hard, offering adequate grip, but leaving considerable room for improvement.

Our goal was to create a comfortable ride, a look that was sporty, and cornering performance that rivaled the elite sports cars costing many times more than the S-15. Fun driving and an occasional autocross were the prime parameters.

The cornering improvement was remarkable.

Here is the beefy Suspension Techniques replacement. The reduction in roll results in less camber change and better tire contact with the road in a turn.

With Yokohama A-008R tires, the GMC improved from a puny 0.75 g two-way average on the skid pad to 0.936 g, enough to frustrate many owners of true sports cars. In fact, the S-15 even outran a fully prepped Corvette on the skid pad. And we even towed a race car with the project truck.

GMC S-15 Sport Truck Specifications

Springs: Suspension Techniques 3 in. lowering front, Suspension Techniques 3 in. lowering blocks rear, one leaf removed, fifteen percent spring rate increase

Antiroll bars: Suspension Techniques standard front, adjustable rear

Shocks: Bilstein gas shocks

Bushings: Suspension Techniques urethane

Tires: Yokohama A-008R 225/50VR16 front, 245/50VR16 rear

Wheels: Elite Billet Star 16x7 front, 16x8 rear

Camber: 2.5 degrees negative front

Castor: Stock

Toe: 1/16 in. out front

A 1.0 g ride through the pylons in the modified Camaro. The lack of body roll and outside front negative camber are major reasons for the IROC-Z corner prowess. The BFGoodrich Comp T/A R1 tires worked superbly. Dan Sanchez

Chevy Camaro IROC-Z

The front-engine, rear-drive Chevrolet Camaro IROC-Z project car turned out to be the best overall performer for the road of all the project cars. But it didn't start out that way. After Suspension Techniques replaced the bushings, antiroll bars and springs, we tackled the set-up. Alignment was straightforward, but corner balancing the weights was time consuming. On the initial drive the car felt solid, but maintained a comfortable ride. For some reason, however, the balance and feel of the car were not quite right. Overall grip was good on the BFGoodrich Comp T/A R1 tires, but the car was twitchy on the mountain road going to the test track.

On the skid pad, the initial numbers were disappointing at 0.89 g, barely up to the stock IROC-Z numbers. The car was then run on the test track, and still felt off. Next, a series of tests and minor changes were made to toe settings, tire pressures and shocks settings on the rear Konis. Each change saw an improvement of grip, feel and drivability. By the end of the day, the Camaro was averaging 1.0 g left and right on the skid pad, and turning quick laps with ease.

One Showroom Stock Camaro racer drove the

The Sport Pak antiroll bars and springs from Suspension Techniques worked hard to keep the IROC level in 1.0 g turns.

car and could not believe how easy to drive and forgiving this IROC was. The car could be overdriven into a turn, but still saved. The response to inputs was excellent and total traction was incredible with the R1 compound Comp T/A tires.

On the return trip over the same mountain road, driving the Camaro was like driving a completely different car. Tuning the suspension and tires made a phenomenal difference in the feel and balance of this car, as it can with most cars. Overall, the project, originally designed for a street application, would make a very good racer.

Ford Mustang GT 5.0 Liter

One of the more challenging projects is the front-engine, rear-drive Mustang GT. Our goal was to create a comfortable street package that would outrun the stock Camaro IROC-Z in the handling department, and spend less than $3,000 doing it.

We replaced the stock springs with the Eibach Pro Kit, lowering the car 1.5 in. The SVO electronic shock system was above the budget, but the same damping characteristics are found with the Tokico five-way-adjustable Illumina system, which has the same workings as the SVO without the electronic cockpit-adjustable feature, and remains within the budget restrictions. The antiroll bars were replaced with Suspension Techniques Sport bars, and wider wheels and tires installed.

All of the changes worked together to transform the GT. The excessive steady state understeer disappeared, with only a touch remaining. The transition to oversteer during power application at the exit of corners was reduced to a much less radical degree. Even with the relatively hard Pirelli P Zero tires, skid pad times improved from about 0.80 g average to 0.89 g average, nipping at the

---

Chevrolet Camaro IROC-Z Specifications

Springs: Suspension Techniques Sport, lowering
Antiroll bars: Suspension Techniques front and rear
Shocks: Bilstein gas shocks front, Koni gas adjustable rear
Bushings: Suspension Techniques urethane
Tires: BFGoodrich Comp T/A R1 245/45VR16 front and rear
Wheels: Momo 16x8 front and rear
Camber: 2.0 degrees negative front
Castor: Stock
Toe: 1/16 in. out front

Stock versus rock! The stock GT rolls around the skid pad. The project car is rock solid and hooked up. Even with the modifications, the Mustang could use a little

more negative camber in the front for better tire contact in the turns. Bob McClurg

The trick pieces: Suspension Techniques antiroll bars, Eibach springs and SVO/Tokico cockpit-adjustable electronic shock absorber system. Bob McClurg

---

Ford Mustang GT Specifications
Springs: Eibach Pro Kit
Antiroll bars: Suspension Techniques front and rear
Shocks: Ford SVO (Tokico) electronic adjustable front and rear
Bushings: Energy Suspension urethane
Tires: Pirelli P Zero 245/45VR16 front and rear
Wheels: Shelby 16x8 front, 16x9 rear
Camber: 2.0 degrees negative front
Castor: Stock
Toe: 1/16 in. out front

---

heels of the IROC-Z. Lap times dropped by over 2 sec. on our test at Willow Springs.

Both the skid pad numbers and lap times improved by simply switching to ultra-high-performance tires like the Yokohama A008RTU, the BFGoodrich Comp T/A or the General XP 2000 Z. We found a gain of about 0.05 g and a time savings of 1.0 sec. on the track. The Pirelli P Zero was hard to beat for overall performance in all conditions.

Continuing development is scheduled, including the use of Eibach Autocross springs with the rear Suspension Techniques antiroll bar modified for some adjustment, or at least stiffened. A locker rear end will help the car off the corners. The SVO rear disc brake package and rear trailing arms will also aid performance. These modifications will gain a little more corner force on the skid pad, nearing 1.0 g lateral acceleration. Lap times will hopefully drop a total of about 3.5 sec. over the stock configuration around Willow Springs.

Shelby CSX IMSA International Sedan

The front-engine, front-drive Shelby CSX was an interesting and challenging project. The car was originally raced by the Shelby factory team in the IMSA International Sedan series. Skip Pipes pur-

chased the car, and the suspension was completely redesigned to improve grip and control. The car was weighed, and all suspension points measured for entry in the computer. Geometry was plotted, and roll rates calculated to minimize

The wiring for the electronic shock absorber system is installed in the GT driver compartment. A Hurst shifter is also installed to reduce shift time. Bob McClurg

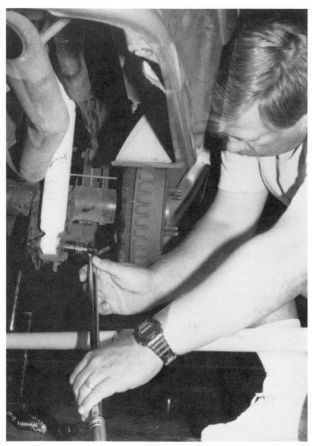

Installing the rear suspension components on the Mustang GT. Bob McClurg

Installing the front suspension components on the Mustang GT. Bob McClurg

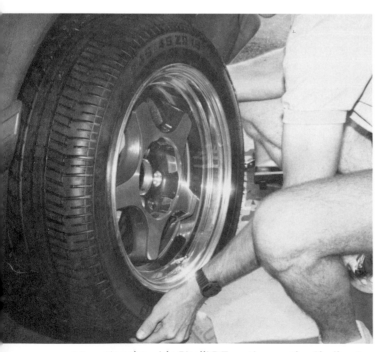

Mounting the wide Pirelli P Zero tires on the Shelby rims to the GT. Bob McClurg

The Shelby CSX races in the IMSA International Sedan class. The car runs on street radials and is allowed some suspension modifications. The Shelby is the only project car used here that is a race-only vehicle. Every other car is easily streetable.

camber change due to body roll. The original front-rear weight distribution for the front-drive Shelby was sixty-five percent front, an excessive amount. At that front weight bias, the two front tires were doing more than eighty percent of the work.

The first step was to alter the weight distribution by moving weight to the rear of the car. Our

The front suspension of the front-drive CSX. Struts are Bilstein racing units, with Eibach Springs on adjustable collars, allowing quick ride height adjustment and corner weight setting.

Rear suspension is a beam axle with trailing arms. Bilstein shocks are mounted upside down.

goal was fifty-seven percent front weight bias, with equal left to right weight, all with the driver in place. To achieve this would have required starting from scratch with a new car, so we were only able to achieve a sixty percent front weight bias—still a major improvement over the original configuration.

Next, suspension frequencies were calculated and spring rates determined. The front struts were replaced with Bilstein coil-over struts with adjustable ride height. A larger front antiroll bar was used in the stock location with stock mounts. At the rear, a tubular Speedway Engineering bar was installed for easy adjustment of roll couple. Roll couple was biased to the rear and the total was stiff enough to keep body roll below 2 degrees at 1.0 g cornering force. This was done to keep camber change below 3 degrees and minimize roll center movement during cornering.

The first test of the modified Shelby was on the Willow Springs test track. Off the trailer, with no time on the car, the first laps on the skid pad were at 1.07 g on BFGoodrich Comp T/A R1 compound tires. With some tuning, the car reached 1.09 g average left and right on the skid pad. On the test track, the car worked well, especially at the corner exit. The only problem was heavy torque steer when the turbo boost came on; driver anticipation made the problem easier to live with.

The first race for the new configuration was at the Mid-Ohio racetrack course. Shane Lewis drove the car up to 6th place in the race, the best-placed independent car. The day ended early, however, when the overstressed engine self-destructed at

Shelby CSX International Sedan Specifications
Springs: Eibach front, Direct Connection rear
Antiroll bars: Suspension Techniques front, Speedway Engineering rear
Shocks: Bilstein gas shocks and struts front, Koni gas adjustable rear
Bushings: Custom hard
Tires: BFGoodrich Comp T/A R1 245/45VR16 front and rear
Wheels: Jongbloed 16x8 front and rear
Camber: 3.0 degrees negative front
Castor: Stock
Toe: 1/16 in. out front

the three-quarter point in the event. Further development should have the Shelby in the top five positions, fighting with the factory teams.

Shogun

The Shogun consisted of a Ford Festiva body with the front-drive drivetrain removed and replaced with a Ford Taurus SHO drivetrain in the backseat. To call this mid-engine, rear-drive package a rocketship is an understatement. At 2,400 lb.,

A Speedway Engineering tubular rear antiroll bar is used. The bar itself is easy to change, and the aluminum arms allow easy adjustment of bar rate to fine-tune roll couple distribution. The link from the bar arm to the axle allows easy neutralizing of the antiroll bar. It is important to eliminate any preload from the bar so that it has the same characteristics in both left and right turns.

The Panhard rod on the rear axle keeps the rear axle from moving laterally during cornering. The vertical adjustments on the left allow the Panhard rod to mount in different locations. This changes the roll center at the rear, which is located at the point where the Panhard rod crosses the centerline of the vehicle.

The Shogun is based on a Ford Festiva chassis with a Taurus SHO drivetrain in the back seat.

During testing, the Shogun corners at 1.0 g with excellent response.

The neutral handling of the Shogun can be seen here. The Shogun responds well to driver inputs, doing exactly what it is asked to do.

Here is the front antiroll bar arrangement. The stock Festiva bar is retained, since it is an active link in the lower control arm, providing longitudinal location.

To control roll, an additional bar was added. It is adjustable to allow tuning of roll couple distribution. It attaches to the strut with a long link.

The front strut is modified to use a Koni insert.

and 220 stock horsepower, the performance potential is close to that of the ZR-1 Corvette. That is the fun part of the equation. The challenge comes with harnessing the power and getting it to go around corners.

The Shogun was the brainchild of Chuck Beck, builder of the 550 Spyder kit car and a former Can-Am driver, and Rick Titus, racer, writer and 1987 SCCA Escort Endurance Champion.

When we started the suspension development program on the Shogun, the car had not turned a wheel. The starting point was to determine spring rates, which turned out to be close off the trailer. The stock Taurus struts and inserts were used for initial testing, and the front Taurus antiroll bar was modified for use at the rear. The stock front Festiva antiroll bar was retained.

The initial tests predictably resulted in some undesirable handling characteristics, but overall, the results were exceptional. Off the trailer, running on Goodyear Gatorback S compound tires, 205/50-15 front and 245/45-16 rear, the Shogun averaged 0.97 g on the Willow Springs skid pad. The primary problems were a significant steady state understeer and excessive trailing throttle oversteer. The understeer was partly camber, inadequate shock absorber damping and excessive front body roll. With the rear antiroll bar stiffened enough to reduce understeer, the inside rear tire was being unloaded too much. A stiffer front antiroll bar was needed.

The trailing throttle oversteer was caused by a substantial change in rear toe to a toe-out condition during rebound. When the throttle was released, the rear suspension would move into toe-out, creating considerable oversteer. The cause of this, we later learned, was primarily compliance in the rear suspension system. The Taurus

Here is the modified rear antiroll bar on the rear suspension, which is part of the Taurus front suspension. The tie rod from the front of the Taurus is used to set rear toe. Rod ends and solid bushings are used in the rear to eliminate compliance.

The rear strut uses adjustable collars to set ride height. The Taurus SHO units are modified for Koni inserts.

Special Editions Shogun Specifications
Springs: Eibach front and rear
Antiroll bars: Suspension Techniques front and rear
Shocks: Koni adjustable struts front and rear
Bushings: Custom
Tires: Goodyear Gatorbacks 205/50ZR15 front, 245/45ZR16 rear
Wheels: BBS 15x8 front, 16x9.5 rear
Camber: 1.0 degree negative front and rear
Castor: Stock
Toe: 1/16 in. out front, 1/16 in. in rear

SHO front suspension is designed to nearly eliminate torque steer feedback to the driver. This is done with soft rubber bushings at every joint of the suspension. At the front, on a front-drive car, this situation enhances stability. At the rear, with rear-drive, the compliance reacts in the wrong direction, causing undesirable handling characteristics.

The understeer problem was corrected with a heavier front antiroll bar, limiting body roll and camber change considerably. The strut cartridges were replaced with Konis, designed for the Porsche 911. These struts improved response and damping considerably, but they are still not correct. Koni is designing strut cartridges especially for the Shogun. These changes instantly allowed the Shogun to corner in excess of 1.0 g on the skid pad. At the rear, replacing the rubber bushings with solid mounts reduced the trailing throttle oversteer. The car will always have some amount of trailing throttle oversteer, however, due to the mid-engine design.

The next phase of testing was completed with the Konis, improved roll control, and solid bushings throughout the rear suspension. The improvements included a major reduction in trailing throttle oversteer, with only a slight tendency remaining, and higher cornering force, in excess of 1.04 g lateral acceleration on the skid pad. The Shogun now transitions extremely well and is predictable. The brakes function superbly, and power from the SHO engine accelerates the Shogun from 0 to 60 mph in just under 5 sec. Overall, the performance is outstanding, and certainly challenges all production cars for handling and performance.

Sources

Suspension components

ADDCO Industries, Inc.
700 East St.
Lake Park, FL 33403
  Antiroll bar kits.

Autotech Sport Tuning Corporation
3 Argonaut
Laguna Hills, CA 92656
  Suspension springs, safety equipment.

Bilstein Corporation of America
8845 Rehco Rd.
San Diego, CA 92121
  Gas pressure shock absorbers, suspension kits,
  sway bars.

Boge of America, Inc.
2658 Atlanta Industrial Dr., Suite E
Atlanta, GA 30331
  Shock absorbers for European cars.

Carrera Shocks
5412 New Peachtree Rd.
Atlanta, GA 30341
  Shock absorbers, springs, struts and coil-over
  components.

Doetsch Tech, Inc.
10728 Prospect Av., #A
Santee, CA 92071
  Shock absorbers.

Eibach North America, Inc.
15311 Barranca Parkway
Irvine, CA 92718
  Eibach Pro-Kit Spring sets, ERS race springs, custom
  springs, oval track race springs, antiroll bars.

Energy Suspension
960 Calle Amanecer
San Clemente, CA 92672
  Polyurethane suspension bushings.

Fiberflex Suspension Technologies
2872 S. Santa Fe Av.
San Marcos, CA 92069
  Fiber-reinforced composite suspension leaf springs
  and components.

Flex-A-Form, Inc.
2060 Frontage Rd.
Anderson, SC 29621
  Fiberglass leaf springs.

Guldstrand Engineering, Inc.
11924 Jefferson Blvd.
Culver City, CA 90230
  Complete line of suspension components for
  Corvette, Camaro, Firebird and other GM models.

HRE Suspensions, Inc.
5928 Balfour Ct.
Carlsbad, CA 92008
  Sway bars and urethane products.

Hellwig Products Company, Inc.
16237 Av. 296
Visalia, CA 93291
  G-Tech and Sport-Tech antiroll bars, springs.

HYPERCO, Inc.
7606 Freedom Way
Ft. Wayne, IN 46818
  Rockwell coil springs, mag racing wheels.

KBD
320 Thor Pl.
Brea, CA 92621
  Suspension and aerodynamic components.

KYB Corporation of America
901 Oak Creek Dr.
Lombard, IL 60148
  Shock absorbers.

Koni America, Inc.
8085 Production Av.
Florence, KY 41042
  Shock absorbers and suspension kits.

Monroe Auto Equipment Company
1 International Dr.
Monroe, MI 48161
  Shock absorbers.

Moroso Performance Products, Inc.
80 Carter Dr.
Guilford, CT 06437
  Herb Adams suspension components.

Penske Racing Shocks
150 Franklin St.
PO Box 301
Reading, PA 19603
  Racing shock absorbers.

Progressive Suspension, Inc.
11129 G Av.
Hesperia, CA 92345
  Shock absorbers.

Sway-A-Way
7840 Burnet Av.
Van Nuys, CA 91405
  Suspension components.

Suspension Techniques
13546 Vintage Pl.
Chino, CA 91710
  Suspension kits, springs, bushings, antiroll bars,
  shock absorbers.

Tilton Engineering, Inc
25 Easy St.
PO Box 1787
Buellton, CA 93427
  Hydraulic brake proportioning valves.

Tokico America, Inc.
1330 Storm Parkway
Torrance, CA 90501
  Shock absorbers and suspension kits.

Tires

BFGoodrich
600 South Main St.
Akron, OH 44397

Bridgestone
One Bridgestone Park
Nashville, TN 37214

Firestone
1200 Firestone Parkway
Akron, OH 44317

General
One General St.
Akron, OH 44329

Goodyear
1144 East Market St.
Akron, OH 44316

Hoosier
One General St.
Akron, OH 44329

Michelin
PO Box 19001
Greenville, SC 29602

Mickey Thompson
PO Box 227
Cuyahoga Falls, OH 44222

Pirelli
500 Sargent Dr.
New Haven, CT 06536-0201

Riken
1113 E. 230th St.
Carson, CA 90745

Toyo
300 W. Artesia Bl.
Compton, CA 90220

Yokohama
601 S. Acacia Av.
PO Box 4550
Fullerton, CA 92634-4550

Aerodynamics

A & A Specialties
220 E. Santa Fe Av.
Placentia, CA 92670

Aeroform
6300 St. John Av.
Kansas City, MO 64123

American Best Car Parts
7400 Greenbush Av.
North Hollywood, CA 91605

Erebuni Corporation
158 Roebling St.
Brooklyn, NY 11211

FOHA Corporation
75A Konrad Crescent
Markham, Ontario L3R 8T8 Canada

GST Industries
815 Stewart St.
Madison, WI 53713

Kaminari, Inc.
15 Argonaut
Aliso Viejo, CA 92656

Lucky Makers, Inc.
5730 Morgan Av.
Los Angeles, CA 90011

Pacer Performance Products, Inc.
5345 San Fernando Rd. W.
Los Angeles, CA 90039

Pacific Auto Accessories, Inc.
15241 Transistor Ln.
Huntington Beach, CA 92649

Priority Precision Products, Inc.
1600 Stewart Av.
Westbury, NY 11590

Razzi Corporation
1050 Branch Dr.
Alphatetta, GA 30201

Spoilers, Etc.
1102 Hub St.
Houston, TX 77023

Transeuro Group, Inc.
14506 S. Garfield Av.
Paramount, CA 90723

Zender North America
700 Pressley Rd.
Charlotte, NC 28217

Wheels

ATS America, Inc.
100 N. Delaney Rd.
PO Box 976
Owosso, MI 48867

Aluett Wheels, Inc.
15721 E. Railroad St., Unit E
City of Industry, CA 91744

American Racing Equipment
19067 S. Reyes Av.
Rancho Dominguez, CA 90221

Amtech Wheel Company
9921 Hayward Way
S. El Monte, CA 91733

Boyd's Billet Wheels, Inc.
8402 Cerritos Av.
Stanton, CA 90680

Centerline Tool Corporation
13521 Freeway Dr.
Santa Fe Springs, CA 90670

Elite Wheel Corporation
1260 W. Pioneer St.
Brea, CA 92621

Empco Custom Wheels
900 Allen Av.
Glendale, CA 91201

Epsilon Wheel Corporation
580 S. Douglas St.
El Segundo, CA 90245

Fagix Wheel Company
3357 Miraloma St., Suite 156
Anaheim, CA 92806

Fittipaldi Motoring Accessories Inc.
1425 NW 82 Av.
Miami, FL 33126

K.M.C. Wheel Company
7633 Cypress Av.
Riverside, CA 92503

Momo, USA, Inc.
2100 NW 93 Av.
Miami, FL 33183

Monocoque Wheel
10658-C Prospect
Santee, CA 92071

Motor Sport Wheels, Inc.
725 Fee Fee Rd.
Maryland Heights, MO 63043

Ronal Wheel Company
15692 Computer Ln.
Huntington Beach, CA 92649

Senter Engineering
3600 E. Olympic Bl.
Los Angeles, CA 90023

Speed Star, Inc.
12631 E. Imperial Highway, C-117
Santa Fe Springs, CA 90670

Topline Wheels, Inc./Etoile Wheels
2872-A Walnut Av.
Tustin, CA 92680

U.S. Wheel Corporation
728 W. Ester St.
Long Beach, CA 90813

Ultra Wheel Company
12350 Edison Way
Garden Grove, CA 92641

Weld Racing, Inc.
933 Mulberry
Kansas City, MO 64101

Safety Equipment

Bell Racing
Route 136
Rantoul, IL 61866

Deist Safety Equipment
641 Sonora Av.
Glendale, CA 91201

Driving Impressions
5-B Hamilton Business Park
Dover, NJ 07801

Filler Products, Inc.
9017 San Fernando Rd.
Sun Valley, CA 91352

Fuel Safe Systems
5271 Business Dr.
Huntington Beach, CA 92649

Shoei Safety Helmet Corporation
2228 Cotner Av.
Los Angeles, CA 90064

Simpson Race Products
22630 S. Normandie Av.
Torrance, CA 90502

Worth Racing
301 N. Harrison St.
Alexandria, IN 46001

Tuning Equipment

REB-CO
70 W. Easy St. #4
Simi Valley, CA 93065
    Scales, tire pyrometers, pressue gauges, watches.

Ruggles'cales
1747 E. Av. Q, Unit D-5
Palmdale, CA 93550
    Corner weight scales, tire protectant.

g.Analyst
10280 Alliance Rd.
Cincinnati, OH 45242

Index